The Tea Party Explained

IDEAS EXPLAINED™

Daoism Explained, Hans-Georg Moeller
Frege Explained, Joan Weiner
Luhmann Explained, Hans-Georg Moeller
Heidegger Explained, Graham Harman
Atheism Explained, David Ramsay Steele
Sartre Explained, David Detmer
Ockham Explained, Rondo Keele
Rawls Explained, Paul Voice
Phenomenology Explained, David Detmer
Ayn Rand Explained, Ronald E. Merrill,
Marsha Familaro Enright
The Tea Party Explained, Yuri Maltsev and
Roman Skaskiw

IN PREPARATION

The Occupy Movement Explained, Nicholas Smaligo
Deleuze and Guattari Explained, Rohit Dalvi

The Tea Party Explained

From Crisis to Crusade

YURI MALTSEV
and
ROMAN SKASKIW

OPEN COURT
Chicago

Volume 12 in the Ideas Explained™ Series

To order books from Open Court, call toll-free 1-800-815-2280,
or visit our website at www.opencourtbooks.com.

Open Court Publishing Company is a division of Carus Publishing Company,
dba ePals Media

Printed and bound in the United States of America.

ISBN: 978-0-8126-9831-2

Library of Congress Control Number: 2013944052

Contents

Preface   vii

1. Two Elections   1

2. How the Tea Party Began   25

3. A Big Government Power Grab Energizes
   the Tea Party   53

4. The Tea Party Landscape   77

5. God and War   105

6. The Tenth Amendment Movement   123

7. The Tea Party and Occupy Wall Street   151

8. Battling the Beast   167

Epilogue: The Future of the Tea Party   193

Index   197

Preface

We have paid close attention to the Tea Party since its inception. As we explain below, the modern Tea Party movement began with a fundraiser by Ron Paul supporters on December 16th 2007 (the 234th anniversary of the pre-revolutionary Boston Tea Party). This event followed the unprecedented Ron Paul 'money bomb' of November 5th. The Tea Party suddenly became a focus of media attention and a major political force following the now-famous impromptu speech by CNBC commentator Rick Santelli on February 19th 2009.

The Tea Party has transformed the face of American politics, politicized many apolitical people, and excited the imaginations of millions. It attracted wide support because of its message of fiscal conservatism and constitutionally limited government. As soon as it became both popular and powerful, the Tea Party struggled with issues it had not anticipated and which divided its supporters: social conservatism, foreign policy, and the role of the Republican Party. As a demonstrably powerful movement, the Tea Party also became something to join, co-opt, capture, exploit, or identify with, for a variety of folks with a variety of different motives.

We have attended many tea parties, spoken at many Tea Party events, and gotten to know numerous Tea Party organizers and activists. We have tried to give an accurate picture of what the Tea Party is and to combat various misrepresentations.

We would like to thank Jacob Huebert for his dedicated research, his insights, and his other contributions to this work. It would not have been possible without him. We would also like to thank David Ramsay Steele for his valuable critical input. Neither of them is responsible for our own opinions on a range of matters.

1

Two Elections

The Tea Party movement began without much fanfare in 2007, as part of a libertarian protest against big government and over-taxation. It suddenly caught fire in February 2009, fueled by the government's bailout of major financial institutions and taxpayer-funded 'mortgage relief'. The leaderless and uncentralized move-ment grew rapidly and soon had thousands of chapters across the country.

As the movement grew, its internal differences of opinion on many political matters became more conspicuous, and numerous existing organizations and political careerists sought to join it, rep-resent it, and influence it. But the Tea Party always remained united on the narrow issues of lower taxation, smaller government, and respect for the U.S. Constitution. As all observers agree, the Tea Party had a huge impact on the midterm elections of 2010.

The Tea Party movement in 2009–2010 and the Occupy Wall Street movement in 2011–2012 politicized many Americans who had formerly preferred to stay out of politics. In earlier years, Teddy Roosevelt, George Wallace, Ross Perot, Patrick Buchanan, and Ralph Nader had all accomplished something similar, with varying degrees of success.

If the two major parties drift too far away from the concerns of real people, the opportunity to tap into the indifferent or disaf-fected is there, which is one of the reasons the Tea Party remains active despite its disappointing election impact in 2012.

Before 2008 most political pundits were under the illusion that there were almost no swing voters left, but as the elections have now proved, there are still plenty of them out there. Barack

Obama found the disaffected in 2008 and made many former non-voters into his enthusiastic supporters. Even more dramatically, the Tea Party showed in 2010 that thousands of formerly apolitical people could become dedicated activists. Lacking any central direction, the Tea Party threw into prominence many inexperienced individuals, as well as attracting the support of a motley crew of minor political careerists, and naturally the media had some fun with both of these spectacles.

Rattling the Establishment: The 2010 Elections

For Republicans and conservatives, the setbacks of 2008 signaled the need for new ideas and faces, so the Tea Party filled a niche in the political marketplace. In the 2010 elections candidates supported by the Tea Party movement won decisive victories in Congress and in many states.

In polls at the beginning of the 2010 election season, 41 percent of the electorate had a favorable view of the Tea Party movement.[1] Though this positive public perception soon began to erode, politicians sensed the movement's influence and many claimed various levels of allegiance. An August 2010 CNN poll found that 2 percent of Americans considered themselves active Tea Party members, and a Rasmussen poll calculated that 29 percent of Americans were "tied to" the Tea Party movement (for example by having a family member who was a Tea Party activist).[2]

The first big story came in January during a special election in Massachusetts for the vacant seat of the late Senator Ted Kennedy. After initially trailing in the polls by as many as 30 percentage points,[3] Scott Brown won the election over Martha Coakley, the Massachusetts Attorney General.

It was the first time in almost thirty years that a Republican from Massachusetts had won election to the U.S. Senate. Many

---

[1] Susan Davis, "WJS/NBC News Poll: Tea Party Tops Democrats and Republicans," *The Wall Street Journal* (December 16th 2009).

[2] Frank Rich, "The Grand Old Plot Against the Tea Party," *New York Times* (October 30th 2010).

[3] "Poll: Coakley has Early Lead in U.S. Senate Race," Suffolk University (September 16th 2009).

conservatives rejoiced, citing the come-from-behind victory as evidence that the Tea Party was winning the argument over smaller government.[4] Others decried Scott Brown's past support for government-controlled health care (at the state level) while in the Massachusetts House of Representatives, as well as his seeming support of the neoconservative military agenda. They considered the frenzy of attention he received to be a compromise of Tea Party principles:

> . . . the Right continues to go gaga for Brown. Let us remember that it was national disenchantment with Bush that led to the election of Obama. Now that Obama is governing pretty much like Bush—and the nation is still disenchanted—why are so many conservatives eager to rally around a Republican who isn't much different than Bush or Obama?[5]

The fervently libertarian originators of the Tea Party could see a stark contrast between how big-government candidates like Scott Brown, who managed to run under the Tea Party banner, were heralded, and the suspicion and skepticism which greeted true fiscal conservatives, like the 'unelectable' and 'dangerous' Rand Paul, whose victory in the Kentucky Senate race was later scarcely mentioned by Rush Limbaugh or Sean Hannity.[6]

Tea Party ire was directed at both parties. At a small protest in Iowa City, organizer Jeff Shipley said:

> You have the stupid party on the right and the evil party on the Left. Sometimes they do something that's both stupid and evil; they call that bipartisanship. . . . I see no difference between Obama and Bush.[7]

---

[4] Patrick Buchanan, "Is America Moving Right?" http://buchanan.org/blog/is-america-moving-right-3494.

[5] Jack Hunter, "Scott Brown's One-Night Stand," *The American Conservative* (January 21st 2010).

[6] Jack Hunter, "Dangerous Rand Paul," *The American Conservative* (March 29th 2010); Robert Schlesinger, "The Problem With Rand Paul's Convictions," *US News* (May 22nd 2010); Jack Hunter, "Left and Right Try to Stop the Rand Paul Revolution," *Charleston City Paper* (May 26th 2010).

[7] Adam B Sullivan, "Iowa City Tea Party Draws Diverse Crowd," *Daily Iowan* (April 16th 2010).

Shipley's assumption that the two-party system is a combination of stupid and evil parties was widely shared in the Tea Party.

> Every once in a while the stupid party and the evil party get together and do something that is both stupid and evil. In Washington, that is called bipartisanship.[8]

Yet inevitably the Tea Party has generally allied itself with Republicans because the language of small government, low taxes, and free markets finds a warmer reception among Republican Party supporters.

If the two parties represent truly opposing ideas, we might expect Democrats to rejoice at the turmoil that the Tea Party wrought within Republican ranks. While a few left-leaning pundits applauded disruptions of the Republican status quo, like Ron Paul's 2008 fundraising success, almost all left-of-center media acted as if the Tea Party assault on Republican ideology was an assault on their own ideology, and really, with the two parties having grown indistinguishable, it was. Many pundits found themselves defending not one political party against the other, as usual, but both parties against the terrifying threat of smaller government.

MSNBC's Chris Matthews denounced the Tea Party defeats of several establishment Republican candidates as "Stalinesque."[9] On the eve of the 2010 election, Keith Olbermann appealed to any indifferent voters on the NBC program *Countdown*. In a nearly twenty-minute rant, he singled out the Tea Party movement as reactionary amateur comedians and puppets of Karl Rove, Dick Armey, Rush Limbaugh, and Glenn Beck whose instructions are "to elect a group of unqualified, unstable, individuals who will do what they are told in exchange for money and power."[10] Karl Rove was a critic, not a supporter, of the Tea Party.

On the same day, the *New York Times*'s Paul Krugman published a column entitled "Divided We Fail," deriding the Tea

---

[8] http://www.redstate.com/barrypopik/2011/04/13/origin-of-stupid-party-evil-party.

[9] Jack Kelly, "The Media's Primary Double Standard," *Real Clear Politics* (May 16th 2010).

[10] "Watch: Olbermann's 20 minute rant against the Tea Party: Only a 'cabal of corporations' are laughing," *Raw Story* (October 28th 2010).

Party's unwillingness to compromise. He wrote, "Future historians will probably look back at the 2010 election as a catastrophe for America, one that condemned the nation to years of political chaos and economic weakness."[11]

Whether one agreed with their views or not, the Tea Party people were clearly the non-conforming newcomers. Despite this, the *New York Times* honored big-government Republican Senator Lindsey Graham with the headline "This Year's Maverick."[12] Senator Graham, a very ordinary Republican politician, had clashed repeatedly with Tea Party supporters in town hall meetings, on the editorial pages of newspapers, and elsewhere. He had said: "The problem with the Tea Party, I think it's just unsustainable because they can never come up with a coherent vision for governing the country. It will die out."

The defense of big government came not only from Democrats. Earlier, in the days following President Obama's election, neoconservative writer David Brooks, and former Bush speechwriter David Frum advised conservatives to ditch their small-government rhetoric.[13] Once the Tea Party arrived, defying the advice of neoconservatives and demonstrating popular support for smaller government, many other establishment Republicans including Mitt Romney, Dick Cheney, and Karl Rove reproached the Tea Party. Many assumed that the Tea Party movement couldn't affect American politics by winning elections, but could only act as spoiler by taking votes from Republicans.

Despite venom in the press, approximately 140 candidates for the U.S. Congress were considered "Tea Party candidates" during the 2010 elections. Ten of those ran for the Senate.[14] This alone is testimony to the movement's influence. Forty House candidates and five Senate candidates (32 percent of congressional Tea Party candidates) were ultimately victorious. Of the sixty seats in the

---

[11] Paul Krugman, "Divided We Fail," *New York Times* (October 28th 2010).

[12] Robert Draper, "Lindsey Graham, This Year's Maverick," *New York Times Magazine* (July 1st 2010).

[13] Jack Hunter, "Scott Brown's One-Night Stand," *The American Conservative* (January 21st 2010).

[14] "Where Tea Party Candidates Are Running," *New York Times* (October 14th); Alexandra Moe, "Just 32% of Tea Party Candidates Win," MSNBC (November 3rd 2010).

House which swung from Democratic to Republican control, Tea Party candidates won twenty-eight.[15]

In gubernatorial elections, seven Republican Tea Party candidates won their party nominations.[16] Four of them went on to win the general election: Rick Scott, a former hospital executive in the Florida race; Paul Richard LePage, a former mayor in Maine who prevailed over six other candidates in the primary; Nikki Haley in South Carolina, who distinguished herself from her three better-funded, better-connected primary rivals by taking uncompromising fiscal conservative positions during the first debate;[17] and John Kasich in Ohio who defeated incumbent Democratic governor Ted Strickland. Tom Tancredo who failed in his bid for the Colorado governorship on the Constitution Party ticket also enjoyed some Tea Party endorsements.

Democratic and Independent Tea Parties

In electoral politics, the Tea Party movement has operated mostly within the Republican Party. While Tea Partiers are aware that Republicans have been as guilty, or almost as guilty, as Democrats, of fiscal irresponsibility and massive expansion of government, Republicans more often adopt fiscally conservative and small government rhetoric. Though this rarely translates into action, it makes them ideologically closer to the Tea Party movement.

However the Tea Party movement has not been entirely Republican. A July 2010 Gallup poll found 15 percent of Tea Party supporters to be Democrats.[18] A small number of Democratic candidates enjoyed at least partial Tea Party support.

U.S. House candidate Mike McIntyre, a Blue Dog Democrat, won in North Carolina's Seventh District with endorsements from

[15] Lisa Lerer, "Tea Party Wins House for Republicans, Wants Rewards in Congress," Bloomberg (November 3rd 2010).

[16] Dan Maes in Colorado, Rock Scott of Florida, Paul LePage in Maine, Tom Emmer in Minnesota, Carl Paladino in New York, Nikki Haley in South Carolina, John Kasich in Ohio. Pamela M. Prah, "Tea Party Could Sway Key Governors' Races," *Stateline* (October 26th 2010).

[17] Jack Hunter, "Haley Stands Out from the Rest of the Republican Pack," *Charleston City Paper* (June 2nd 2010).

[18] Frank Newport, "Tea Party Supporters Overlap Republican Base," *Gallup*, (July 2nd 2010).

a prominent Tea Party activist. The endorsement drew outrage from Tea Party Express, a newly-formed national Tea Party organization founded by two GOP consultants. The outrage reflected the split between ideology and partisanship within the Tea Party movement. After winning the election, McIntyre also received praise from a North Carolina Tea Party organization for his call to repeal NAFTA.[19]

Incumbent Democratic Idaho representative Walter Minnick did receive the endorsement of Tea Party Express (despite their GOP bias) for his votes against cap-and-trade, the Obama economic stimulus, and Obamacare. Minnick reluctantly accepted the endorsement but later rejected it after a scandal surrounding a racially charged article written by a Tea Party Express figure. He lost the election to his Republican challenger.

A West Virginia Tea Party group backed Democrat Michael Oliverio who successfully defeated fourteen-term incumbent Allen Mollahan in the primary. He went on to lose a close general election. Several state-level Democrats also received endorsement from Tea Party groups.[20] Likewise, independent and third-party candidates received a modicum of Tea Party support.

Most notably, former Republican representative Tom Tancredo of Colorado quit his party and ran for the governorship with the Constitution Party, drawing from Tea Party groups first an ultimatum to end his candidacy, then endorsements.[21] He finished a distant second to Democrat John Hickenlooper, but far outpaced Republican Dan Maes who received only 11.1 percent of the vote.

Four candidates for the U.S. House and sixteen for state offices were ballot-listed as Tea Party candidates, almost all of them in Florida. One of the four House candidates ran in New Jersey, the rest in Florida. One of the sixteen state-level candidates ran in New York, the rest in Florida. All of these received less than

---

[19] "Mike McIntyre (NC7) Says, 'We Need to Repeal NAFTA!'," *NC Tea Party* (February 18th 2011).

[20] Tiffany Stanley, "Meet 2010's Tea Party Democrats," *The New Republic* (October 27th 2010).

[21] Allison Sherry, "Colorado Tea Partyers say Tancredo betrayed them," *Denver Post*, (July 26th 2010); Paul Steinhauser, "Tancredo Gets Big Tea Party Endorsement," CNN (October 25th 2010.

11 percent of the vote, and none seemed to affect the outcome of their election.[22]

Politics, of course, is a dirty business. Some independent Tea Party candidates have been accused of being imposters. Two Democratic Party officials in Michigan pleaded no contest to felony charges related to their attempts at putting fake Tea Party candidates on the ballot to siphon votes from Republicans.[23] Similar accusations were made in Florida where almost all of the ballot-listed Tea Party candidates competed.[24]

The Tea Party Versus the Republican Party Establishment

Though almost all of the Tea Party's electoral activism takes place within the Republican Party, it doesn't necessarily help the Republican establishment. This is evidenced by the neoconservative criticism of the Tea Party's small-government ideology.

In October 2010, 87 percent of local Tea Party organizers canvassed by the *Washington Post* expressed dissatisfaction with mainstream Republican Party leaders.[25] Tea Party candidates have clashed with and challenged the Republican establishment, even unseating incumbent Republicans.

In Alaska, incumbent Republican Senator Lisa Murkowski lost in the primary election to Tea Party candidate Joe Miller; however she won the general election as a write-in candidate.

Republican Utah Senator Robert Bennett lost in the primary to Tea Party–backed lawyer Mike Lee who won the general election in a landslide victory.

In Kentucky, Ron Paul's son, Rand Paul, defeated Trey Grayson in the primary. Although Trey Grayson wasn't an incumbent, he enjoyed overwhelming support from establishment Republicans

---

[22] "Ballot-Listed Tea Party Candidates Did Not 'Spoil' Any Election for the Republican Nominee," *Ballot Access News*, (January 21st 2011).

[23] Rachel Rose Hartman, "Second Michigan Democrat Pleads No Contest in 'Fake' Tea Party Scheme," *Yahoo! News* (November 22nd 2011).

[24] Rachel Rose Hartman, "Florida Tea Party Hopeful Denies Backing from Democratic Rep. Grayson" (June 22nd 2011).

[25] "An Up-Close Look at the Tea Party and Its Role in the Midterm Elections," *Washington Post* (December 19th 2011).

despite being a former Democrat. Rand Paul went on to win election to the Senate.

A similar situation occurred in Florida where Tea Party–backed Marco Rubio defeated one time GOP star, Governor Charlie Crist, who decided to run in the general election as an independent. Rubio won easily.

In Delaware, after Republican voters chose Tea Party–supported Christine O'Donnell over Michael Castle, Bush advisor Karl Rove criticized her as unelectable and the voters who chose her as damaging to the Republican cause, further highlighting the rift between the Tea Party and establishment Republican figures, who sought ways to criticize the Tea Party without appearing unconservative.

Reason Magazine's Nick Gillespie and Matt Welch wrote in a *Los Angeles Times* column:

> Rather than serving as shock troops for GOP incumbents against Democrats, Tea Party activists have demonstrated a willingness to unseat even electable Republicans in favor of candidates who take seriously their mostly single-issue concern of limited government.[26]

The American Spectator's James Antle wrote:

> Rank-and-file conservatives no longer trust the Republican establishment. They don't trust big-spending incumbents. They don't even trust conservative magazines, websites, and commentators who in their view run down conservative candidates.[27]

The tension between allegiance to party and allegiance to the idea of small government continued within the Tea Party movement in the 2012 election cycle.

Another ideological tension also became hard to miss, the tension between fiscal conservatives and the many social conservatives who flocked to the Tea Party banner, either as the most ready venue for expressing frustration, or for solidarity with the basic

---

[26] Nick Gillespie and Matt Welch, "In U.S. Politics, the Independents Have It," *Los Angeles Times* (July 26th 2011).

[27] James Antle, III, "Crossing the Delaware," *American Spectator* (September 15th 2010).

message, or to co-opt the movement's energy for their own aims. This dynamic was already visible before the 2010 elections. As Danielle Bean wrote in the *Washington Post*:

> Both the religious right and the Tea Party movement might find themselves backing many of the same candidates, but that does not necessarily make then political allies. In fact, as November elections grow nearer, I expect we'll see a fair number of push and pull between these two groups, as they compete to influence the political stances and win the attention of conservative candidates. The most successful candidates will be those who manage to please both kinds of conservatives, using good old-fashioned politics to convince each other that their concerns are a priority. Can a candidate truly prioritize both social issues and fiscal ones?[28]

These tensions notwithstanding, most Republicans found enough common ideological ground with the Tea Party to harness their support. They dusted off their rhetoric of limited government and used it with great success, delivering one of the most stunning Republican electoral victories ever.

Though some in the media tried to downplay the Tea Party's impact, for example by headlines like "Just 32% of Tea Party Candidates win,"[29] the Tea Party movement largely defined the 2010 midterm elections. For any new movement, 32 percent electoral success is spectacular! The effectiveness of the candidates elected under the Tea Party banner, however, remained to be seen.

Even before the 2010 elections, many long-time small-government advocates were doubtful. In September 2010, libertarian writer Lew Rockwell expressed his skepticism about victorious Tea Party candidates in an article entitled "Prepare to Be Betrayed." Though he applauded the spread of small-government ideology, he pointed out that many within the Tea Party now promoted authoritarian ideas:

> Just as with old-time conservatives, there are many issues on which the Tea Party tends toward inconsistency. The military and the issue

---

[28] Danielle Bean, "Conservative Conflicts Are Brewing," *Washington Post* (September 22nd 2010).

[29] Alexandra Moe, "Just 32% of Tea Party Candidates Win," MSNBC (November 3rd 2010).

of war is a major one. Many have bought into the line that the greatest threat this country faces domestically is the influx of adherents of Islam; in international politics, they tend to favor belligerence toward any regime that is not a captive of U.S. political control. On immigration, the Tea Party ethos favors national IDs and draconian impositions on businesses rather than market solutions like cutting welfare. On social and cultural issues, they can be as confused as the Christian right, believing that it is the job of government to right all wrongs and punish sin.[30]

The Left shared this skepticism. In a *New York Times* column entitled "The Grand Old Plot Against the Tea Party," leftist columnist Frank Rich wrote:

> But whatever Tuesday's results, this much is certain: the Tea Party's hopes of actually effecting change in Washington will start being dashed the morning after. The ordinary Americans in this movement lack the numbers and financial clout to muscle their way into the back rooms of Republican power no matter how well their candidates perform. . . .
>
> What the Tea Party ostensibly wants most—less government spending and smaller federal deficits—is not remotely happening on the country club GOP's watch. The elites have no serious plans to cut anything except taxes and regulation of their favorite industries.[31]

Following the Republican successes of 2010, the attitude of the GOP changed almost immediately. Perhaps the most candid of comments came from former Republican Senate Majority Leader Trent Lott, who spoke to the *Washington Post* about the incoming class of GOP freshmen: "We don't need a lot of Jim DeMint disciples. As soon as they get here, we need to co-opt them." The grand strategists of the GOP echoed the sentiments of Lott. Karl Rove told his interviewer from *Der Spiegel* that the Tea Party members are "not sophisticated" and "It's not like these people have read the economist Friedrich August von Hayek."[32] In fact quite a number of Tea Partiers have indeed read *The Road to Serfdom*.

---

[30] Llewellyn H. Rockwell, Jr. "Prepare to Be Betrayed," LewRockwell.com (September 22nd 2010).

[31] Frank Rich, "The Grand Old Plot Against the Tea Party," *New York Times* (October 30th 2010).

[32] "Obama Has Turned Out to Be an Utter Disaster," *Spiegel* (October 19th 2011).

Whether through hypocrisy or co-opting, the Tea Party politicians in Congress were quick to live down to these expectations. Their greatest success was a very modest one. Tea Party pressure likely intensified the debate in the summer of 2011 over raising the debt ceiling prior to its passage—with the support of many formerly Tea Party–identified candidates.

The left claimed that not raising the debt ceiling would cause a government shutdown. Tea Party favorite Senator Rand Paul, along with others, claimed that raising the debt ceiling gave the government yet another pass on their irresponsibility, which only made the United States debt problems more severe and temporarily delayed their consequences.

Nick Gillespie and Matt Welch wrote:

> The only reason Washington is even talking about proposals to slow the growth of government spending, instead of robotically jacking up the nation's credit line for the 11th time in a decade, is that a large, decentralized group of citizen activists has spent the last few years loudly telling politicians from both parties one consistent message: restrain your own power or face our wrath.

Gillespie and Welch succinctly stated: "It's becoming more and more clear to Tea Party activists and their analogues on issues from education reform to drug legalization that success in politics is directly proportional to independence from the two major political parties." They explain why the GOP and specifically Speaker John Boehner might take the Tea Party seriously:

> Boehner is not holding the line on debt ceiling negotiations out of any evidence of sense of principle, he's doing it because the Tea Party helped send more than 90 brand-spanking new representatives and senators to Washington last fall, and those people are talking and acting differently than the 21st-century Republicans Americans have grown to hate. He knows that if he continues to disrespect the limited government tradition, these activists will punish him and his party come 2012.
>
> This is the enduring lesson of the Tea Party, and it's one that any sort of political group would do well to emulate: by refusing to be cowed by one of the major parties, and promising to inflict damage if its aims are ignored, this grassroots uprising shows how political independents can force mainstream parties to do their bidding.[33]

---

[33] Nick Gillespie and Matt Welch, "In U.S. Politics, the Independents Have It," *Los Angeles Times* (July 26th 2011).

This is high praise for merely delaying a decision antithetical to the Tea Party movement. The increased debt ceiling passed after the media had been saturated by hysterical accusations of uncompromising Tea Party fanatics attempting to blow up government. A majority of the House of Representatives Tea Party Caucus voted in favor of it.[34]

President Obama signed the Budget Control Act of 2011 into law on August 2nd 2011, raising the debt ceiling. After the vote, the proportion of people with an unfavorable view of the Tea Party soared to 40 percent.[35] This is likely because of *both* the apoplexy in the media about radical Tea Partiers attempting to destroy the government *and* the betrayal felt by many Tea Party sympathizers. Another increase to the debt ceiling passed in January 2012 with no media attention or public debate.

Ron Paul, who had refused to join the Tea Party Caucus when it was formed after the 2010 election, anticipated the 'betrayal'. His chief of staff wrote: "Congressman Paul decided not to join the Tea Party Caucus. . . . He strongly believes the Tea Party movement should remain a grassroots phenomenon, rather than being co-opted by Washington or any political party."[36]

The smell of a sell-out wasn't confined to the debt ceiling issue. Thirty-one out of forty newly elected Tea Party candidates in the House supported extending the Patriot Act, in February 2011.[37] Though this move was likely supported by the growing faction of the Tea Party which favored American greatness through interminable military intervention, other elements of the Tea Party felt betrayed.

The Tea Party candidates offered no noticeable resistance to the National Defense Authorization Act of 2012, which authorized indefinite detention of American citizens without trial or probable cause, nor to what was effectively a bailout of European banks by the U.S. Federal Reserve in October 2011.

---

[34] Pat Garofalo, "Tea Party Bluffers: Tea Party Caucus Votes to Raise the Debt Ceiling Despite Not Receiving Demands," *Think Progress* (August 2nd 2011).

[35] "Documents: The Full Results from the New York Times and CBS News Poll," *New York Times* (August 4th 2011).

[36] Patrick Brendel, "Report: Ron Paul Not Joining House Tea Party Caucus," *American Independent* (November 17th 2010).

[37] John Tyner, "How Did (Tea Party) Patriots Act?" LewRockwell.com (February 10th 2011).

The 2012 Elections

The Tea Party had secured the Republicans' victory in the 2010 midterm elections. Before those elections both Democrats and Republicans may have underestimated the power of the Tea Party to mobilize voters. Members of Congress elected with Tea Party support in 2010 were united in their professed intention to implement deep cuts in federal spending along with lower taxes.

In 2012 the situation was very different. The Tea Party's involvement in the 2012 GOP presidential primaries was minimal, owing to divisions over whom to endorse as well as lack of enthusiasm for all the candidates. Overall Tea Party activities declined steeply following the 2010 elections.

Tea Party groups across the nation have shifted their focus away from national politics to local action. A shift in the focus and operational activities of the Tea Party has also affected the movement's national visibility and influence. Most Tea Party chapters, rather than staging public events, are in the process of integrating into the Republican Party's structures and electing their own candidates. The presidential candidates closest to the Tea Party were Ron Paul, whose candidacy was blocked by the Republican establishment, and Herman Cain and Michele Bachmann, both furiously vilified by the mainstream media.

The 'moderate' (left) wing of the Republican Party, brutalized the previous November, returned to Capitol Hill completely demoralized. It was unlikely to collude with Democrats to maintain that party's favorite social programs. These Republicans, however, were still very vocal in supporting the Democrats' interventionist foreign policy. Some, like Senators McCain and Graham, were even more interventionist than the President and his foreign policy establishment.

Among the most visible liberal Republicans, as seen from the Tea Party's perspective, are Mitt Romney, John Boehner, Rudy Giuliani, Scott Brown, Peggy Noonan, Chris Gibson, Joseph Cao, Jon Huntsman, Jr., Amo Houghton, Colin Powell, Charlie Dent, Michael Grimm, Chris Smith, Senators John McCain, Chuck Grassley, Susan Collins, and Lindsey Graham, to name a few. Some long-time Republicans have spoken out for more progressive taxation than the Tea Partiers can stomach, including Arnold Schwarzenegger, Jim Jeffords, Olympia Snowe, David Stockman, Newt Gingrich, Paul O'Neill, Bruce Bartlett, and Sheila Bair.

Many Tea Party members did not vote on Election Day due to their disappointment with the Romney-Ryan ticket. Ron Paul's supporters shared his pessimistic assessment of the elections:

> I don't think there's enough difference between the two candidates, and I assume the victor today will be the status quo. We're going to continue with basically the same policies that we've had for a long time, so I don't see the election, the way it's turning out, to be very crucial at all.[38]

According to libertarian journalist Justin Raimondo:

> Conservatives will claim it's because Romney stood for nothing—and that's true in terms of domestic policy. He reversed himself on every major domestic issue, from health care to abortion and tax policy. But on foreign policy he *did* stand for something: a huge increase in the military budget in spite of our looming bankruptcy, unconditional support for Israel on each and every issue, and war with Iran. This was the main dividing line between the Ron Paulians and the Romneyites, and the main reason why no endorsement from Paul (the elder) was forthcoming. Given the closeness of the election in several key states, particularly Ohio—the state that put the President over the top—support from Paul's voters would have made the difference. Ron got over 113,000 votes there in the GOP primary. And that made all the difference.[39]

In the 2012 elections, not only did President Obama, the nemesis of the Tea Party, win an impressive re-election with a 3.5 percent advantage but several congressional candidates closest to the Tea Party lost, such as Allen West in Florida and Richard Mourdock in Indiana.

On the other hand, both the House and the Senate became more fiscally conservative with only five Tea Party caucus congressmen losing their seats. It's a pretty good survival rate with the country moving decisively to the left. With the election to the Senate of Ted Cruz of Texas and Jeff Flake from Arizona, the Tea Party caucus is stronger in the Senate than ever. A prominent Tea

---

[38] http://politicalticker.blogs.cnn.com/2012/11/06/ron-paul-foresees-2012-outcome.

[39] http://original.antiwar.com/justin/2012/11/06/election-2012-ron-pauls-revenge.

Party figure, Republican Senator Jim DeMint, left the Senate to become president of the influential Heritage Foundation, a policy think tank of the Republican Party. "The Tea Party is not a political party; it's an informal community of Americans who support a set of fiscally conservative issues," says FreedomWorks Tea Partier Matt Kibbe. "And when you take a look at the roster of new fiscal conservatives being sent to Congress next year, it's clear our issues are winning."[40]

The Tea Party's followers in Congress have made dramatic federal spending cuts the centerpiece of an economic message that has dominated the national debate. It was expected that reductions in domestic and defense spending in a process known as sequestration would make some progress toward the Tea Party's goal of cutting government spending.

No Tea Party Candidate

There was no clear Tea Party candidate for the presidency. There was a procession of short-lived Tea Party favorites one after another, as Michele Bachmann, Ron Paul, Herman Cain, Donald Trump, Rick Perry, and even Newt Gingrich were the preference of most Tea Partiers at one time or another. The nomination of Mitt Romney symbolized, however, that the Tea Party influence over the GOP was very limited.

As soon as the Tea Party appeared as a formidable force, conservative groups like Americans for Prosperity, TheTeaParty.net, and FreedomWorks—staffed by experienced political organizers offered training and organizational support. This institutional support allowed the Tea Party to build up a formidable political force, but it has been far less successful at achieving its substantive goals. The Tea Party couldn't stop the passage of Obamacare, and while the Tea Party pushed deficit reduction to the top of the agenda, it has not succeeded in doing anything to reduce the size of government.

Most Republican candidates received some announcement of Tea Party support: Newt Gingrich got the support of one hundred Tea Party leaders from twenty-five states who announced that they

---

[40] Meredith Jessup, "Tea Party vs. Progressive Republicans: Battle for the Soul of the GOP," *The Blaze* (December 3rd 2012).

would form a coalition called Tea Partiers with Newt.[41] Occasionally, these endorsements would be condemned as a betrayal by other Tea Partiers, as when a Tea Party star, South Carolina Governor Nikki Haley, endorsed Mitt Romney. Many see it as a testimony to the Tea Party's diluted image and confused message that such ideologically disparate candidates as Romney and Gingrich could receive Tea Party support. As a result, many of the early Tea Partiers who were exclusively libertarian or fiscal conservative now pursue their goals independent of any Tea Party affiliation. They believe either that the Tea Parties have strayed too far from their message, or that the Tea Party image has become too divisive and tarnished—too much of a burden to whatever legislation or process they are attempting to effect.

Why were Tea Party members disappointed in the Romney-Ryan ticket? Republican frontrunner, Mitt Romney, an establishment figure who tried to please everyone, could not energize the Tea Party followers. As BlogTalkRadio (popular among Tea Partiers) emphasized before the 2012 elections:

> . . . everyone seems to be jumping for joy, celebrating and acting like our country is going to be saved by 'America's Comeback Team'. The real question for the day is, will Tea Partiers ignore the past history of both Mitt Romney and Paul Ryan and vote for a new liberal progressive administration to replace the existing liberal progressive administration? That really is the question of the day! The addition of Paul Ryan to the GOP Presidential platform did not suddenly make the GOP a Constitutional or Conservative establishment. The selection of Paul Ryan for Mitt Romney's VP did not change the fact that the GOP's chosen child Mitt Romney is very much a liberal progressive and so is Paul Ryan. Paul Ryan's voting record, supports a liberal progressive agenda. . . . Paul Ryan is the wrong Paul![42]

The theory that Republicans could win elections if their nominee were conservative enough to fit the Tea Party ideology was challenged by critics of the Tea Party who noted that

---

[41] Read more: http://dailycaller.com/2012/01/19/exclusive-100-tea-party-leaders-to-announce-support-for-newt/#ixzz2Utr5KT2u.

[42] "America's Comeback Team: Another Liberal Progressive Agenda," *American Statesman* (August 13th 2012).

The Religious Right and Tea Party groups are making the case that Romney could have won if he had more clearly and unambiguously embraced their policies. They are determined to force the Republican Party to stop nominating 'moderates', on the shaky premise that compromise has cost the party at the polls.[43]

At the local level, however, the Tea Party movement remains dedicated to fiscal conservatism and limited government. In some regions, particularly the Bible belt and Texas, it is also socially conservative, but a movement calling itself a 'Tea Party' is unlikely ever to stray completely from fiscal conservatism.

Though they have a less visible presence after the setback of 2012, many continue to organize and gain experience in political activism, fundraising, and the legislative process. They continue to infiltrate the Republican Party, at times finding themselves welcome, at times not. They are preparing for tomorrow's political struggles and will surely continue to make themselves heard.

Most Tea Party followers were angered by President Obama being re-elected to provide even more to his constituencies of the poor and crony capitalists alike and to enact more than $600 billion in tax increases on the 'wealthy', while Republican leaders agreed to allow him more federal borrowing without anything in return. Although Democratic and Republican establishment leaders are pointing fingers, Tea Party supporters in Congress are happily accepting credit for the cuts. As Clinton's Labor Secretary and liberal guru Robert Reich pointed out, sequestration was being heralded as a victory by Tea Party members of Congress. He quotes Republican Congressman from Kansas Tim Huelskamp, a Tea Partier elected in 2010, who said of the cuts: "This will be the first significant Tea Party victory in that we got what we set out to do in changing Washington." Reflecting the views of many leftist Democrats Reich continued:

> Sequestration is only the start. What they set out to do was not simply change Washington but eviscerate the U.S. government—"drown it in the bathtub," in the words of their guru Grover Norquist—slashing Social Security and Medicare, ending worker protections we've had since the 1930s, eroding civil rights and voting rights, terminat-

---

[43] "Which Way Is Right? With Chris Ladd, the Tea Party vs. Math: A Detailed Look at the 2012 Results," *GOPlifer* (November 26th 2012).

ing programs that have helped the poor for generations, and making it impossible for the government to invest in our future.[44]

This is a pyrrhic Tea Party victory, however, as sequester does not mean real spending cuts, but only small reductions of two or three percent in the amount of the *increases* in the budgets of federal agencies and departments. Each and every agency and department of the federal government will actually have more money to spend in 2013 than they had in 2012, and in every year following through 2021.

Veronique de Rugy of the Mercatus Center at George Mason University writes:

> A further breakdown of the percentage of budget programs reveals that sequestration provides relatively small reductions in spending rates across the board. With sequestration, defense increases 15% (vs. 23%); nondefense discretionary increases 6% (vs. 12%); Medicare increases 62% (vs. 74%); and net interest increases 160% (vs. 179%).[45]

Many Tea Partiers as well as most Americans are misled by the fact that while the sequester projections are spending increases; the Obama Administration and most of the media always call them 'cuts'. When people hear 'cuts', they think that spending has been reduced below current levels, not that spending has increased. Thus, calling a reduced growth rate of projected spending a 'cut' by government leads to a false feeling of victory for Tea Partiers and other fiscal conservatives. In reality it means a growing deficit, increases in the national debt, an even larger burden for future generations of Americans, and the remorseless approach of the hyperinflation-or-default moment.

While Tea Party organizers have insisted that they created a nonpartisan grassroots movement, left-leaning Democrats have argued that Tea Parties were largely created by conservative billionaires like the Koch brothers as well as well as Fox News, as a fake grassroots movement ('astroturf') to combat Obama's vision of the future. We look at this issue in Chapter 4.

---

[44] http://robertreich.org/post/44259531689.

[45] Veronique de Rugy, "Federal Spending Without and With Sequester Cuts" (November 7th 2011), http://mercatus.org/publication/federal-spending-without-sequester-cuts.

Toward the Precipice

Tea Party supporters' fierce animosity toward Washington, and the president in particular, is rooted in deep pessimism about the economic direction of the country and the conviction that the policies of the Obama administration are directed towards destruction of the market economy, disarming of the populace, and creating a permanent majority of minorities based on redistribution of income to political clients (both poor and rich) plundered from the productive middle class and the rich. Most Tea Party supporters believe that Mr. Obama does not share traditional American values and is a 'great divider', irresponsibly exacerbating racial problems and cynically fueling class hatred.

Followers of Ron Paul in the Tea Party movement embrace arguments that government should not provide what individuals can provide for themselves. Most (but not all) consider police and public safety acceptable functions of government, but government should not take from one person's income to provide for another's health or well-being. Many Tea Partiers advocate abolishing the Federal Reserve and Internal Revenue Service entirely. As most Republican candidates are not even close to endorsing these views, so "most of Paul's voters stayed home on Election Day, or else voted for Gary Johnson, the Libertarian standard-bearer this time around."[46]

As far as the Tea Party goes, it always has worked by applying pressure in a more local manner. It runs candidates for the House and Senate. It is the reason, and knows it is the reason, that the Republicans have their majority in the House. If the Tea Party becomes indifferent or sits out an election, the Republicans will lose any hope of a decisive advantage.

The issue still uniting and motivating the mainstream Republican Party and the Tea Party is the deficit-debt crisis—a national debt over one hundred percent of gross domestic product and a budget deficit of over ten percent of GDP. If the deficit continues to grow as it has been doing, then there must be a run on the dollar, double-digit inflation, or even a general government default on its obligations. The deficit cannot be brought under control without shrinking government expenditure. Tea Partiers

---

[46] http://original.antiwar.com/justin/2012/11/06/election-2012-ron-pauls-revenge.

believe it is now too late to avoid disaster merely by limiting the rate of growth of the deficit. The Tea Partiers take the view—shared by the great majority of rank-and-file Republicans—that higher taxes cannot close the deficit.

The Tea Party is an anti-big-government, grass-roots movement. Its supporters believe in the free market solutions to our financial crisis in general and sequestration in particular. Richard Rahn put it this way:

> The debate over sequestration has caused a renewed focus on all of the waste, duplication and inappropriate or nonessential things the federal government does. . . . at some point, the ability of the government to borrow at low cost will run out. At that time, the government will have no choice but to make many activities self-supporting and privatize them. Smart politicians will begin proposing such solutions now—rather than pushing for more destructive tax increases.[47]

Tea Partiers vowed to purge the Republican Party of officials they consider 'sellouts' or not rightwing enough and to oust the Democrats perceived by most Tea Partiers as socialists. Most Tea Party supporters are united in their belief that the Obama administration has curtailed individual liberty and grossly overstepped its constitutional powers, that it is destroying the America we love, is fiscally irresponsible, and is serving its rich supporters, solidifying the crony socialism emerging as the new political and economic system of America. They do not see any viable alternative in the present Republican leadership.

Rank-and-file Tea Party supporters insist that if they lost any chance of repealing federal legislation like Obamacare on the federal level, they would press states to nullify or ignore it. Most radical Tea Party branches also plan to focus on the hard-core libertarian issue of secession from 'unconstitutional federal tyranny'.

The Tea Party's focus on individual liberty, fiscal conservatism, and limited government remains a powerful driving force in shaping Republican policies. The Tea Party's agenda has not been implemented: no agencies, bureaus, commissions or departments have

---

[47] Richard Rahn, "Privatize Almost Everything. With Money Running Low, Government Functions Become Unviable," *Washington Times* (April 30th 2013).

been shut down, Obamacare has not been repealed, and federal spending has only increased.

At the state and local levels, however, there is more reason for optimism. The Tea Party movement has been a palpable influence for tax cuts, budget discipline, and gun rights in various states.[48] The full extent of Tea Party influence is difficult to gauge. Sometimes its efforts are indistinguishable from those of other Republicans, and sometimes initiatives and politicians receive mixed support from Tea Party groups.

According to Bill Bike, "The history of the Republican Party shows that the effort of Karl Rove and his Conservative Victory Project and Crossroads political groups to neutralize the Tea Party wing of the GOP likely is doomed."[49] The Tea Party movement won and kept Congressional seats in 2010 and 2012. The GOP establishment was unable to destroy or control this grass roots conservative and libertarian movement. It is noteworthy that Crossroads GPS, the Karl Rove–affiliated group that Senate Majority Whip Dick Durbin asked the IRS Commissioner Shulman in a letter to investigate, escaped the "special scrutiny" the IRS reserved for Tea Party groups.[50] Obama's apparatchiks don't see neoconservatism as the enemy—why should they?—but they do have the Tea Party in their sights.

The Tea Party movement remains primarily centered on advocacy of small government, with no consensus on foreign policy or social and cultural issues, though one issue that does also unite them is defense of gun rights. The identity of the Tea Party is still developing. Local groups struggle with national ones, and libertarian factions struggle with those who advocate social conservatism and American exceptionalism. A surprising alignment between evangelicals and libertarians is clearly visible under the banner of the Tea Party.[51] Rand Paul is supported by both evangelicals and libertarians.

---

[48] Louis Jacobson, "Gauging the Effect of the Movement on the 2011 Legislative Sessions Is a Little Like Reading Tea Leaves," *National Conference of State Legislatures* (September 2011).

[49] William Bike, "Rove Effort to Destroy Tea Party May Be Doomed," OpEdNews (March 13th 2013).

[50] http://news.investors.com/ibd-editorials/060413-658777-stephanie-cutter-met-with-douglas-shulman-at-white-house.htm#ixzz2VMQYZAbN.

[51] For an illuminating and distinctively evangelical take on the Tea Party, see David Brody, *The Teavangelicals* (Zondervan, 2012).

Yet most Tea Partiers have not given up all hope of effective political leadership in national politics. For example, Wisconsin Governor Scott Walker endeared himself to the Tea Party when he and the GOP-led state legislature stripped collective bargaining privileges from the state's public employees and successfully survived a recall election against the assembled forces of the left.

"Gov. Walker has a lot going for him and he'd be a very appealing candidate in a state like Iowa for the caucuses," says Bob Vander Plaats, an influential player in the Iowa Tea party movement, where Walker recently spoke. "Not only is he right on a lot of issues, he's been very bold and courageous on his leadership on a lot of those issues. And being a neighbor to Iowa doesn't guarantee you success but it certainly doesn't hurt."[52]

---

[52] Nicole Debevec, "Politics 2014: Roads to 2014, 2016 Become Rocky as Retirements Mount," http://www.upi.com/Top_News/US/2013/06/02/Politics-2014-Roads-to-2014-2016-become-rocky-as-retirements-mount/UPI-94391370161800/#ixzz2VNsF6yPo.

2

How the Tea Party Began

As with most vital historical movements, the ideas, the discontent, the agitation existed long before they coalesced into anything you could give a name to. Before the modern Tea Party movement, its ideas already existed and were promoted explicitly by literally hundreds of different organizations, including Citizens for a Sound Economy, the Foundation for Economic Education, the Cato Institute, and the National Rifle Association. The Tenth Amendment Center was formed in 2006, a few years before the emergence of the Tea Party.

So when did the Tea Party begin?

Many commentators point to February 19th 2009, when Rick Santelli, a CNBC commentator, appeared on television raging against the federal government's bailout of irresponsible borrowers in the country's ongoing mortgage crisis. "The government is promoting bad behavior," he declared, standing on the trading floor of the CME Group in Chicago. Turning to the traders working behind him, he said, "This is America! How many of you people want to pay for your neighbor's mortgage that has an extra bathroom and can't pay their bills?" The traders around Santelli stopped their work and booed. Santelli then looked back at the camera, "President Obama, are you listening?"

He added: "We're thinking of having a Chicago tea party in July. All you capitalists that want to show up to Lake Michigan, I'm going to start organizing!"[1] The video of his rant went viral that same day and led to protests in at least forty cities across the coun-

---

[1] "Santelli's Tea Party," CNBC (February 19th 2009). It's telling that Santelli didn't need to explain what he meant by "a tea party."

try on February 27th.[2] According to many prominent accounts, this marked the birth of the modern Tea Party movement.[3]

Scott Rasmussen and Douglas Schoen declare: "we believe it [the Tea Party Movement] began in 1992, with the unprecedented electoral success of Ross Perot [*sic*]." They observe that "One could see the beginning of this resurgence on December 16th, 2007, in Boston" when "2008 presidential candidate and right-wing populist leader Ron Paul led supporters from the State House to Faneuil Hall." This isn't entirely accurate. The event was organized and promoted without any initiative from Ron Paul or his campaign. Ron Paul did not attend the event either, though his son, future Senator Rand Paul, accepted the organizers' invitation to speak at Faneuil Hall. The authors go on to assert "The Tea Party movement as we know it today was set in motion on February 19th, 2009, when CNBC financial analyst Rick Santelli made an impromptu speech on the floor of the Chicago Mercantile Exchange."[4]

In *Give Us Liberty: A Tea Party Manifesto*, Dick Armey and Matt Kibbe begin: "It's difficult to say exactly when the modern Tea Party movement came into being." They then discuss growing outrage and the government's financial irresponsibility in 2009, culminating in Rick Santelli's rant.[5]

Kate Zernike's *Boiling Mad: Inside Tea Party America*, begins with a mention of Santelli's rant then notes: "In fact, the first tea party had already taken place three days earlier in Seattle, led by a twenty-nine-year-old woman named Keli Carender." Zernike makes frequent mention of the prominence of Ron Paul supporters in Tea Party events,[6] but no mention of the first modern polit-

---

[2] Judson Berger, "Modern-Day Tea Parties Give Taxpayers Chance to Scream for Better Representation," Fox News (April 9th 2009).

[3] See for instance Jim Geraghty, "A Short History of the Tea Parties," *National Review Online: The Campaign Spot* (January 28th 2011); Jill Lepore, *The Whites of Their Eyes: The Tea Party's Revolution and the Battle Over American History* (Princeton: Princeton University Press, 2010), 3; Susan Page and Naomi Jagoda, "What Is the Tea Party? A State of Mind," *USA Today* (July 8th 2010).

[4] *Mad as Hell: How the Tea Party Movement Is Fundamentally Remaking Our Two-Party System* (New York: Harper, 2010), 116, 120.

[5] Dick Armey and Matt Kibbe, *Give Us Liberty: A Tea Party Manifesto* (New York: HarperCollins, 2010), 11–19.

[6] Kate Zernike, *Boiling Mad, Inside Tea Party America* (New York: Times Books, 2010), 2, 19, 26, 65, 151, 154.

ical event which called itself a tea party—a 2007 online fundraiser for Ron Paul, coupled with protests which mimicked the original 1773 Tea Party.

Santelli's rant did prompt many people to action and did draw a lot of media attention, but the earlier event has a better claim to being the first incarnation of the modern Tea Party. On December 16th, 2007, over a year before the now-famous rant, a crowd of protesters braved below-freezing temperatures for a "tea party" in Columbus, Ohio, to hear speeches and watch activists throw boxes representing the IRS, the Federal Reserve, and other symbols of big government into the Scioto River.[7] Similar protests occurred in cities across the country that day, including Boston—home of the original tea party. These were the first modern political events to embrace the title "Tea Party."

Those 2007 tea parties were conducted by supporters of the libertarian Texas Congressman Ron Paul who was seeking the Republican presidential nomination. Much of the rhetoric of these protests matched that of the later, 2009 protests which attracted so much more media attention. Although some participants of the later Tea Party movement have important disagreements with Ron Paul and his supporters, the Ron Paul campaign marks the beginning of the Tea Party's story.

The Ron Paul Revolution Begins, Quietly

The Ron Paul presidential campaign of 2008 produced the first modern Tea Party event, and many Ron Paul supporters later became prominent in the Tea Party.[8] Both the Paul Campaign and the Tea Party were largely fueled by individual activism—at least in their earliest days—and both considered themselves to be unfairly treated by the media.

When Ron Paul announced his entry into the 2008 presidential race on March 12th, 2007, many long-time critics of big government were thrilled. For the mainstream media, however, it was a nonevent. More airtime was given to Nebraska Senator Chuck

---

[7] Jacob Huebert, "As Ohio Goes . . .," *LRC Blog* (December 16th 2007), www.lewrockwell.com/blog/lewrw/archives/17780.html.

[8] Kate Zernike, *Boiling Mad: Inside Tea Party America* (New York: Times Books, 2010), 2, 19, 26, 65, 151, 154.

Hagel's announcement that he would not run for president and former Senator Fred Thompson's declaration that he might run.[9] Most voters didn't pay much attention either; a poll taken later that month by McLaughlin and Associates showed Paul's support among Republicans and independents at a statistical 0 percent, putting him below non-candidate Hagel and former New York Governor George Pataki, who also wasn't running.[10]

Little reason existed for high expectations. In fact, when friends urged him to run, Paul himself was, in his words, "not at all convinced that a sizable enough national constituency existed for a campaign based on liberty and the Constitution" to sustain a viable campaign.[11] Many of Paul's supporters at that time hoped his campaign would be useful primarily for introducing libertarian ideas to a broader audience. Dr. Paul had already been through that once as the Libertarian Party presidential candidate in 1998, when he received about 0.5 percent of the popular vote.[12]

While the mainstream media mostly ignored Paul's campaign for months,[13] Paul's fans did what they could to compensate by taking to the Internet to spread the word. His popularity spread by word of mouth. Eventually, whenever there was an online poll, Paul's fans would co-ordinate their activities on blogs and Internet forums, and swoop in, ensuring his success. If there was an online news story about the election which ignored Ron Paul, his supporters made themselves heard in the reader comments wherever these were available.

Accusation of outright censorship against him were not uncommon and perhaps not entirely without merit. He was excluded from a *Los Angeles Times* poll,[14] unmentioned in the *Washington*

---

[9] Murray Sabrin, "Can Ron Paul Win?" LewRockwell.com (March 14th 2007).

[10] "White House 2008: Republican Nomination (p.2)" Polling Report.com.

[11] Ron Paul, *The Revolution: A Manisfesto* (New York: Grand Central, 2008), 4.

[12] David Leip, "1988 Presidential Election Results," *Dave Leip's Atlas of U.S. Presidential Elections.*

[13] See for instance Eric Garris, "MSM's 'Ron Paul Eraser' Hard at Work," LewRockwell.com.

[14] "Los Angeles Times EXCLUDES Ron Paul from 'On the Trail' Politics Section," *Ron Paul Forums* (December 31st 2007).

Post's post-debate commentary,[15] minimized in a *Miami Herald* article,[16] and omitted from the *BCC News*'s election guide and later Gallup and Rasmussen Polls.[17] He was ignored in a *New York Times* column lamenting the GOP's militancy[18]—very strange given his vociferous and long-standing opposition to undeclared wars. A pool run by future Tea Party icon Glenn Beck, who then worked for CNN, also excluded Ron Paul.[19] He received by far the least amount of time in televised debates.

Using the social networking website meetup.com (Facebook was much less prominent than it is today), Paul's supporters formed local clubs which worked to promote Ron Paul and his campaign. Supporters held signs by interstate highways during rush hours. They created their own advertisements and placed them in newspapers, on billboards, or in backyards. They unfurled homemade banners at public events and sought exposure anywhere they could find crowds or cameras. Ron Paul became wildly popular on YouTube where videos related to him were viewed many more times than those featuring any other candidate. According to a study by law professor Edward Lee, the second most popular candidate on YouTube, Hillary Clinton, received about half as many views as Dr. Paul.[20]

These activities occurred at the initiative of Ron Paul's supporters with no direction from his campaign. People felt inspired to promote him, so they organized and did so. Supporters in different parts of the country shared ideas with each other online, but no central authority co-ordinated their efforts.

Ron Paul's support rose steadily, though he continued to receive either minimal attention or open hostility from the mainstream press. Pundits on MSNBC's *Hardball* at first reviewed all

---

[15] Michael D. Shear and Dan Balz, "In Debate, Romney and Giuliani Clash on Immigration Issues," *Washington Post* (November 29th 2007).

[16] *Miami Herald*, "Miami Herald Poll: McCain rising, Giuliani fading," Beth Reinhard, Breanne Gilpatrick and Marc Caputo (January 23rd 2008).

[17] "Censoring Ron Paul (Then and Now)," lostrepublic.us (August 8th 2009).

[18.] Bob Herbert, "Rombo and the G.O.P.," *New York Times* (December 1st 2007).

[19] "Glenn Beck at It Again," dailypaul.com (November 16th 2007).

[20] J.H. Huebert, "Little-Known Candidate Big on YouTube," *Columbus Dispatch* (August 25th 2007).

the candidates except Ron Paul. They discussed helping the American voters "focus on the real candidates," by trimming the field which would be a "great service to the American people." When they eventually mentioned Ron Paul, *New York Magazine*'s Jennifer Senior called him a freeloader, and Chris Matthews talked about how much Rudy Giuliani's campaign benefited from bringing up 9/11 in response to Ron Paul's libertarian arguments.[21]

Among the multitude of Ron Paul–related videos on the web, one called for a website where supporters could pledge donations to Paul's campaign on November 5th, 2008. November 5th had significance for some Paul supporters who associate it with the quasi-libertarian graphic novel and movie *V for Vendetta*.

V for Vendetta makes allusions to Guy Fawkes, well known in Britain as the man who allegedly tried to blow up Parliament with gunpowder on November 5th, 1605 (though some historians now say the whole thing was a frame-up). Supposedly, Guy Fawkes's "gunpowder plot" was part of a conspiracy to put a Catholic on the throne. To this day, November 5th is celebrated across hundreds of thousands of British streets as "Bonfire Night," with effigies of Guy Fawkes burned in the flames. The anarchist-flavored *V for Vendetta* made Guy Fawkes a more general symbol of discontent, disobedience, resistance, and rebellion.

In October 2008, Trevor Lyman, a Florida musician, launched the website ThisNovember5th.com where people made pledges to the Ron Paul Campaign. By November 5th, some 37,000 Ron Paul supporters went to his campaign website and donated more than $4.2 million, setting the single-day record for any GOP candidate thus far in the campaign and the single-day record for online fundraising by any 2008 candidate.[22] The average donation was slightly over a hundred dollars.

Ron Paul's fundraising success at last won the attention of the political and media establishment, some of it quite hostile. Ron Paul supporters were called terrorists on the basis of one fundraiser being held on Guy Fawkes Day.[23]

---

[21] See for instance Sarah Lai Stirland, "'Criminal' Botnet Stumps for Ron Paul, Researchers Allege," Wired.com (October 31st 2007).

[22] "Ron Paul Sets Online Fundraising Record with $4.2 Million in One Day," Fox News (November 6th 2007.

[23] "Kirchick and Sieradski: Factually Wrong on Ron Paul," *The Atlantic*

The *Chicago Tribune*'s Mark Silva noted that the fundraising success would give Paul what he needed to "convince 'the mainstream media'" that he is a viable candidate. Silva added that this served as "proof" that "there may well be big money to be raised, indeed record money, outside the walls of the major parties' castles."[24] Paul even received congratulations from the left, which celebrated his ability to defeat the establishment. *The Nation*'s John Nichols said his readers "can and should be encouraged by the fact that a candidate is breaking the rules and getting a resounding response from grassroots donors."[25]

Political website Politico sought out Trevor Lyman, the November 5th money bomb organizer, to ask how he pulled it off. Other politicians hoping to replicate Paul's success were likely disappointed by his answer: "There's really no officialness about it in any sense. It's just a website that said, 'Hey, let's all donate money on this day.' And once the [online advertising] banners were in place and people could start spreading links, it just propagated virally. And that's really it."[26]

When asked about his fundraising success, Ron Paul was not inclined to take credit for a brilliant stroke. He said that many observers considered his success a technological innovation, when in actuality it was testimony to the power of his ideas.

The December 2007 Tea Party

Other candidates might not have been able to duplicate Ron Paul's fundraising phenomenon, but Lyman intended to not only duplicate, but surpass his original effort. What would be the date of the next event? Joe Bozzi, a co-ordinator of the Columbus, Ohio,

---

(November 13th 2007); David D. Kirkpatrick, "Candidate's Pleased to Remember This Fifth of November," *New York Times* (November 6th 2007); "Glenn Beck at It Again . . ." (November 16th 2007); Glenn Greenwald, "The Ron Paul Phenomenon," Salon.com (November 6th 2007); Peter Glaskowsky, "A Penny for the Guy, a Hundred Bucks for Ron Paul" (November 5th 2007).

[24] Mark Silva, "Ron Paul's 'Money Bomb,' Records and Lessons," *The Swamp* (November 6th 2007).

[25] John Nichols, "The Real Ron Paul Revolution," CBS News (December 18th 2007).

[26] Kenneth P. Vogel, "The Man, the Technique Behind Ron Paul's Haul," *Politico* (November 6th 2007).

Meetup group, made a suggestion on an online Ron Paul forum: December 16th, the anniversary of the Boston Tea Party.[27] The date was soon fixed.

Then another supporter, Bob Dwyer of Dartmouth, Massachusetts, had an additional idea: to hold an event at Boston's Faneuil Hall, where some of the country's founders had hatched plans to respond to British oppression, including the Boston Tea Party. In three weeks, the Boston Ron Paul Meetup group registered a political action committee, raised more than ten thousand dollars, bought radio ads, set up a live webcast, and arranged to use the hall.[28] Meanwhile, Meetup groups in many other cities across the country made their own plans to hold their own tea party themed events.

Ron Paul himself didn't actually attend these rallies. They weren't official campaign events, but at the invitation of organizers, his son, future Senator and Tea Party hero Rand Paul, who until that time had made no appearances of note on the national political stage, came to speak at the Boston event. When the day arrived, more than a thousand people braved a blizzard to pack the hall to hear the candidate's son speak.

The scene looked much like the Tea Party events that would spring up in 2009, complete with "Don't Tread on Me" Gadsden flags and tricorne hats. Rand Paul wasted no time in breaking out the revolutionary rhetoric. He began:

> I'd like to welcome you, sons and daughters of liberty, to the revolution. They say the British scoffed at the American rabble and laughed at the Americans, their imperfect uniforms, their imperfect tactics. They laughed at retreat after retreat of the American army. They laughed right up until Yorktown. Today, you are that American rabble: the disgruntled, the disillusioned, the cynical, the bereaved—bereaved at the loss of liberty. The establishment in their high-rise penthouse laughs at you, they laugh at us . . . but you know what? They're not laughing today.[29]

---

[27] See the post by "jb4ronpaul" at http://www.ronpaulforums.com/showthread.php?26371-November-5th-BLOWBACK.-THINK./page10.

[28] Ben Van Heuvelen, "How Rand Paul Became the Tea Party's Obama," Salon.com (May 14th 2010).

[29] "Rand Paul at Faneuil Hall" (video), http://www.youtube.com/watch?v=oZYs4cNVKqs.

Although it was still relatively early in the day, the younger Paul predicted the money bomb would break records and have a far-reaching effect: "We're going to give them a money bomb so big, so undeniable that it will resonate throughout the political landscape."

Then he marveled at the do-it-yourself nature of the event:

> We had a meeting like this in Nashville, and the woman who was in charge of it is a dentist. She organized a big rally, and it was wonderful, but, you know, the neat thing about it is no one selected her. The campaign didn't pick her. The Meetup group picked her. They got together and formed a Meetup group in Nashville; they hold signs on the Interstate; they are so committed. But they picked their own leader. And I think consequently you may get a better variety of people.

Rand Paul's prediction about the Tea Party money bomb's success and its impact were correct. Some thirty thousand individuals made donations totaling more than $6 million—the most raised on the web in a single day by any candidate, ever.[30]

This sent the campaign's total fundraising for the fourth quarter of 2007 to $18 million—far surpassing its ambitious $12 million goal. The December 16th money bomb also gave Paul the highest fundraising total for the quarter of anyone seeking the Republican presidential nomination.[31]

All of this led to much more media attention, but for all his fundraising, increased media exposure and improved poll numbers, Fox News excluded him entirely from the pre-New Hampshire primary debate in January 2008, breaking from their tradition of the New Hampshire primary by saying they'd only admit candidates with double-digit support.[32] Blogs and alternative news media sources exploded with anger, claiming the exclusion was not so much about the level of Paul's support, but about his ideas. He stood alone among the Republican field in his opposition to war, the Patriot Act, and the Federal Reserve system, and in his belief

---

[30] Jose Antonio Vargas, "Ron Paul Beats Own Fundraising Record," *The Trail* (December 17th 2007).

[31] Andrew Malcolm, "News Shocker: Ron Paul Was the Biggest GOP Fundraiser Last Quarter," *Los Angeles Times* (February 1st 2008).

[32] James Joyner, "Ron Paul Excluded from Fox Debate," Outside the Beltway.

that America's economy was due for a crisis (a belief which would soon prove accurate).

Ron Paul's Ideas

Ron Paul's message has always been rooted in libertarianism, a political philosophy that promotes maximum individual liberty. It holds that people should be allowed to do "anything that's peaceful," as libertarian thinker Leonard E. Read put it.[33] In the words of libertarian theorist and economist Murray Rothbard, "no man or group of men may aggress against the property of anyone else."[34]

In everyday life, almost everyone observes this basic libertarian rule. We don't kill and steal. If we want our neighbor's property we don't threaten him with violence and take it. Instead, we try to persuade him, perhaps offering something in exchange, and if he remains unwilling, we're out of luck. We cannot initiate force against our neighbor to change his personal habits either.

In its purest philosophical form, libertarianism insists simply that force may never be initiated against a person or a person's property by anybody. We probably would not consider this a radical uncompromising stand until we admit to ourselves that all laws, are ultimately backed by a threat of force and that taxes are collected under threat of force.

Some might read this and think: "But then government wouldn't be able to do anything, it wouldn't even exist," to which the most radical libertarians would reply: "Exactly." This small minority of libertarians do indeed call themselves anarchists, though they distinguish themselves from the violent leftist anarchists of the turn of the previous century by calling themselves "anarchocapitalists," "free market anarchists," or "rational anarchists," emphasizing their profound respect for private property. Some libertarian anarchists prefer the term "voluntarists," emphasizing the non-initiation of force principle, or "advocates of a private-law society."[35]

---

[33] Leonard E. Read, *Anything that's Peaceful* (Irvington-on-Hudson: Foundation for Economic Education, 1964).

[34] Murray N. Rothbard, *For a New Liberty: The Libertarian Manifesto* (Auburn: Ludwig von Mises Institute 2006 [1978]), 27.

[35] Hans-Hermann Hoppe, "State or Private-Law Society" (May 9th 2011).

Ron Paul, however, has never been an anarchist. He believes a minimal level of government is appropriate to provide for the common defense against foreign invaders and domestic criminals. He remains a devoted advocate of the United States Constitution.

Like all congressmen, Paul took an oath to uphold the Constitution of the United States. He applies the Constitution according to what he sees as its original meaning and believes modern courts have interpreted it too loosely. He maintains that his fellow lawmakers have disregarded the constitutional limits on their power, leading to an explosive growth of government over the past century. As he explained in his book *The Revolution: A Manifesto*:

> To be sure, the U.S. Constitution is not perfect. Few human contrivances are. But it is a pretty good one, I think, and it defines and limits the scope of government. When we get into the habit of disregarding it or—what is the same thing—interpreting key phrases so broadly as to allow the federal government to do whatever it wants, we do so at our peril.[36]

Paul believes that Congress is only permitted to do the rather short list of things authorized in Article I. Otherwise, the Tenth Amendment reserves all other government power for the states. Although as a moral matter Paul believes in individual rights, he believes that greater legal recognition of so-called "states' rights" would place an urgently needed check on federal power. The Tenth Amendment is discussed in greater detail below in Chapter 4.

Paul appears to be a libertarian first and a constitutionalist second. For example, he begins the chapter on conscription in his latest book, *Liberty Defined*, by invoking the libertarian principle of self-ownership, then uses constitutional arguments to back up his claim.

In the same chapter, he makes a purely libertarian argument against the income tax, even though the power to tax is enshrined in the Constitution.[37] He also demonstrates a willingness to entertain

---

[36] Ron Paul, *The Revolution: A Manifesto* (New York: Grand Central, 2008), 67.

[37] Some tax protesters such as Irwin Schiff dispute whether the income tax as currently implemented is constitutional, though Article I section 8 clearly gives Congress the power "to lay and collect taxes."

the seldom-heard argument that the U.S. Constitution was a step backward for liberty. Namely that the Articles of Confederation which came before it and allowed for almost no major central authority were superior:

> The transition away from the original notion upon which we were founded, that government was to be strictly limited to the protection of individuals from out-of-control government authoritarians, has been going on a long time. . . . The erosion started early, and it could be argued that even the Constitution itself weakened this principle that was embedded in the Articles of Confederation.[38]

Limiting Government

Ron Paul's philosophy calls for greatly reduced taxation, government spending, and regulation—positions commonly associated with "small-government conservatives" and various Republican politicians. However Ron Paul often criticizes other proponents of small government, saying their plans only cut the rate of growth of government or make tiny reductions in the deficit.

Ron Paul seems devoted to meaningfully reducing the size of government. For example, he announced he would repeal the federal income tax and replace it with nothing. In October 2011, in the midst of his campaign for the Republican nomination for president, he unveiled a plan to eliminate five cabinet-level agencies: the Departments of Education, Commerce, Energy, Interior, and Housing and Urban Development.

His supporters consider him exceedingly credible. Long before his fame of recent years, Paul was known in Congress as "Dr. No" for his practice of voting "no" on any bill he considers to be unconstitutional, which was nearly everything. This serves as strong evidence that, if elected President, he would exercise his veto power in the same way.

Opposition to the Federal Reserve

Dr. Paul has said numerous times that he entered politics because of his interest in monetary policy and his concern about fiat money

---

[38] Ron Paul, *Liberty Defined: 50 Essentials Issues that Affect Our Freedom* (New York: Grand Central, 2011), 210–11.

and the Federal Reserve system. He has made opposition to the Federal Reserve Bank (or "Fed") a central part of his message.

As a libertarian, Paul believes money needn't be determined by government, and that allowing government to print (and spend) as much money as it wants—as the Federal Reserve essentially does—is extremely dangerous.[39] As a constitutionalist, Paul also thinks that the Fed is unconstitutional, because the Constitution gives the power to coin money to Congress alone.[40]

Paul's economic views are based in the Austrian school of economics (so named because its early leading thinkers, such as Ludwig von Mises and Friedrich Hayek, happened to be from Austria).

According to Austrian economists, government creation and spending of excessive amounts of fiat money (money that can't be redeemed for gold or some other commodity) creates unsustainable "booms" that eventually result in "busts"—economic recessions or depressions. Excessive expansion of the money supply creates false economic signals and causes resources—land, labor, and capital goods—to become invested in projects which do not reflect true consumer demand. The bust must ensue, to free those resources and allow the economy to restructure.

This view stands in stark contrast to that of mainstream economists, both on the left and on the right, who believe that government control of the money supply is essential for economic growth and stability.

For example, even Milton Friedman's "Chicago" or "Monetarist" school of economics, which is generally considered libertarian, differs from the Austrian school on the issue of money, believing that government should have a limited role, controlling and modestly inflating a national currency. Toward the end of his career, however, Milton Friedman repudiated this view:

> I have attempted to persuade the Federal Reserve System that it was doing the wrong thing and it ought to adopt a different policy. This time was ill-spent because the public-interest characterization of government is basically flawed. . . . We do not regard a businessman as

---

[39] For a concise presentation of this view, see Murray N. Rothbard, *What Has Government Done to Our Money?* (Auburn: Ludwig von Mises Institute, 2008 [1991]).

[40] U.S. Constitution, Art. I Sec. 8.

selflessly devoted to the public interest. We think of a businessman as in business to improve his own welfare, to serve his own interest. . . . Why should we regard government officials differently? They too aim to serve their own interest, and in government as in business we must try to set up institutions under which individuals who intend only their own gain are led by an invisible hand to serve the public interest. The Federal Reserve System puts a great deal of power in the hands of a few people and it is so constructed that it has been in their self-interest to pursue a policy which, I believe, has been very harmful for the public rather than helpful. . . . Clearly, it was not in the self-interest of the Federal Reserve hierarchy to follow the hypothetical policy [of a monetary rule]. It was therefore a waste of time to try to persuade them to do so.[41]

In an essay co-authored by Friedman and Anna J. Schwartz, they stated: "Our own conclusion . . . is that leaving monetary and banking arrangements to the market would have produced a more satisfactory outcome than was actually achieved through government involvement."[42]

Early in his campaign, some of Ron Paul's admirers understandably wondered if monetary policy was the best issue to put at the forefront of a presidential campaign. After all, most people don't understand how the Fed works, and a political campaign doesn't seem like the ideal forum for educating them on this complicated topic.

It turned out, however, to be an extremely popular issue. Even Paul was stunned by how much interest this issue drew, especially when, on a visit to the University of Michigan, some students in the crowd set dollar bills on fire and held them in the air chanting "End the Fed!"—a phrase that would provide the title for a *New York Times* bestselling book by Paul in 2009.[43]

Why did the Federal Reserve issue take off? The recession which began in late 2007 seemed to send many people looking for answers. Some found the predictions of a housing bubble made by

---

[41] Milton Friedman's address at the Western Economic Association, "Economists and Economic Policy," published in *Economic Inquiry* (January 1986).

[42] Milton Friedman and Anna Schwartz, "Has Government Any Role in Money?" *Journal of Monetary Economics* (January 1986), 37–62.

[43] Ron Paul, *End the Fed* (New York: Grand Central, 2009), 4.

Ron Paul in 2001 and 2003.[44] Others found compilations of video clips called "Peter Schiff was right" which went viral during the housing collapse. It shows investor and follower of the Austrian school of economics Peter Schiff being ridiculed on major news programs as he warned of a housing crisis in the years before it began. The video received millions of views.[45]

For those coming from a populist or libertarian background, the secretive Federal Reserve provided an egregious example of an institution protecting the interests of the politically connected elites, socializing the losses of major commercial banks while their profits remained private.

Paul urged his growing number of followers to learn about Austrian economics, which had recently become much easier to do than it ever had been before because of the vast online library of the Ludwig von Mises Institute (mises.org), an organization dedicated to promoting Austrian economics and libertarian thought.[46] Through these and other resources, people learned, became outraged, and joined Paul's opposition to the Federal Reserve System.

Opposition to War

Ron Paul was a staunch opponent of the ongoing U.S. wars in Afghanistan and Iraq. These were main issues in his campaigns in both the 2008 and 2012 presidential races. The issue of foreign policy later divided the Tea Party. To the extent that it was a descendant of the Ron Paul campaign, the Tea Party was anti-war, but this quickly changed to agnosticism toward foreign policy in order to include more people on economic issues. Later a "strong national defense" became a staple of protests organized under the Tea Party banner.

Paul's first and foremost objections to war were moral. Libertarianism is anti-war because modern wars involve killing innocent people—libertarians believe that war entails legalized

---

[44] MSNBC, *Morning Joe* (May 15th 2009); C-Span, Ron Paul's testimony on House floor.

[45] "Peter Schiff Was Right," www.youtube.com/watch?v=2I0QN-FYkpw.

[46] Full disclosure: One of the authors, Dr. Maltsev, is a senior fellow at the Ludwig von Mises Institute.

mass murder.[47] Paul also subscribes to the idea of "just war theory," which he has summarized in this list of principles:

1. War should be fought only in self-defense
2. War should be undertaken only as a last resort
3. A decision to enter war should be made only by a legitimate authority
4. All military responses must be proportional to the threat
5. There must be a reasonable chance of success, and
6. A public declaration notifying all parties is required.[48]

Paul thought that no U.S. foreign intervention in recent decades has satisfied these criteria, and certainly not the wars that began under President Bush, a fellow Republican. Paul didn't believe that these wars were fought in self-defense because the Taliban in Afghanistan and Saddam Hussein in Iraq, evil though they were, never attacked the United States and could not have posed a serious threat to the United States if they had wanted to.

In his campaign, he emphasized the concept of "blowback"— the idea that terrorists have attacked the United States not because "they hate our freedoms," as some politicians would have it, but because, as Paul puts it, "we're over there." Stop meddling, Paul argues, and their primary motivation to attack will go away. He has consistently argued that starting more wars in the Middle East will only encourage more terrorism.[49]

Bush Backlash

One reason that so many people were ready to hear Paul's message in 2008 was because they were angry at President George W. Bush who had promised smaller government but delivered the opposite. As Paul often points out, when Bush ran in 2000, he spoke as though he really wanted a smaller government; even on the ques-

---

[47] See Jacob H. Huebert, "Why Libertarians Oppose War," Antiwar.com (September 10th 2010).

[48] Ron Paul, "Why Are Americans So Angry?" LewRockwell.com (June 29th 2006).

[49] "Republican Debate Transcript, South Carolina," CFR.org (May 15th 2007).

tion of war, the candidate Bush promised a "humble foreign policy" and "no nation building." The reality of the Bush presidency
turned out to be quite different, and the anger of his liberty-
minded supporters was not sated by the often-repeated assertion
that the September 11th attacks 'changed everything'.

For a supporter of limited government, President George W.
Bush was one of the worst presidents ever, making government
bigger and more intrusive in practically every area. For example,
when Bush took office, the federal government spent $1.9 trillion
per year; his final budget was over $3 trillion.[50] From fiscal years
2001 through 2007, Bush increased spending an average of four
percent per year, making him the biggest overall spender, in terms
of annual increase, since at least Jimmy Carter. He increased military spending an average of 6.7 percent per year, making him the
biggest military spender since Franklin Delano Roosevelt.[51]
Meanwhile, the Federal Register, in which federal regulations are
published, continued to grow, from 64,438 pages in 2001 to
78,090 in 2007.[52]

As recently as 1996, abolishing the Department of Education
(which was created relatively recently, under the Carter
Administration) was part of the Republican Party platform.[53]
Bush, however, not only failed to seek its abolition, he promoted
and signed the No Child Left Behind Act, which asserted unprecedented federal control over America's classrooms. President Bush
also promoted and signed the Medicare Part D, a massive new
entitlement that will cost $1 trillion over the course of a decade.[54]
As *Weekly Standard* editor Fred Barnes approvingly noted, Bush
practiced "big-government conservatism"—that is, "using what
would normally be seen as liberal means—activist government—
for conservative ends," and being "willing to spend more and

---

[50] Michael D. Tanner, "A Repudiation, but of What?" *Star-Telegram* (November 10th 2008).

[51] Chris Edwards, "Presidential Spending," *Cato-at-Liberty* (September 27th 2007).

[52] Veronique de Rugy, "Bush's Regulatory Kiss-Off," *Reason* (January 2009).

[53] "Republican Party Platform of 1996," *The American Presidency Project*, www.presidency.ucsb.edu/ws/index.php?pid=25848#axzz1WvwSLe7V.

[54] James Bovard, "The Biggest Medicare Fraud Ever," LewRockwell.com (September 1st, 2005).

increase the size of government in the process."[55] Few small government advocates accepted the contradictory, perhaps even Orwellian, idea of "big-government conservatism."

From 2003 to 2007, Bush did all of this with the eager co-operation of Republican majorities in the House and the Senate. Throughout Bush's two terms, popular conservative commentators—Rush Limbaugh, Sean Hannity, Ann Coulter and others—spent most of their time defending Bush against his Democratic critics and very little time criticizing Bush's big-government ways. Writers at such higher-brow conservative venues as *National Review* and *Weekly Standard* took the same approach, mostly defending the president and attacking his critics. With all prominent political and media figures in agreement, the conservative rank and file mostly went along with Bush's policies; from the beginning of his presidency through the 2008 Republican primary season, Bush averaged an 85 percent approval rating among Republicans.[56]

How was it possible for Republicans, apparently so fiercely opposed to big government both before and after George W. Bush—both in the 1990s and under Obama—to be such servile supporters of Bush's unprecedented expansions of government? The immediate causes were September 11th and the wars that followed; the larger causes are the neoconservatism and religious-rightism which gained prominence in the conservative movement and the Republican Party during the last part of the twentieth century.

Ron Paul Versus the Republican Party

Many in the Republican Party were not receptive to Paul's message, particularly his opposition to America's wars.

This was most dramatically demonstrated at a debate in May 2007, where Paul stated his view that terrorists "attack us because we're over there. We've been bombing Iraq for ten years" and advised, "We need to look at what we do from the perspective of what would happen if somebody else did it to us."

---

[55] Fred Barnes, "A 'Big Government Conservatism,'" *Opinion Journal* (August 15th 2003).

[56] Jeffrey M. Jones, "Bush Approval Rating Down to 60% Among Republicans," Gallup (May 8th 2008).

This so incensed fellow candidate and former New York Mayor Rudolph Giuliani that he requested (and was given) time to reply: "That's an extraordinary statement . . . that we invited the [September 11th 2001] attack because we were attacking Iraq [in the 1990s]," Giuliani said. "I don't think I've ever heard that before, and I've heard some pretty absurd explanations for September 11th."[57]

The crowd of GOP faithful roared its approval for Giuliani's response. In a press release issued shortly after the debate, Paul offered Giuliani a reading list of books that showed that the 9/11 attacks were indeed considered by experts to be "blowback" against America's foreign policy in the Middle East. One of those books was the government's own *9/11 Commission Report*, which noted that Osama bin Laden was motivated in substantial part by the presence of U.S. troops in Saudi Arabia as well as other interventions such as sanctions against Iraq.[58]

During Fox News's post-debate analysis, chief political correspondent Carl Cameron referred to the spat: "Rudy Giuliani, the front-runner in national polls took issue with something one of the second tier candidates . . . said." Commentator Michael Steele who, a year later, would become the chairman of the Republican National Committee, said, "I think Ron Paul, for me, basically, it's done."

Fox News then reported the initial results of their text message poll which showed Ron Paul leading. Commentator Sean Hannity was visibly stunned. "In my view, Ron Paul did not win that debate by any stretch," he said. Carl Cameron attempted to minimize the significance of Ron Paul's lead in the text message poll with some logical gymnastics:

> [It was] almost in line with the attraction he's caused for the press. It seems that by getting slapped by Rudy Giuliani for his assertion that the U.S. effectively asked for the 9/11 attacks . . . he's going to get a lot of ink. So Ron Paul, quite, by the actions of Rudy Giuliani's attack, may be doing quite well, and as for the text messaging, maybe he's a little better organized and having his organizers do the necessary dialing.

---

[57] "Republican Debate Transcript, South Carolina," CFR.org (May 15th 2007).

[58] Ron Brynaert, "Paul Campaign Hopes 'Reading for Rudy' Will 'Educate' Giuliani," *The Raw Story* (May 24th 2007).

In the very last report of Fox's post-debate text message poll, Ron Paul slipped to second place behind Mitt Romney, 26 percent to Romney's 27 percent. When asked by co-host Alan Colmes to reconcile Ron Paul's variance with everybody else on stage with his success in the poll, Michael Steele said, "To be honest, it says absolutely nothing. It says he's got a lot of folks out there who are going to text message for him. I think tonight, in my view, there was clear separation between those who should be in this campaign and those who shouldn't . . . based on their responses."

At least Paul got to participate in that debate. As mentioned earlier, Fox News barred him from a January 2008 debate even though his poll numbers had risen substantially and he'd been among the top fundraisers in late 2007.

All of this might lead one to wonder why Ron Paul was in the Republican primary—or the Republican Party—at all. On numerous occasions, Ron Paul faced this question. He points out that he's been elected representative of Texas's Fourteenth Congressional district twelve times. He often tells conservative audiences that he merely wants them to look to their past.

The Old Right

Specifically, Ron Paul encourages conservative audiences to look to the days of Senator Robert Taft, who served in the Senate from 1939 until his death in 1953. Taft, known as "Mr. Republican" in his day, favored a non-interventionist foreign policy, which put him at odds with "establishment" Republicans of the day, including Dwight Eisenhower, who defeated Taft in the race for the 1952 Republican presidential nomination.

Taft was part of what is sometimes referred to as the "Old Right" tradition, which consisted of intellectuals and a few politicians who opposed the New Deal and U.S. interventionism abroad. For the most part, these people weren't quite libertarians, but they were closer than just about anyone else in public life at the time.

The "Old Right" essentially died out soon after World War II, especially once William F. Buckley Jr. founded *National Review* magazine in 1955 and set about creating and shaping a conservative movement that was focused first and foremost on winning the Cold War against the Soviet Union. Taft and other voices of the Old Right began to pass away, and Buckley saw to it that any other anti-war voices, such as that of libertarian Murray Rothbard, were marginalized.[59] When the Vietnam War came, the schism between anti-war libertarians and pro-war conservatives grew even deeper. For the most part, mainstream conservative Republicans have been in the pro-war camp ever since.

Conservative Republican devotion to war increased even more when neoconservatives began appearing on the right in the 1970s. The neocons, led by their intellectual "godfather," Irving Kristol, envisioned a world in which the U.S. military made the world "safe for democracy," as Democratic President Woodrow Wilson had once envisioned. In recent decades, neocons have also promoted "national greatness conservatism," in which the government, through war efforts and other projects, would give the people something (supposedly) greater than themselves to work toward and thus make them virtuous. With respect to domestic policy, the neocons were flexible and "pragmatic," not devotees of any small government or individual liberty philosophy.[60]

Alongside that strand of conservative thought, the "religious right" rose in prominence within the Republican Party, particularly in the early 1980s, largely as a reaction to *Roe v. Wade*, government attacks on religious schools and broadcasting, and the cultural shift to the left during and after the "free-love" era.[61] Religious-right-ism—at least the variety promoted by Reverend Jerry Falwell—seeks to promote, among other things, "family values," school prayer, national defense, and solidarity with the state of Israel.[62] It opposes abortion, homosexuality, and other perceived assaults on traditional religious values.

Some religious conservatives explicitly seek to impose their values on all of America using the force of law—for example, through a constitutional ban on same-sex marriage or a federal ban on abortion, should *Roe v. Wade* be overturned as they desire. Others

---

[59] See Murray N. Rothbard, *Betrayal of the American Right* (Auburn: Ludwig von Mises Institute, 2007), 147–172.

[60] For further details, see C. Bradley Thompson, "Neoconservatism Unmasked," *Cato Unbound* (March 7th 2011).

[61] See Daniel McCarthy, "The Authoritarian Movement," LewRockwell.com (June 30th 2006).

[62] Stephen W. Carson, "Christians in Politics: The Return of the 'Religious Right'," LewRockwell.com (October 30th 2003).

favor allowing state and local governments to do the same. The latter group's beliefs overlap Ron Paul's constitutional, Tenth Amendment view, as well as the personal view he often expresses, though they occasionally contradict the libertarian philosophy underpinning his constitutionalism.

By the George W. Bush years, the pro-war and religious-conservative factions united to dominate the Republican Party. They were largely responsible for the lack of restraint on government spending and power during that time. The neocons supported endless war and substantial domestic interventions. Many of the religious-rightists supported government to advance their moral cause. Neither group devoted much effort, if any, to opposing taxation, spending, or regulation on principle.[63]

Ron Paul's Movement

Ron Paul ultimately failed to win the 2008 Republican nomination because most Republicans did not share his philosophy, but he placed a respectable fourth with more than a million votes—far more than his debate rival, Rudy Giuliani, who flopped early, attracting far fewer votes than Ron Paul in Iowa, New Hampshire, South Carolina, and Nevada. He dropped out after failing to win in Florida, ending up with a total of less than 600,000 votes.[64]

The legacy of Ron Paul's 2008 "revolution" is a revitalized libertarian movement. His presidential campaign founded the political organization, Campaign for Liberty, with over $4.7 million left from his presidential campaign. That fact that his campaign had money left over at all is itself strong evidence of Ron Paul's fiscal prudence. Hillary Clinton's failed presidential campaign of the same year, by contrast, ended $9.5 million in debt, even after she spent $11.4 million of her own money.[65]

The Campaign for Liberty is different from what in recent decades has been the most visible elements of the libertarian movement: institutions based in Washington D.C., most notably

---

[63] See McCarthy, "The Authoritarian Movement."

[64] "2008 Presidential Republican Primary Results," *Dave Liep's Atlas of U.S. Presidential Elections.*

[65] Michael Luo, "For Clinton, Millions in Debt and Few Options," *New York Times* (June 10th 2008).

the Cato Institute, funded in substantial part by billionaires Charles and David Koch. Later in the Tea Party era, they would become favorite targets of the left. These Washington-based organizations made an effort to appear "respectable" and "serious" to the Washington establishment. They take a top-down approach, striving to influence policymakers, including legislators and judges.

In contrast, the Ron Paul movement took libertarianism to a much wider audience that was interested in advancing its ideas—especially the ones about war and the Federal Reserve system—without fear of offending Washington elites. They promoted liberty from the bottom up, among ordinary people.

Ron Paul prompted countless young people to begin discovering the works of Austrian economists Ludwig von Mises and Murray Rothbard, radical thinkers whom Beltway-based free-market institutions had mostly downplayed for years in the interest of appearing respectable to the mainstream. This was an enormous leap forward for libertarianism which no one could anticipate when Ron Paul first announced his candidacy.

Another part of Ron Paul's legacy was the network of Meetup groups and their successor organizations all across the country who had supported his campaign. Many of them sought out other projects after Paul's campaign. One of the first was support of Ron Paul's bill in Congress to audit the Federal Reserve, which, thanks to the economic crisis, received 319 co-sponsors in the House before finally being quashed by Congressional leadership.[66] Campaign for Liberty supporters called Congressmen and held demonstrations outside Federal Reserve buildings in numerous cities.

The other important legacy of Ron Paul's movement—for better or worse—is the Tea Party movement, which closely imitated the Ron Paul movement's structure, strategies, and message, but with some important differences, as we'll see in the chapters ahead.

Revisiting Rick Santelli's Rant

Rick Santelli's complete rant went as follows:

---

[66] See Gary North, "On Auditing the Fed: The Doddering Senate," LewRockwell.com (May 3rd 2010).

SANTELLI: . . . the government is promoting bad behavior, because we certainly don't want to put stimulus forth, and give people a whopping eight or ten dollars in their check, and think that they ought to save it.

And in terms of modifications, I'll tell you what, I have an idea. You know the new administration's big on computers and technology. How about this, Mr. President and new administration—Why don't you put up a web site to have people vote on the Internet as a referendum to see if we really want to subsidize the losers' mortgages, or would we like to, at least, buy cars and buy houses in foreclosure and give them to people who might have a chance to actually prosper down the road, and reward people that could carry the water, instead of drink the water.

TRADER: [*sitting nearby*] What a novel idea! What? Who thought of that!
[*Traders in the pit start clapping and cheering.*]

JOE KERNEN: [*in studio*] Rick, they're like putty in your hands. Did you hear . . .

SANTELLI: No they're not, Joe. They're not like putty in our hands! This is America! [*turns around to address pit traders*] How many of you people want to pay for your neighbors' mortgage that has an extra bathroom and can't pay their bills? Raise their hand. [*traders boo; Santelli turns around to face CNBC camera*] President Obama, are you listening?

TRADER: [*sitting nearby, goes over to Santelli's mike.*] How about we all stop paying our mortgage? It's a moral hazard.

KERNEN: It's like mob rule here, I'm getting scared. I'm glad . . .

SANTELLI: Don't get scared, Joe. They're already scaring you. Y'know, Cuba used to have mansions and a relatively decent economy. They moved from the individual to the collective. Now they're driving '54 Chevys, maybe the last great car to come out of Detroit.

KERNEN: They're driving 'em on water too, which is a little strange to watch, at times.

SANTELLI: There you go.

KERNEN: Hey Rick, how about the notion that Wilbur pointed out, you can go down to two percent on the mortgage . . .

SANTELLI: You can go down to minus two percent, they can't afford the house!

KERNEN: . . . and still have forty percent not be able to do it, so why are we trying to keep them in the house?

SANTELLI: I know Mr. Summers is a great economist, but boy I'd love the answer to that one. [*some cross-talk*]

QUICK: Wow. You get people fired up.

SANTELLI: We're thinking of having a Chicago tea party in July. All you capitalists that want to show up to Lake Michigan, I'm going to start organizing.

QUICK: What are you dumping in this time?

SANTELLI: We're going to be dumping in some derivative securities. What do you think about that?

WILBUR ROSS: [*in studio*] Mayor Daley is marshalling the police right now. . . .

KERNEN: The rabble rousers.

ROSS: . . . the National Guard. You know Rick, one of our producers says if Roland Burris steps down, man, Senator Santelli, the junior senator from Illinois. It's a possibility. I'm just sayin' . . .

SANTELLI: Do you think I want to take a shower every hour? The last place I'm ever going to live or work is DC.

KERNEN: Have you raised any money for Blago? [*laughter*]

SANTELLI: No, but I think that somebody's going to have to start raising money for us. . . . Listen, all I know is that there's only about five percent of the floor population here right now, and I talk loud enough they can all hear me. So if you want to ask them anything, let me know. These guys are pretty straightforward, and my guess is, a pretty good statistical cross section of America, the silent majority.

QUICK: Not so silent majority today.

KERNEN: Yeah, not so silent.

QUICK: So Rick, are they opposed to the housing thing, to the stimulus package, to everything out there?

SANTELLI: You know, they're pretty much of the notion that you can't buy your way into prosperity, and if the multiplier that all of these Washington economists are selling us is over one, that we never have to worry about the economy again. The government should spend a trillion dollars an hour because we'll get $1.5 trillion back.

QUICK: Wilbur?

ROSS: Rick I congratulate you on your new incarnation as a revolutionary leader.

SANTELLI: Somebody needs one. I'll tell you what, if you read our Founding Fathers, people like Benjamin Franklin and Jefferson, what we're doing in this country now is making them roll over in their graves.[67]

Many of those who approved of Ron Paul did not approve Santelli's message.

At the libertarian-leaning financial website, *The Daily Reckoning*, Dave Gonigam found this argument "pretty hard to respond to—unless you actually opposed the Wall Street bailouts, thus proving your laissez-faire *bona fides*." The trouble was, Santelli had not expressed this sort of outrage over the TARP—so, as Gonigam put it, the Santelli view seemed to be "billions for bankers, but not one cent for homeowners."[68]

John Amato wrote in the generally liberal *Huffington Post*: "Watching Santelli's embarrassing diatribe at the expense of the American people made me realize that these Wall Street frat boys still don't get it. America is sick and tired of the riches they have manipulated out of the system and then be lectured by people who make more money than a hundred middle class workers combined."[69]

---

[67] Tom Blumer, "Rant for the Ages: CNBC's Rick Santelli Goes Off; Studio Hosts Invoke 'Mob Rule' to Downplay," *News Busters* (February 19th 2009).

[68] Dave Gonigam, "Why I'll Sit Out the Chicago Tea Party," *Daily Reckoning* (February 23rd 2009).

[69] John Amato, "Clueless Rick Santelli Doesn't Understand His Attitude Is

While the early tea parties held in support of Ron Paul focused their anger on federal institutions and the elites who profited from the Federal Reserve, Goldman Sachs, Henry Paulson, the IRS, many of the people who joined the Tea Party movement later focused more of its anger on the welfare state and its clients existing at the expense of productive middle-class Americans.

In other words, there was a shift from condemning all government privilege to condemning only the privileges of the poor at the expense of the rich.

Critics of President Obama often cited class warfare as running theme of his speeches and the focus of his re-election campaign—playing groups of people against one another to win support. Rick Santelli's rant is viewed by critics as playing into the class-warfare paradigm, and distracting from the Tea Party's simpler and more universal message of simply wanting to be left alone.

Why America Loathes Wall St. and Bankers," *Huffington Post* (February 21st 2009), www.huffingtonpost.com/john-amato/clueless-rick-santelli-do_b_168878.html.

3

A Big Government Power Grab Energizes the Tea Party

The surprising and spectacular growth of the Tea Party movement was a response to the perception that Big Government was taking advantage of the problems it had generated to grow even bigger. Not only was the government intruding into more and more areas of our lives, but by its irresponsible spending policies it was sleepwalking toward a fiscal crisis of apocalyptic proportions.

The recession which began in 2008 was the predictable consummation of years of government policies to contrive that millions of people would acquire mortgages they ultimately couldn't afford. These polices began no later than the Clinton administration, but were pursued with equal vigor under George W. Bush.

When the recession broke, the story on the left was that this was the outcome of Bush's free market policies. In fact Bush's policies were anything but free market. The administration's response to 9/11 had become a cover for a huge expansion of government spending. As a candidate, Bush had some kind words to say for the free market, but in office he was a big spender over the entire course of his two terms.

In reaction to the recession, for which his administration bore a major part of the responsibility, Bush took government spending to unprecedented heights in late 2008, claiming, "I've abandoned free market principles to save the free market system."[1] His successor, Barack Obama, took it to even dizzier heights after that. Judging by what Bush did and said, and by what McCain said during the campaign, we can't be confident that a Republican

---

[1] "Bush: 'I've Abandoned Free Market Principles to Save the Free Market System'," Thinkprogress.org (December 16th 2008).

administration would have been any better than Obama, but as it turned out, Obama became the target of the Tea Party's wrath.

Following numerous bailouts, stimulus measures, and other expansions of government spending, we have witnessed a higher level and faster increase of the national debt than under any previous president.[2]

> As a result of policy corruption, specifically failing to make sure government spending and regulations meet reasonable cost-benefit tests, employment and income growth have lagged, with most Americans reporting lower after-inflation adjusted incomes than four years ago.[3]

Millions of Americans joined the Tea Party movement on concerns about an unholy alliance between government and big business. Frustrated by the petty partisan games played by Republicans and Democrats they felt an urgent need to defend their right to self-governance, their right to be left alone, and other basic American values and constitutional liberties.

Many Tea Party supporters drew the conclusion that Obama is a "socialist," impelled by socialist, even Marxist, ideology to expand the government and topple the capitalist system. Whatever the merits of this analysis, the depiction of Obama as socialist, communist, or fascist was certainly well represented in posters, bumper stickers, T-shirts and other visual propaganda conspicuous at Tea Party rallies, picnics, and meetings.

No doubt many Tea Partiers became incensed by Obama policies that might well have been implemented just the same by a Republican. Yet most Tea Partiers believe that under the Obama Administration we've taken bigger and more resolute steps away from the free enterprise and individual self-reliance that made this country strong and prosperous. Ultimately, it is not a matter of personalities or even parties, but strictly a matter of policies and programs.

Bailouts

Asked about the economy at a January 2008 Republican presidential debate, Ron Paul said he believed "we're in a recession" and

---

[2] Mark Knoller, "National debt has increased $4 trillion under Obama," CBS News (August 22nd 2011).

[3] Richard W. Rahn, "Intellectual and Policy Corruption," *Washington Times* (February 7th 2012).

that "it's going to get a lot worse if we continue to do the things we've done in the past." John McCain declared: "I don't believe we're headed into a recession. I believe the fundamentals of this economy are strong, and I believe they will remain strong."[4]

By the end of that year, however, economic reality proved that Ron Paul was right. The housing market collapsed and with it, the market for mortgage-backed securities—risky instruments that many financial institutions had invested in—creating a major financial and economic crisis from which the economy was not to escape for some years. (The National Bureau of Economic Research later pinpointed the start of the recession as December 2007, a month before Ron Paul's comments.)

The federal government responded to the crisis in two main phases: Bush administration bailouts of firms harmed by the downturn and more bailouts and so-called "stimulus" spending under President Obama. The bailouts first occurred under Bush in Fall 2008. On September 16th 2008, the Federal Reserve announced a rescue of insurance company American International Group Inc. (AIG) from collapse with an $85 billion loan (later increased), in exchange for which the Fed took an equity interest of about 80 percent in the company. Then Bush's Secretary of the Treasury, Henry Paulson, proposed what would become the Emergency Economic Stabilization Act of 2008.

This legislation was originally intended to allow the government to purchase up to $700 billion of financial institutions' "troubled assets," particularly mortgage-backed securities, to prevent the institutions from failing and, the theory went, stabilize the economy. The new law created the Troubled Asset Repurchase Program (TARP), which supposedly existed to buy banks' unsalable assets, but the TARP's mission quickly changed from simply buying banks' troubled assets to government spending on essentially anything that, in the Treasury Secretary Hank Paulson's view, would help the economy. Technically, the law's language allowed the Treasury Secretary to do this—but few expected at the time the bill was passed that he actually would use his power in this way, though some critics speculated the loose language was a deliberate political calculation, allowing members

---

[4] "Republican Debate Transcript, Myrtle Beach, South Carolina," CFR.org (January 10th 2008).

of Congress to deflect anticipated voter outrage by criticizing the plan's implementation.[5]

Polls taken before Congress voted on the legislation showed that a majority of Americans opposed it. Many saw this as little more than a government handout to politically connected firms, such as Paulson's former employer, Goldman Sachs, which had gambled on risky investments. Many observed that with a government bailout, these firms simply avoided the consequences of their irresponsibility, forcing taxpayers to pay for it instead. Anti-bailout demonstrations occurred across the country. On September 25th the left-wing activist group TrueMajority.com reported that it held 251 protest events.[6] Activists associated with Ron Paul's Campaign for Liberty also staged protests.

In a Pew poll, only a third of Americans (34 percent) correctly said that TARP was enacted by the Bush administration. Nearly half (47 percent) incorrectly believed TARP was passed under President Obama.[7] This is a good example of the way many people exaggerate the difference between the two parties and assume that the Republicans are more free market than they really are.

Pundits, left and right, came down on both sides of the bailout issue. Many self-styled conservatives, who until then had supported Bush's unprecedented spending considered this too much for them. Many liberal commentators objected to what they saw as crony capitalism—President Bush helping his wealthy friends while the rest of America suffered. At the same time, many voices in the mainstream media argued in support of the bailout. The *Economist* endorsed it;[8] so did talk-show host and future Tea Party poster boy Glenn Beck before changing his position.[9]

Major left-leaning newspapers, such as the *New York Times* and *Washington Post*, as well as government owned media—National

---

[5] Joe Weisenthal, "Congress to Hank. Thanks for Flip-Flopping on the TARP!" *Business Insider* (November 13th 2008).

[6] Ben Rooney, "Bailout Foes Hold Day of Protest," CNNMoney.com (September 25th 2008).

[7] "34% Was TARP Passed Under Bush or Obama?" *Pew Research Center.*

[8] "A Shock from the House," *Economist* (September 29, 2009); "Lifelines," *Economist* (October 9th 2008); "A Helping Hand to Homeowners," *Economist* (October 23rd 2008).

[9] Colby Hall, "Glenn Beck for Office? TARP Flip-Flop Shows Why He Can Never Get Elected," Mediaite.com (December 3rd 2009).

Public Radio and the Public Broadcasting System—also lined up behind TARP.[10] They may have found the bailout distasteful but argued, as the measures' proponents in Washington did, that it was necessary to avoid greater economic disaster.

Because of the public's opposition, the legislation initially failed in the House of Representatives on September 28th 2008. It passed a few days later on October 3rd, after $150 billion of government 'pork' was added to the bill to persuade some congressional 'no' voters to change their minds. Beneficiaries included Burger King Holdings Inc., London-based Diageo PLC, which produces Captain Morgan rum, builders of NASCAR auto-racing tracks, and movie and television producers.[11] President Bush promptly signed it into law.

This change in the TARP allowed the federal government to bail out Chrysler and General Motors, in exchange for a 60 percent ownership share. Polls showed that a majority of Americans opposed bailing out automakers,[12] and an auto bailout proposal in Congress failed in December 2008,[13] but the TARP enabled the Bush Administration to achieve the same result despite disapproval from both the people and Congress.

President Obama continued bailouts of the automotive industry in 2009 and still believes (or wants others to believe) that it prevented another Great Depression and that his bailout was the only way to prevent the closure of General Motors and Chrysler Group and the collapse of the nation's supplier base.[14] This view is not shared by the Tea Party movement. Mark Meckler, co-founder of Tea Party Patriots, said in an interview[15] that a central Tea Party objection to the White House's process was that the car companies

---

[10] Paul Krugman, "The World According to TARP," *New York Times* (September 28th 2008); Joseph E. Robert, "If the Bailout Doesn't Pass . . ." *Washington Post*, (October 3, 2008).

[11] Ryan J. Donmoyer, "Bailout of U.S. Banks Gives British Rum a $2.7 Billion Benefit," *Bloomberg* (June 26th 2009).

[12] Ben Rooney, "61% of Americans Oppose Auto Bailout," CNNMoney.com (December 4th 2008).

[13] "Auto Bailout Bill Dies in Senate," CNN.com (December 11th 2008).

[14] Chris Isidore, "The Comeback of the American Car: Auto Bailouts Worked," CNN Money (February 28th 2012).

[15] Benjy Sarlin, "D'oh! Romney's Auto-Bailout Dance Enrages Tea Party Too," talkingpointsmemo.com (February 18th 2012).

received government loans and special treatment rather than going through a normal private sector bankruptcy. "We have a bankruptcy system that applies to everyone else," Meckler said. Bailout of automakers and United Auto Workers Union is still unpopular among the majority of Americans. A more recent Gallup poll found 51 percent of those surveyed still disapproved of the $85 billion rescue effort, with only 44 percent saying they approved.[16]

The Stimulus

Upon taking office in January 2009, President Obama began to promote the American Recovery and Reinvestment Act of 2009, otherwise known as the "stimulus bill." This bill was premised on the ideas of economist John Maynard Keynes, who in the 1930s argued that very large amounts of government spending are necessary to keep an economy going during a recession.

Many of today's economists agree with Keynes and believe government spending can stimulate the economy. Regarding Keynes's famous book, *The General Theory of Employment, Interest and Money*, the leftist *New York Times* columnist Paul Krugman said "It's the most amazing work and it's held up remarkably well. . . . It's probably, even more than Adam Smith, I would say, the most important book in the history of economics."[17]

Free-market economists, however, particularly from the Austrian School of economics, strongly disagree and believe such spending can only harm an economy.[18] Many economists outside the Austrian school are also somewhat skeptical of the impact of stimulus spending.

Whether we thinks it's a good idea or not, we might expect such "stimulus" spending to emphasize immediate spending on projects such as government buildings and infrastructure—things that the government would presumably spend money on sooner or later anyway, and which would visibly put people to work. The

---

[16] Paul A. Eisenstein, "Public Still Opposes Auto Bailout, Gallup Poll Finds," *Detroit Bureau* (February 23rd 2012).

[17] Paul Krugman discussing his introduction to *The General Theory of Employment, Interest and Money* for publisher Palgrave Macmillan, YouTube, posted June 30, 2008.

[18] George Reisman, "Economic Recovery Requires Capital Accumulation, Not Government 'Stimulus Packages'" (February 25th 2009).

Obama stimulus did include some such spending, but it also devoted hundreds of billions to what critics have described as left-wing pet political endeavors and cash prizes for special interest groups supporting the President.

The bill included:

- $87 billion for Medicare outlays and related spending

- $20 billion toward nutrition assistance program (food stamps)

- $3 billion for grants to fund science and technology research

- $1 billion for periodic censuses and programs

- $2 billion for "other activities"

- $43.9 billion for the Department of Energy (DOE)

- $1.1 billion for a variety of programs administered by the Department of Homeland Security

- $20.4 billion for programs administered by the Department of Health and Human Services

- $4.6 billion for employment and training programs administered by the Department of Labor

- $17.6 billion for Pell grants and other student financial assistance and facilities at post-secondary institutions including federal student loan programs

- $29.1 billion for other education programs aimed particularly at elementary and secondary education

- $11.2 billion for housing assistance programs administered by HUD

- $39.5 billion available to states each twice a year to help them balance their books

- $2.3 billion "emergency" spending for the Temporary Assistance for Needy Families (TANF) program

- A $246 million tax break for Hollywood movie investors in big budget movie projects over an 11-year period

- $248 million for furniture at the new Homeland Security headquarters

- $600 million to buy hybrid vehicles for federal employees

- $400 million for the Centers for Disease Control to screen and prevent STD's

- $650 million for the digital television converter box coupon program

- $850 million for Amtrak

- $1.2 billion for "youth activities," including youth summer job programs

- $4.19 billion for the Neighborhood Stabilization Program allocation, of which, $3.44 billion would be competed for by nonprofit groups as well as states and localities

- $7.5 billion in each year would be reserved for incentive grants to be given to states on a competitive basis in fiscal year 2010, based on states meeting specified criteria in how they spent their initial allocations

- $193,956 to researchers at Houston's Rice University and the University of Texas in Dallas, to gauge how people and municipalities feel about the stimulus

- $500,000 for blue, 96-gallon, microchip-embedded recycling bins in Dayton, Ohio which will spy on citizens' recycling habits, plus another $500,000 to promote recycling

- $294,958 for researchers at Wake Forest University to study the effects of yoga on menopausal women

- $456,663 to University of California, Berkeley for a study of Neptune's atmosphere

- $712,883 for researchers at Northwestern University who will attempt to use artificial intelligence to compile jokes from the internet into hilarious comedy routines

- $677,462 to researchers at Georgia State University to study inequality and unfairness among monkeys

- $554,763 to the U.S. Forest Service to renovate a visitors' center at Mount St. Helens, Washington, which is currently closed and which the Forest Service has no plans to re-open

- A variety of tax credits for desired behavior[19]

Adding fuel to the firestorm of criticism which the bill received, then White House Chief of Staff Rahm Emanuel proclaimed, "Never let a serious crisis go to waste. What I mean by that is it's an opportunity to do things you couldn't do before." A column in the *Wall Street Journal* reflected: "now that Democrats have finally released the details we understand Rahm's point much better. This is a political wonder that manages to spend money on just about every pent-up Democratic proposal of the last 40 years."[20]

The version which President Obama signed into law on February 17th 2009 totaled over a thousand pages and cost $787 billion.[21] Just as most self-described conservatives supported President Bush's early big-government policies (it wasn't until TARP that most abandoned their support), the left raised little objection despite there being as much crony capitalism built into this bill as there had been with TARP. The Obama stimulus followed the left's favored economic theories and spent unprecedented recourses on projects they supported, so most Obama supporters were satisfied.

Nominal conservatives, on the other hand, whether truly opposed to big government or merely partisan, became more united than ever in their opposition to out-of-control government spending. There were exceptions: future 2012 Republican Presidential candidate Jon Huntsman charged that the bill wasn't big enough,[22] sharing this view with the leftist Paul Krugman.[23] In

---

[19] Mike Miller, "Pork Galore: Obama's Stimulus Bill Does Little to Stimulate the Economy," *Liberty Maven* (January 28th 2009); Johanna Neuman, "Pork for Hollywood? Obama Stimulus Package Includes Film Tax Write-Off," *The Wrap* (February 2nd 2009); Matthew Vadum, "ACORN's Stimulus," *The American Spectator* (January 27th 2009); Peter Roff, "10 Wasteful Stimulus Projects," *US News and World Report*, http://www.usnews.com/opinion/ slideshows/10-wasteful-stimulus-projects.

[20] "A 40-Year Wish List," *Wall Street Journal* (January 28th 2009).

[21] Laura Meckler, "Obama Signs Stimulus into Law," *Wall Street Journal* (February 18th 2009).

[22] David Weigel, "Huntsman in 2009: Stimulus 'Probably Wasn't Big Enough," Slate.com (May 23rd 2011).

[23] Paul Krugman, "On the Inadequacy of the Stimulus," *The New York Times* (September 5th 2011).

Congress, no Republican representatives and only three Republican Senators voted for the bill. A Rasmussen poll showed public support for the stimulus package had fallen to 37 percent by February 4th 2009, a week and half before it was signed.[24]

Under the Obama Administration, central government continued its manipulation of the failing economy through the Federal Reserve's near-zero interest rate policy. "The Fed," wrote eminent economist and Tea Party supporter Paul Prentice in the *Wall Street Journal* "never injected real "capital" into the system, it merely injected fiat bank reserves. Real capital comes from real savings, not from the printing press. Until the geniuses who run the central bank, and the professors who enable them, understand this, there will be no end to the malinvestment and the credit-driven booms and busts."[25]

Additional stimulus packages and jobs programs followed shortly after, creating even more Tea Party outrage with Obama's policies. "Above all, Tea Party followers share a profound objection to unchecked spending and expanding credit, as successive administrations and the Federal Reserve have done to the tune of trillions of dollars. This effort to stimulate the economy, they believe, has not only failed to end the recession but made it worse."[26]

The Solyndra Debacle

The most scandalous of the stimulus provisions and an arrogant example of "crony capitalism" is the Solyndra loan debacle directly involving both President Obama and Vice President Biden. For Tea Partiers it was yet another example of pervasive corruption in Washington. Both President Obama and Vice President Biden backed a $535-million loan guarantee to Solyndra Corporation in 2009 as part of their goal of "green" energy. Solyndra investors and major Democrat donors presented the case that such guarantees for Solyndra would create four thousand new jobs. This loan guarantee, from the Tea Party's perspective, was the most obviously wasteful part of the American Recovery and Reinvestment Act of 2009 (ARRA) which provided Obama donors with massive handouts of

---

[24] "Support for Stimulus Package Falls to 37%," *Rasmussen Reports* (February 4th 2009).

[25] *Wall Street Journal* (February 6th 2012).

[26] Joshua Green, "The Tea Party's Brain," *Atlantic* (November 2010).

taxpayers' money. In September 2011 Solyndra filed for bankruptcy, fired almost all its workforce, and discontinued operations. American taxpayers had to repay the loan the government had guaranteed.

Tea Party critics maintained that the Obama administration was overly influenced by awarding loan guarantees to their cronies and donors. It turned out that President Obama's top fundraiser Steven Spinner had demanded the Department of Energy bureaucrats' fast approval of a loan guarantee for Solyndra, even as his wife's law firm was working for Solyndra.

> "How hard is this? What is he waiting for?" wrote Steven J. Spinner, a high-tech consultant and energy investor who raised at least $500,000 for Obama before being appointed to a key job helping oversee the energy loan guarantee program. "I have OVP [the Office of the Vice President] and WH [the White House] breathing down my neck on this."[27]

In December 2011 the *Washington Post* published a thorough examination of the Solyndra scandal and the Obama green technology program in general. It concluded that politics played a key role in the decision-making process with Solyndra and other projects. The *Post* showed that Obama Administration officials had disregarded warnings about the credibility of government loan recipients. They were fully aware that administration officials were mostly concerned about negative political repercussions of Solyndra's default and bankruptcy and exerted influence so that key layoffs would be delayed until after the 2010 election.[28]

The global warming policies and cap-and-trade initiatives of the Obama Administration are the most attacked and ridiculed at Tea Party rallies. There is no consensus over the issue of global warming among Tea Partiers. A September 2011 CNN/ORC poll found that 58 percent of Tea Party Republicans don't believe global warming is a proven fact[29] and according to our interviews, very few believe that government should do anything about the

---

[27] Matthew Mosk and Ronnie Greene, "Obama Fundraiser Pushed Solyndra Deal from Inside," ABC News and iWatch News (October 7th 2011).

[28] Joe Stephens, and Carol D. Leonnig, "The Solyndra Scandal: Politics Infused Obama Energy Programs," *Washington Post* (December 25th 2011).

[29] Dan Mercia, "Poll: Tea Party Opinions of Global Warming, Evolution Problematic for GOP," CNN (September 22nd 2011).

climate. Many Tea Party supporters are science buffs who follow the arguments of Richard Lindzen, Judith Curry, Anthony Watts, and other climate scientists skeptical of the IPCC doom-and-gloom purveyors. Most Tea Partiers believe that we need to remove government restrictions to free up the development of domestic gas, oil, and nuclear resources.

The Stimulus Didn't Work

In 2009 and 2010, big claims were made for the stimulus. It would quickly kick-start the economy and within a few years unemployment would fall dramatically. There is now abundant evidence that the stimulus made matters worse and delayed recovery.

Since the 'recovery' was so much slower than the Obama administration confidently predicted, and much slower than recoveries from comparable earlier recessions, the administration's only remaining argument was that things would have been worse without the stimulus. There is no scientific basis for any such assertion, and plenty of indications that the opposite is true: the economy would have rebounded quicker and more soundly without any stimulus measures.

John Lott has summarized much of the evidence in his book *At the Brink*. A comparison of countries which adopted 'stimulus' measures and those which chose 'austerity' clearly shows that 'austerity' works, while 'stimulus' is counterproductive. For example, Canada was hit by the recession just like the U.S., and all the unemployment and output numbers tracked closely with the U.S. until the implementation of the U.S. stimulus. From that point, Canada recovered much better and much more quickly than the U.S. Exactly the same picture emerges when comparing the U.S. with European countries. Those that responded to the recession by 'austerity' have recovered much better and much quicker than the U.S.[30] Obama publicly chastised European leaders for not 'stimulating' their economy. But in fact, since prosperity in one country always tends to enhance prosperity in its trading partners, European statesmen who refrained from stimulus measures were

---

[30] John R. Lott Jr., *At the Brink: Will Obama Push Us Over the Edge?* (Regnery, 2013), 102–112.

helping to reduce the ill-effects of Obama's stimulus spending even in the U.S. itself.

'Stimulus' sounds encouraging while 'austerity' sounds grim. Why wouldn't 'stimulus' have stimulating effects? Government spending is always at the expense of productive industry. All government spending is paid for by taxation, by borrowing, or by printing money. Taxation is a burden on productive people and reduces their spending by the same amount as the government spending. Printing money drives up prices, and is thus a concealed form of taxation: productive people have to pay higher prices for goods, because of what the government is doing. Borrowing seems to postpone the decision and does in fact impose a burden on future generations. However, borrowing immediately restricts what productive people can do. This is because the government uses the borrowed money to buy resources which would otherwise be available to productive people. No matter how things are arranged, increased government spending must always be a deduction from the resources available to the productive part of the economy, the part that alone is the engine of growth and future higher living standards.

If we could arrange things so that some of the negative impact on the productive sector could be concealed from view, while the government was spending money freely, then there might possibly be a brief burst of prosperity caused by the government spending. Eventually the reality of the negative impact would become clear, and we would be back in a slump. However, in a modern economy, with its savvy traders and digital technology, this kind of lag is much less likely. The negative impact hits at the same time as the new government spending. And the negative impact must be greater than the benefits of the new spending, because the negative impact cuts into the most profitable opportunities, while the government spending is simply ladeled out to clients and dependents of the government, who are not under the same competitive pressure to find profitable opportunities.

'Austerity' sounds grim, but it simply means cutting back the operations of government. (Very often it simply means cutting back the rate of growth of government operations.) This can only lead to comparatively more resources becoming available for generators of wealth in the productive part of the economy.

The Government as Job Creator

The Obama Administration continued its manipulation of the economic system through the Federal Reserve's near-zero interest rate policy. "The Fed", writes eminent economist and Tea Party supporter Paul Prentice in the *Wall Street Journal*,

> never injected real 'capital' into the system, it merely injected fiat bank reserves. Real capital comes from real savings, not from the printing press. Until the geniuses who run the central bank, and the professors who enable them, understand this, there will be no end to the malinvestment and the credit-driven booms and busts.[31]

The Tea Party case against government jobs programs is straightforward.[32] The government cannot create jobs because it has nothing which is not taken coercively from the citizenry. To provide a government project with resources, these must be denied to private projects. Net jobs are not created, but only redirected from the private to the public sector.

Though most people would describe taxes as part of a "social contract," or "the price we pay for a civilized society,"[33] the fact that they are collected coercively is undeniable. Ongoing refusal to pay your taxes will result in force being initiated against you. Austrian economist and Nobel laureate Friedrich von Hayek frequently distinguished between the coercive and voluntary economies, arguing that the former should be minimized: "the 'substitution of political for economic power' now so often demanded means necessarily the substitution of power from which there is no escape for a power which is always limited."[34] Henry Hazlitt put the point succinctly in a criticism of Keynesian economist John Kenneth Galbraith: "The 'private sector' of the economy is, in fact, the voluntary sector; and . . . the 'public sector' is, in fact, the coercive sector." He continued:

---

[31] *Wall Street Journal* (February 6th 2012).

[32] For another great explanation of this and other free market principles, see Henry Hazlitt, *Economics in One Lesson* (Harper, 1946). Chapter IV covers public works.

[33] This Oliver Wendell Holmes Jr. quote is inscribed above the doors to the Internal Revenue Service in Washington D.C.

[34] F.A. Hayek, *The Road to Serfdom, the Definitive Edition* (University of Chicago Press, 2007), 166.

The voluntary sector is made up of the goods and services for which people voluntarily spend the money they have earned. The coercive sector is made up of the goods and services that are provided, regardless of the wishes of the individual, out of the taxes that are seized from him. And as this sector grows at the expense of the voluntary sector, we come to the essence of the welfare state. . . . The welfare state, as Bastiat put it with uncanny clairvoyance more than a century ago, is the great fiction by which everybody tries to live at the expense of everybody else. This is not only a fiction; it is bound to be a failure. . . . for the energetic and able lose their incentive to produce more than the average, and the slothful and unskilled lose their incentive to improve their condition.[35]

Private endeavors are driven by economic considerations, while public endeavors are driven by political ones. They can never be efficient because political endeavors are by definition, centrally planned, and central planners lack the intricate knowledge which is normally dispersed in the individual minds of all the market participants.

Government spending grows each year, but what is most relevant is whether it is increasing or decreasing as a percentage of gross domestic product (GDP) and how it relates to the percentage of the adult labor force at work. As was demonstrated by Richard W. Rahn, chairman of the Institute for Global Economic Growth, there is a strong inverse relationship between increasing the size of government and job creation. What is typically ignored by the neo-Keynesians, writes Dr. Rahn, is that there is an enormous tax extraction cost for the government to obtain each additional dollar. . . . Thus, the real deadweight loss of additional government taxing and spending is estimated to be in the $3 to $4 range.[36] One 2011 calculation using the job-creating rhetoric from the White House which accompanied President Obama's Stimulus found that each job "created" cost the U.S. taxpayer over a quarter of a million dollars.[37]

---

[35] Henry Hazlitt, *Man vs. the Welfare State*, ed. Bruce Caldwell (Ludwig von Mises Institute: Auburn, 2007), 121–22.

[36] Richard W. Rahn, "Government Spending Jobs Myth. Facts Show Keynesian Model Is Wrong," *Washington Times* (December 19th 2011).

[37] Tyler Durden, "The Cost of Obama's Stimulus Plan: $312,500 Per Job (Vote) Created or Saved (And Guess Who Is Paying It)," *Zero Hedge* (September 12th 2011).

What concerns Tea Partiers is that the government may be reaching the limits of the ability to tax and borrow. If so, we may soon be faced with a tough choice: either massive cutback in government spending or the recourse to printing money, generating a high and escalating rate of inflation. The immediate response of Obama and the Democrats is to call for higher taxation on "the wealthy." Unlike the other major populist movement, Occupy Wall Street, the Tea Party movement rejects social envy and class warfare rhetoric and policies. One of the major accusations of the Tea Party against Barack Obama is that he is a 'great divider'.

Government Corruption

The bigger the government gets, the more corruption proliferates. Any society with an over-powerful state is automatically riddled through and through with corruption.

Corruption takes many forms. Most of those forms could be seen in the actions of both Bush and Obama administrations, from the most primitive—government officials simply taking bribes for special favors, to covering up wrongdoing, to using taxpayer money to pay off political supporters, to using government prosecutors to punish enemies, to failing to fulfill its fiduciary duty to citizens by not performing cost-benefit analyses before taking actions.

Promulgating policies that knowingly hurt millions of people, because this benefits the political ruling class, is far more serious than a government official requesting a cash bribe—as despicable as that may be. Pushing for tax increases without first getting rid of counterproductive or useless programs and cleaning up mismanagement is an example of policy corruption.[38]

To many Tea Partiers, the Obama administration seems to disregard the rule of law. "Pinal County (Arizona) Sheriff Paul Babeu is hopping mad at the federal government. Babeu told CNSNews.com that rather than help law enforcement in Arizona stop the hundreds of thousands of people who come into the United States illegally, the federal government is targeting the state and its law enforcement personnel."[39] At the same time, in hear-

---

[38] Richard W. Rahn, "Intellectual and Policy Corruption," *Washington Times* (February 7th 2012).

[39] Penny Starr, "Arizona Sheriff: 'Our Own Government Has Become Our Enemy'," cnsnews.com (August 1st 2010).

ings before Congress Obama's Attorney General Eric H. Holder Jr. was reticent about the Fast and Furious guns-to-drug-dealers scandal, in which the American taxpayer footed the bill for the purchase of firearms which were then provided to Mexican drug gangs.

The Obama administration gave grants to the Association of Community Organizations for Reform Now (ACORN) which was exposed to be thoroughly corrupt, causing Congress to prohibit it from receiving any more grants. "Many Democrats used to advertise their ACORN connections. Now, however, the Democratic-led Senate has voted to cut off its [ACORN's] grants from the Department of Housing and Urban Development. . . . Republicans are using ACORN to portray Democrats as corrupt."[40] In the wake of the exposure of ACORN, Richard Rahn pointed out that the Justice Department was requiring Bank of America, as part of its settlement for alleged "lending discrimination," to make large contributions to leftist groups unconnected to the government lawsuit against Bank of America, including groups that are little more than renamed ACORNs. Other banks also were being pressured to make similar "settlements" to groups with close ties to Democrats.[41]

Barack Obama's personal involvement with ACORN as its attorney and community organizer as well as his close friendship with William "Bill" Ayers a co-founder of the Weather Underground, a self-described communist revolutionary group implicated in a campaign of bombing of police departments and other public buildings during the 1960s and 1970s convinced many Tea Party members that the President is a Marxist. Another piece of evidence, to Tea Partiers, of Obama's anti-Americanism was his open microphone gaffe on March 19th 2012, promising Russian President Dmitry Medvedev "more flexibility" on missile defense after the election. "On all these issues, but particularly missile defense, this can be solved, but it's important for him to give me space," Mr. Obama could be heard saying to Mr. Medvedev, according to a reporter from ABC News, who was traveling with the president. Mr. Obama then elaborated in a portion of the

---

[40] Sharon Theimer and Pete Yost, "Did ACORN Get Too Big for Its Own Good?" MSNBC (September 29th 2009).

[41] Rahn, "Intellectual and Policy Corruption."

exchange picked up by the cameras: "This is my last election. After my election I have more flexibility." "I understand," replied Medvedev, "I will transmit this information to Vladimir," referring to Vladimir Putin, who succeeded Medvedev.[42] These comments, ignored or treated lightly by much of the media, "sent shivers down the spines of conservative who already believed the president is a not-so-closeted socialist. They recall his criticism of the Founding Fathers for constitutionally limiting a president's ability to bring about change unilaterally. They fear that, unconstrained by the need to run again, Obama will perform a political version of *Girls Gone Wild*, with the Constitution shredded and America transformed beyond recognition," wrote columnist Cal Thomas, a writer close to the Tea Party's outlook.[43]

The Tea Party Responds to the Power Grab

SEATTLE

Watching the stimulus make its way toward passage, Keli Carender, a 29-year-old living in Seattle, felt frustrated. Half-Mexican, with a pierced nose, and employed as a teacher of math to welfare recipients, Carender did not meet the later stereotypical image of a Tea Partier, but she had been a conservative in a not-so-conservative part of the country for her entire life. She became increasingly concerned over the direction the country was headed. She was disturbed by TARP and the auto bailout. The pending stimulus bill pushed her to action.

"I felt like it was just running right over me and I didn't have any say in it at all," she later told the *New York Times*'s Kate Zernike.

> So I basically thought to myself, I have two courses. I can give up, go home and crawl into bed, and be really depressed and just let it happen, or I can do something different and find a new avenue to get my voice out.[44]

---

[42] David Goodman, "Microphone Catches a Candid Obama," *New York Times* (March 26th 2012).

[43] Cal Thomas, "A Second Term: Obama Unleashed," *Washington Examiner* (March 28th 2012).

[44] Zernike, *Boiling Mad*, 13–19.

Carender decided to take the latter course and on January 5th 2009 started a blog, *Redistributing Knowledge*, writing under the pseudonym "Liberty Belle." The first few days of posts were the sort of thing one might expect from a first-time conservative blogger with thoughts about strategy and various issues. Then on February 10th she announced a President's Day "protest against the Porkulus" to be held in downtown Seattle. ("Porkulus" was conservative talk-radio host Rush Limbaugh's name for the stimulus bill.) "The idea," Carender wrote, "is to use what we've learned about dissent over the last eight years [from anti-war protesters]. We need loud protests with lots noise [*sic*] and visuals." She urged would-be attendees to paint signs and "imagine that you are a left-wing college student with nothing else to do and that should help get you started."[45] Presumably her blog, like any new blog from someone who's not an established writer, had few readers at the time, but Carender nonetheless attracted attention to her event. She managed to get a plug from local conservative radio host Kirby Wilbur,[46] and one from Steve Beren, a former Republican candidate for Congress.[47] Then, the day before the event, she saw her event promoted by popular conservative blogger Michelle Malkin.[48] Just before the event, Carender blogged her hopes for it:

> Make no mistake, the President will be signing that bill tomorrow, I have no illusions that he will actually listen to us. BUT, maybe, just maybe we can start a movement that will snowball across the nation and get people out of their homes, meeting each other and working together to redirect this country toward its truly radical founding principles of individual liberty and freedom.

Carender's anti-Porkulus event on February 16th drew just over one hundred people. Many carried signs protesting the stimulus,

---

[45] "Liberty Belle," "It's On!! President's Day Protest at Westlake Park in Seattle!" *Redistributing Knowledge* (February 10th 2009).

[46] Zernike, *Boiling Mad*, 18.

[47] "Seattle Protest Against Obama Stimulus Plan!" *TCUNation* (February 12th 2009).

[48] Michelle Malkin, "Taxpayer Revolt: Porkulus Protest in Seattle, Obama to Sign Theft Act in Denver," MichelleMalkin.com (February 15th 2009).

calling President Obama a socialist, and telling him to spare us his "change," a sarcastic reference to his campaign slogan. President Obama did sign the bill a day later, but a movement like the one Carender hoped for was set in motion. At her rally, she collected many email addresses for an initial mailing list for further action. She wrote on her blog:

> I got most, if not all, of their email addresses in order to start a Seattle Action Network. If every city and town had one too, then we could be more effective in fighting Obama and his dictatorial tendencies. I remembered something I heard during the buildup to the election: whenever Obama held [an event], they collected email addresses and phone numbers. . . . So I thought, boom, that's it. That's what we have to start doing too, so that we can actually meet up in real life, rather than just online.[49]

In this way one of the first Tea Party groups not related to the Ron Paul movement was born. It was called the "Seattle Sons and Daughters of Liberty."

DENVER

On February 17th, the day after the Seattle event, President Obama was slated to sign the stimulus bill in Denver before an invitation-only audience at the Denver Museum of Nature and Science. An "anti-Porkulus" protest was organized there to mark the occasion.

The Denver protest, however, was initiated not by a lone concerned citizen but by the Colorado chapter of Americans for Prosperity, a Washington, D.C.–based organization whose funding has derived in substantial part from oil billionaires Charles and David Koch.[50] It was also "spearheaded," according to Malkin, by the Independence Institute, whose funding derives from the Republican Coors beer family; former Republican Congressman Tom Tancredo, known for focusing almost exclusively on restricting immigration; and several Colorado state Republican Party offi-

---

[49] Keli Carender, "So, So Proud: Happy, Satisfied, Tired, RILED UP!!!" *Redistributing Knowledge* (Keli Carender's blog) (February 16th 2009).

[50] Michelle Malkin, "From the Boston Tea Party to Your Neighborhood Pork Protest," MichelleMalkin.com (February 16th 2009).

cials and politicians.[51] Some two hundred people attended.[52] According to the *Denver Post*, attendees ranged from Republican "party operatives" to "moms with children in tow" to "anti-illegal immigration activists" to "self-described libertarians."[53] Malkin spoke and brought a roasted pig to feed the crowd. Other speakers included Jim Pfaff of Americans for Prosperity, Jon Caldara president of the Independence Institute, former Republican Congressman and presidential candidate Tom Tancredo.

CHICAGO

On the heels of a November 22nd demonstration in support of Ron Paul's bill to audit the Federal Reserve, Chicago-based libertarian activists, had been discussing ideas for other big events, specifically a Tea Party–style protest in downtown Chicago that would bring together opponents of the Fed, opponents of the Internal Revenue Service, Libertarian Party members, and others who wanted to reduce the size of the federal government. Organizers shared the idea with other activists, and they began posting it on various liberty-related MeetUp groups' web pages. Soon other groups also picked up on the concept and began forming plans for events in different locations.

Rick Santelli's tirade from the floor of the Chicago Board of Trade created a huge surge of support and participation. At least forty rallies were held in different parts of the country on February 27th 2009.[54] Two months later, on tax day, April 15th 2009, hundreds of Tea Parties were held all across America. The *Wall Street Journal* estimated more than three hundred,[55] the *New York Times*, more than 750.[56] The Tea Party had arrived.

---

[51] Michelle Malkin, "'Yes, We Care!' Porkulus Protests Holler Back," MichelleMalkin.com (February 17th 2009).

[52] "President Signs Massive Stimulus in Denver," ABC 7 News: TheDenverChannel.com (February 17th 2009).

[53] John Ingold, "Anti-stimulus Protest Staged at Colo. Capitol," denverpost.com (February 17th 2009).

[54] Judson Berger, "Modern-Day Tea Parties Give Taxpayers Chance to Scream for Better Representation," Fox News (April 9th 2009).

[55] Glenn Harland Reynolds, "Tax Day Becomes Protest Day," *Wall Street Journal* (April 15th 2009).

[56] Liz Robbins, "Tax Day Is Met with Tea Parties," *New York Times* (April 15th 2009).

The Movement Discovers Itself

What happened in the wake of Santelli's tirade surprised every-one. The most remarkable thing was that the energy of the rap-idly growing Tea Party movement was primarily local. Though prompted by YouTube and other mass media, hundreds of new local groups formed across the country, often by individuals com-ing together who had not previously known of each other's exis-tence. They made use of MeetUp. They met weekly to plan new events and took up frequent collections before some of them instituted regular membership dues. Many, perhaps most, of these new groups had no previous contact with any of the exist-ing nationally-organized associations we describe in the next chapter, though one or more of these organizations would prob-ably soon establish contact with any unaffiliated local group.

As we would expect, Tea Party members were mostly not new converts to an anti-big-government worldview, but people who had long held such beliefs in one form or another without doing much, or perhaps anything, to promote them. This local quality is the great strength of the Tea Party: however much they would come to feel let down by the politicians nominated by the media as 'Tea Party leaders', these new activists knew and still know that politicians and celebrities do not define the movement but at best present a somewhat distorted reflection of it.

The Tea Partiers had little respect for leading Republicans, especially those most closely associated with George W. Bush. They did not even necessarily agree with Rick Santelli, whose tirade helped to ignite their movement. Tea Partiers were more upset about the bailouts to big bankers than about mortgage relief. As people who were themselves too little to be bailed out, they did not take kindly to the contention that financial institu-tions which had committed serious errors were too big to fail.

In areas other than big government, taxation, the deficit, and the debt, the new Tea Party members were all over the map. Many of them quickly concluded that it might be best to keep quiet about the issues that divided them, but for other new members, their opinions on foreign policy, abortion, or immigra-tion seemed so obviously right that they could see no point in being reticent. This variety of opinions on many issues did not at first prove a liability, because the Tea Party was united by opposition to the Obama administration. Whatever might divide the Tea Party, its members were unanimously against the stimulus bill and against Obamacare. Later they would be equally unified in their opposition to Obama's assault on the right to bear arms.

Deficit Terrors

As the Tea Party grew rapidly and began organizing on a more ambitious scale, one of its looming terrors was the sheer size of the budget deficit and the rapid growth of the national debt, projected to grow rapidly from less than a trillion to more than $5 trillion. In one of the objective accounts by an outside observer, Joshua Green wrote of

> the loose affiliation of angry conservatives, disaffected independents, Glenn Beck disciples, strict constitutionalists, and assorted malcontents who gather under the Tea Party banner. This heterodox mass distrusts the political establishment and believes the federal government has grown dangerously large. Some believe that it has usurped powers rightfully reserved for the states, rendering many of its actions illegitimate (the Constitution is the sacred Tea Party text). Above all, Tea Party followers share a profound objection to unchecked spending and expanding credit, as successive administrations and the Federal Reserve have done to the tune of trillions of dollars. This effort to stimulate the economy, they believe, has not only failed to end the recession but made it worse.[57]

---

[57] Joshua Green, "The Tea Party's Brain," *Atlantic* (November 2010).

4

The Tea Party Landscape

What kind of people are Tea Partiers? There seems to be general agreement that they represent a range of different folks of many ethnic groups, religious beliefs, and occupations. However, compared with the total population of American adults they are on average slightly more educated, slightly older, they have somewhat higher than average incomes (without being wealthy), and they are slightly 'more white'.[1] Of course, these qualities tend to be associated anyway: a random sample of people over forty-five years of age is automatically going to be 'more white' than people under forty-five, for example.

Older people in every generation are usually more rightwing than younger people, as individuals learn about the world throughout their lives. As Winston Churchill is supposed to have observed, anyone under twenty-five who is not a socialist has no heart, and anyone over forty who is still a socialist has no brains. The Tea Party is somewhat more male than female, but not extremely so; the highest estimate we've seen is 60 percent male.

Accusations of Racism

Some opponents of the Tea Party movement endlessly reiterate that the Tea Party is about race, calling it a "barely concealed racist

---

[1] *New York Times*/CBS News Poll (April 2010); *USA Today*/Gallup Poll (April 2010). The *USA Today*/Gallup Poll found that 28 percent of the U.S. population identified themselves as Tea Party supporters, and they were "generally representative of the public at large."

movement."[2] To anyone intimately acquainted with the Tea Party, as we are, this is completely ridiculous. It is standard for the left to accuse anyone they disagree with of being racist. For many leftists, this is the only argument they know; facts and evidence have no bearing on it.

Nonetheless, the 'racist' charge has become commonplace in the media both in the U.S. and Europe. For example, Tea Partiers often criticize NPR and PBS, and the leftists who control NPR and PBS naturally respond by denouncing the Tea Party as racist.

From the Tea Party perspective, one of the major abuses of the Constitution is the Public Broadcasting Act of 1967 (47 U.S.C. § 396) which set up public broadcasting in the United States, establishing the Corporation for Public Broadcasting, and eventually the Public Broadcasting Service (PBS) and National Public Radio (NPR).

Many Tea Partiers believe that Congress overstepped its authority in violation of the First Amendment by provided funding to indoctrinate Americans into believing that we need more government spending and socialist schemes. Instead of directly confronting the issues raised by the Tea Party and arguing about facts and ideas, NPR and PBS alike use the traditional and most trusted scare tactics of racial divide, imputation, and name calling to combat the political influence of the Tea Party.

The ideas of democratic socialism and "world revolution" based on the "new majority" (the sort endorsed by the Occupy Wall Street protests) are given credibility by government financed radio and television. As Richard Rahn says, "It has been recognized for decades that NPR has a left-wing agenda and much of its news programming is nothing more than an endless series of demands for more government spending or more regulation."

They use our own tax dollars to do it, calling government radio and TV a public good, a Tea Party member told me in Iowa. Historically, 70 to 80 percent of the aggregate revenues of all public broadcasting stations have been funded from federal, state, and local government sources, principally through CPB, public universities and technical colleges. There is absolutely no reason to treat government broad-

---

[2] drazid.org/ 03-22-2010 or Uwe Schmitt, Mortal Combat in South Carolina, *Die Welt*, translated by Ron Argentati, *Watching America* (20th January 2012).

casting as a 'public good' presumably 'under produced by the market'. The same liberal and socialist messages are also promulgated without any tax subsidy by ABC, NBC, MSNBC, CBS, CNN, and most local Fox stations. There is simply no justification for the government funded and run media. "The Founders, writes Rahn, would decry the use of taxes to lobby for more taxes. . . . What is corrupt is to use taxpayer dollars to lobby for more money for one's favorite program or self-interest.[3]

Former NPR fund-raising executive Ron Schiller has said of the Tea Party: "I mean, basically they . . . believe in sort of white, middle-America, gun-toting. I mean, it's scary. They're seriously racist, racist people."[4]

NPR, in a series of programs designed to discredit the Tea Party movement and its well-known figure Michelle Bachmann, quotes a certain Ryan Lizza who tells NPR *Fresh Air*'s Terry Gross: "To understand her, you have to understand the movement that she came out of. Her early ideological roots were formed by opposition to abortion . . . and she's always been concerned with social issues, the culture war issues. . . . She takes her Christianity very seriously. She comes out of a religious evangelical conservative movement that is very much concerned with developing a biblical worldview and applying it to all corners of one's life."

Then Lizza "noticed this biography of [Robert E.] Lee by [Steven] Wilkins. [I had] never heard of Wilkins and started looking at who he was. And frankly couldn't believe that she was recommending this book. . . . It is an objectively pro-slavery book and was one of the most startling things I learned about her in this piece."[5]

Leftwing comedian Janeane Garofalo called the Tea Partiers "racist rednecks who hate blacks." When Herman Cain enjoyed significant Tea Party support in his short-lived bid for the 2012 Republican presidential nomination, Janeane Garofalo ingeniously managed to attribute his campaign to racism.[6] She said: "People

---

[3] Richard W. Rahn, "Spending for Tyranny," *Washington Times* (February 22nd 2011).

[4] Lazar Berman, "Black Tea," *The American: The Online Magazine of the American Enterprise Institute* (June 2nd 2011).

[5] "The Books and Beliefs Shaping Michele Bachmann," NPR (August 9th 2011).

[6] "Janeane Garofalo, "Racist Republicans Support Herman Cain" RealClearPolitics.com (September 29th 2011).

like Karl Rove liked to keep the racism very covert. And so Herman Cain provides this great opportunity say you can say 'Look, this is not a racist, anti-immigrant, anti-female, anti-gay movement. Look we have a black man."[7] Paul Krugman of the *New York Times* wrote that the Tea Party movement is motivated by "cultural and racial fear."[8]

Replying to these views, a popular radio personality Neal Boortz points out: "Every good leftist Democrat knows if you can't win your argument on any other grounds, you always have race. The one big advantage to playing the race card, of course, is that you can paint any opposing thoughts or viewpoints as being racist."[9] A blogger at the GayPatriot.com, a website for gay Tea Party supporters comments on the media bias against conservatives:

> It always seems as if the media must portray citizens by color when they are "white" especially Republican or conservative. I rarely ever see gatherings or protesters described as "black liberals" or "white liberals" and so forth. It seems to be a way of denigrating the protests by saying they are white and you can sometimes hear the sneers on MSM when they talk about Republicans being white (by white hosts!). There is nothing wrong with being Caucasian or conservative but you wouldn't know that by the press reports.[10]

Pulitzer Prizewinning journalist of the *New York Times*, Kate Zernike, author of *Boiling Mad: Inside Tea Party America*, and definitely no fan of the Tea Party writes:

> The Tea Party started out organized by young libertarian-leaning activists who were concerned about the stimulus and the bailouts. It pretty quickly spread to include people who were more driven by anxiety about the economy—either their own personal situation or just in general. . . . As time moved on and particularly as health-care legislation became a focus for them, older people got involved, and that's why we see polls now showing that the bulk of the Tea Partyers are

---

[7] *The Patriot Post Chronicle* (October 5th 2011).

[8] Andrew Breitbart, "Have You Heard Ken Gladney's Story?" RealClear Politics.com (August 10th 2009).

[9] "Playing the Race Card: Trump or Joker?" BBC News (April 24th 2001).

[10] "AP Finds Anti-ObamaCare Protests Represent Genuine Grassroots," GayPatriot.net (August 13th 2009).

over 45, with a large number of them over 65. . . . What brought most people out for the Tea Party was real concern about the economy, about the debt. I think people need to understand the need to have a conversation around that issue. Also, these are people who feel like they have history and economic arguments on their side. So you need to understand what they are saying. [Those who want to argue with them] will need to [come prepared] to argue on the facts and the ideas. Otherwise, it's just all about anger on both sides. [11]

Tea Party supporters claim these issues have nothing to do with race. Angela McGlowan, a black congressional candidate from Mississippi, told The Associated Press that her Tea Party involvement is "not about a black or white issue . . . It's not even about Republican or Democrat, from my standpoint. All of us are taxed too much."[12]

Another eminent African American activist Wardell Connerly, the founder and the chairman of the American Civil Rights Institute, decried accusations of Tea Party racism and defended the movement in a *National Review* column: "Race is the engine that drives the political Left. In the courtrooms, on college campuses, and, most especially, in our politics, race is a central theme. Where it does not naturally rise to the surface, there are those who will manufacture and amplify it," Connerly said. "I am convinced beyond any doubt that all of this is part of the strategic plan being implemented by the Left in its current campaign to remake America."[13]

The popular TV show, *The Good Wife*, has an occasional minor character, Kurt McVeigh, who is a strong supporter of the Tea Party. He was at first presented as presumptively racist, but as more was revealed about him, became more attractive and clearly not at all racist.

Factually Inaccurate?

Since the Tea Party does not have an official organization or membership list, and anyone who shows up for Tea Party events can

[11] Marjorie Kehe, "Kate Zernike on 'Boiling Mad: Inside Tea Party America'," *Christian Science Monitor* (October 21st 2010).
[12] "Black Tea Party Activists Called 'Traitors'," Foxnews.com (April 5th 2010).
[13] Krissah Thompson, "Some Black Conservatives Question Tea Party's Inclusiveness," *Washington Post* (April 7th 2010).

consider themselves 'members', then obviously there are going to be some people with bizarre or unpleasant views, but in our considerable experience interacting with Tea Party members all over the country, we have found this element to be extremely small. African Americans and other minorities are quite commonplace among Tea Party activists. Atheistic followers of Ayn Rand rub shoulders with Evangelical Christians, and students with small business owners. The few politicians still trusted by many Tea Partiers are ethnically diverse, including Marco Rubio, Alan West, Herman Cain, and Nikki Haley.

In their study of the Tea Party, Skocpol and Williamson provide some information to refute charges of racism, though they leave the general impression that this ugly phenomenon is quite prominent in the Tea Party. This is partly due to a high level of sensitivity to manifestations of supposed racism. The authors give the example of one Tea Party interviewee who remarked that "Some people have a plantation mentality."

Skocpol and Williamson's strong leftist bias pervades their book. They repeatedly state that Tea Partiers hold many beliefs that are factually false:

> Tea Partiers' factually inaccurate beliefs about many policy matters are particularly striking given their relatively high levels of education and overall savvy about the political process. It is hard to escape the conclusion that deliberate propagation of falsehoods by Fox and other powerful media outlets is responsible for mis-arming otherwise adept Tea Partiers, feeding them inaccurate facts and falsely hyped fears.[14]

As an example, they cite the opinion of Tea Partiers that Obamacare will add to the U.S. federal government deficit, commenting that "in fact it is projected to significantly reduce the long-term federal deficit." What is remarkable here is that they do not say 'This is a controversial issue, the Left claims Obamacare will reduce the deficit, while many rightwing economists and analysts claim it will enormously increase it. Perhaps the Tea Party ought to give more attention to the leftist argument, because, after all, it's good enough to convince us'. Instead they take the posi-

---

[14] Theda Skokpol and Vanessa Williamson, *The Tea Party and the Remaking of Republican Conservatism* (Oxford: Oxford University Press, 2012), 202.

tion that the leftist view is a 'fact', and so there must be something wrong with the admittedly intelligent, highly-educated Tea Partiers because they refuse to accept this 'fact'.[15]

A Tool of Powerful Interests?

Aside from accusations of racism, the other popular charge against the Tea Party is that the movement does not represent genuine beliefs and spontaneous activism, but rather the desires of powerful, monied interests. Tea party activists are either unwitting dupes or conscious henchmen promoting the agenda of conservative billionaires or Republican Party insiders.

Popular *New York Times* columnist Paul Krugman, a perpetual critic of both libertarianism and conservatism wrote in April 2009:

> . . . it turns out that the tea parties don't represent a spontaneous outpouring of public sentiment. They're AstroTurf (fake grass roots) events, manufactured by the usual suspects. In particular, a key role is being played by FreedomWorks, an organization run by Richard Armey. . . and supported by the usual group of right-wing billionaires. And the parties are, of course, being promoted heavily by Fox News. But that's nothing new, and AstroTurf has worked well for Republicans in the past.[16]

In the article, he dismisses the Tea Parties in their entirety and predicts the Democrats will benefit if the GOP fails to move on from its sudden, "clueless" preoccupation.

Paul Krugman wrote this just two months after Rick Santelli's famous rant, when the Tea Party movement was still fairly young, before many of the political power brokers even mobilized in reaction to the Tea Party. An August 2011 *New York Times* article entitled "The Monolithic Tea Party Just Wasn't There" by Kate Zernike, author of *Boiling Mad: Inside Tea Party America*, speaks

---

[15] The many analysts who have predicted that Obamacare will add enormously to the deficit do not dispute that it won't do so if the assumptions of its proponents are accepted, but argued that these are unrealistic, and in practice adjustments are bound to be made. In February 2013 the Government Accountability office projected the consequences if Obamacare's unsustainable "cost containment" provisions are phased out, and found that Obamacare would then add $6.2 trillion to the long-term deficit.

[16] Paul Krugman, "Tea Parties Forever," *New York Times* (April 12th 2009).

to the fractured nature of the Tea Party movement even after two years during which various political machines have sought to influence it: "the power of the Tea Party as a singular force may be more phantom than reality." Also, "the Tea Party is no monolith. It is not an official party with policy positions, and its members— some loosely affiliated, some not affiliated with any group but merely sympathetic to what they think the Tea Party stands for— arrived with often different and sometimes incompatible interests."[17] A movement which continues to be made up of small, disparate, fiercely independent subgroups cannot simply be the agent of Paul Krugman's "usual group of right-wing billionaires."

There would be some truth to Krugman's critique if it were applied to a major component of the later Tea Party movement, but in 2009 his criticism was way off the mark and grotesquely unfair to the tens of thousands of Tea Party activists who, for their own reasons and at their own initiative, demonstrated against the reckless economic policies of the federal government. His political assessment of the Tea Party movement strengthening the Democrats also proved to be incorrect. The Republican victory in 2010 was one of the biggest ever.

The Structure of the Tea Party Movement

Different sources have given wildly differing estimates of the Tea Party's size and scope. An attempt at measuring the Tea Party movement was made by the *Washington Post* in 2010. Their months-long effort to contact every Tea Party group in the country culminated in October. They'd succeeded in contacting 647. Most had fewer than fifty members and the median amount of money raised in 2010 was $800. At the time, Tea Party Patriots claimed 2,300 chapters.

A CNN poll around the same time found that 2 percent of Americans considered themselves active members of the movement, while Rasmussen calculated that 29 percent of Americans were, either through friends or family, "tied to" the Tea Party movement.[18]

---

[17] Kate Zernike, "That Monolithic Tea Party Just Wasn't There," *New York Times* (August 1st 2011).

[18] Frank Rich, "The Grand Old Plot Against the Tea Party," *New York Times* (October 30th 2010).

Based on the interactions of this book's authors with dozens of Tea Party activists, it's clear the initial Tea Party protests were locally organized. Each was funded either by a lone affluent member, by member donations, sometimes by local businesses donations. Others were unfunded and covered occasional expenses like the printing of flyers out of pocket as the need arose. Some incorporated as non-profits.

Many Tea Party groups remain local and fiercely independent. More than one Tea Party leader lamented to this book's authors that the left has a huge ideological advantage since they always call for centralization, while the individualism more characteristic of conservatives often divides them and weakens their activism.

Once the Tea Party movement gained prominence, political opportunism abounded. Some political organizers switch the name of their long standing efforts to 'Tea Party' regardless of whether there was ideological overlap. Other Tea Parties formed for the specific purpose of endorsing a particular candidate, provided him or her with vaunted Tea Party credentials.[19] Of course, some of them seem suspiciously opportunistic. There were even accusations of Democrat-created, fraudulent Tea Party campaigns meant to siphon votes from Republican candidates.[20]

A diverse variety of national groups quickly joined the fray. Some of them, most notably FreedomWorks and Americans for Prosperity, pre-dated the Tea Party movement, but their ideology of fiscal conservatism and limited government so closely matched the Tea Party movement, they quickly and naturally became of part of it. They were among the first national organizations with the Tea Party label, hence the target of Paul Krugman's early criticism in April 2009.

Some national organization helped local groups with specific expenses, occasionally in exchange for allegiance or "chapter" status. Alliances were and continue to be tenuous, often arising for a single lobbying effort or political event, then disintegrating. Some states have successfully formed coalitions of Tea Party groups, like the Ohio Liberty Council which formed in June 2009 and has the

---

[19] Interview with Tim Pugh.

[20] Rachel Rose Hartman, "Second Michigan Democrat Pleads No Contest in 'Fake' Tea Party Scheme," Yahoo! News (November 22nd 2011).

mission: "To unite, inform, and empower Ohio freedom loving groups and citizens to affect policy in favor of liberty."[21]

Numerous national organizations joined the Tea Party movement. They all feature advocacy of limited government and lower taxes, but diverge on other issues, and on strategy. National organizations have at times engaged in vigorous infighting which included back and forth accusations of putting profit ahead of advocacy, accusation of Republican Party infiltration, and, the charge made by Paul Krugman, of being astroturf rather than genuine grass roots.

As the Tea Party movement evolved, nationally organized groups gained an increasing share of the media's attention. Some of them were formed and run by former political operatives, including established GOP consultants. In general, national groups are characterized by their large donor bases, extensive political connections and media contacts, and paid staff, sometimes at state level in addition to national level.

The shifting nature of alliances makes it difficult to construct what is perhaps the most important estimate: how much of the Tea Party influence, funding, and volunteer base is on the national rather than local level.

Independent groups continue to be active, and many maintain their suspicion of the GOP as well as national groups.[22] It is likewise difficult to accurately estimate the remaining influence of these national groups as compared to that of the local ones. Their funding and presence remain impressive, but in politics, power is often just the perception of power. Many Tea Party organizations are waiting for new issues to arise.

Some of the fiercely independent Tea Party activists perceive a dilemma between remaining independent and uncompromising, and the allure of stature and money which might won by emulating the practices of the establishment they love to hate. The division was examined by *Politico*'s Ken Vogel in his article on the "Tea Party's Growing Money Problem":

Many Tea Party organizations have shied away from the heavy-handed solicitations that flood the e-mail boxes of political activists.

---

[21] The Ohio Liberty Council, http://www.ohiolibertycouncil.org/.

[22] Interview with Tim Pugh.

And the handful of Tea Party groups that have raised substantial amounts, either by embracing aggressive fundraising or through pre-existing connections to wealthy donors, are viewed suspiciously within the movement. Local groups have been left to literally pass the hat seeking donations at their meetings or rely on their organizers' bank accounts. . . .

The movement's money problems suggest what may be the Tea Party's central paradox—that the very anti-establishment sentiment that spawned it may keep it from having the resources it needs to become a sustainable political force. Many of the newly engaged activists who joined the movement regard traditional political fundraising as representative of the corrupt politics they abhor. "When you start chasing the money, you start having to compromise, and that's where a lot of D.C. organizations go wrong," said Everett Wilkinson, a south Florida financial advisor who helps to run two of the biggest Tea Party groups in Florida. "If we stay trim and we keep our overhead small, we won't have to raise a lot of money and we won't have to compromise. No one owns us."[23]

A Survey of National Organizations Working within or through the Tea Party

THE 9/12 PROJECT

This group was founded by radio and television personality Glenn Beck. He announced its creation during an episode of his Fox News show in March 2009. They helped organize the Taxpayer March on Washington on September 12th 2009, and, a year later, the "Restoring Honor" rally. The events were both criticized and praised as a merging of social conservatism with the fiscal conservatism of the initial Tea Party movement.

In their rhetoric, they promote unity, Christian values, and the idea of strong national defense. Glenn Beck has called the organization an attempt to "bring us all back to the place we were on September 12, 2001," when we stood "together to protect the greatest nation ever created."[24]

---

[23] Kenneth P. Vogel, "Tea Party's Growing Money Problem," *Politico* (August 9th 2010).

[24] Christopher Snow Hopkins, Siddhartha Mahanta, and Theresa Poulson, "12 Tea Party Players to Watch," *National Journal* (November 7th 2010).

On their website, the 9/12 Project claims over five hundred chapters all over the country, though some of them are known to no longer be active. They've co-operated with other Tea Party groups on fiscal issues,[25] and remain active, organizing leadership seminars and promoting support of the military, though their biggest and most influential event (by far) remains the 2009 "Restoring Honor" rally.

AMERICANS FOR LIMITED GOVERNMENT

Americans for Limited Government (ALG) describes itself as "a non-partisan, nationwide network committed to advancing free-market reforms, private property rights and core American liberties."[26]

They've been in existence longer than the Tea Party movement. In 2006, they fought against eminent domain property confiscation in California.[27]

In 2009, they provided database support to the Tax Day protest in Washington DC.[28] That same year, they claimed to have 400,000 members, though this may have been an exaggeration. They were accused of counting an email list bought from a marketing vendor.[29]

They have a ten-thousand-member Facebook page and disseminate press releases and news relevant to the small government cause.

AMERICANS FOR PROSPERITY

Americans for Prosperity (AFP) also pre-date the Tea Party movement. They formed in 2004 when Citizens for a Sound Economy split into two new groups following an internal rift. (The other new organization was FreedomWorks.) Citizens for a Sound Economy had formed twenty years earlier in 1984 and advocated what later became the Tea Party message—less government, less regulation, and lower taxes. Like its predecessor organization, AFP receives a portion of its funding from the Koch brothers, making

---

[25] Interview with Tim Pugh.

[26] From the group's website: http://getliberty.org.

[27] Pamphlet: "More Than Meets the Eye: What Would Proposition 90 Mean For California?" *California Budget Project* (September 2006).

[28] Hopkins, Mahanta, and Poulson, "12 Tea Party Players to Watch."

[29] Scott Shane, "A Critic Finds Obama Policies a Perfect Target," *New York Times* (September 25th 2009).

it the most ready target for accusation of being a front for monied interests.

The AFP Foundation is the grass-roots-activist wing of the organization. According to its spokeswoman, it has chapters in thirty-two states and an email list of 1.6 million, and has received donations from seventy thousand members.[30]

AFP uses state-level co-ordinators to win the support of local, independent Tea Party groups and individuals. They are a regular player in the shifting game of allegiances among Tea Party groups. Local groups can gain "chapter" status with AFP if they so choose. Their tactics have sometimes offended local Tea Party activists:

> The bounty-hunting aspect of AFP's membership drive and its focus on recruiting tea party activists to do the groundwork has rankled some of [Florida's] grassroots conservative activists, who tend to prize their independence. . . . the tea partiers on the ground may not be so amenable to serving as AFP's foot soldiers. Even the former Florida field co-ordinator for AFP, Apryl Marie Fogel, has criticized the initiative. "Incentivizing people with money is no different than what ACORN or other groups are doing," she told Sunshine State News, comparing the process to "Astroturf." "This is the opposite of what AFP stands for."[31]

AFP has organized a "Hands Off My Health Care" bus tour, and participated in a rally in support of embattled, union-fighting Wisconsin governor Scott Walker. Their chapters engage in a wide variety of limited government advocacy. They also run educational and outreach events.

During the 2012 presidential election, their budget totaled over $100 million, at least $27 million of which went toward anti-Obama campaigns.[32]

AMERICAN MAJORITY

American Majority (AM) calls itself "America's Political Training Institute." They are very much focused on identifying, and training activists at local and state levels to promote right-wing causes. On

---

[30] Eric Lipton, "Billionaire Brothers' Money Plays Role in Wisconsin," *New York Times* (February 21st 2011).

[31] Stephanie Mencimer, "Koch-Funded Group Paying Tea Partiers to Collect Voters' Personal Info," *Mother Jones* (January 30th 2012).

[32] Andy Kroll, "Americans for Prosperity Chief: We Don't Know if $27 Million in Anti-Obama Has Any Effect," *Mother Jones* (September 3rd 2012).

their website, as of February 2012, they claim to have trained over nineteen thousand individual and over eighteen hundred candidates in 556 training sessions.

They took to the streets in Wisconsin to support Governor Scott Walker.[33] AM also sponsored Media Trackers, another non-profit launched in Wisconsin to expose unscrupulous liberal activism, including voter fraud, in the effort to recall governor Scott Walker.

In 2011, the group made headlines with a sudden and surprisingly harsh criticism of then-presidential candidate Michele Bachmann, widely considered a Tea Party candidate:

> The group's president, Ned Ryun, said in a blog post entitled "Bachmann's Floundering Can Damage Tea Party" that "It's time for Michele Bachmann to go."
>
> Ryun explained, "Since her meteoric rise this summer and win in the Iowa Straw poll, her campaign has been plagued by losses of top staff, lackluster fundraising, and a seeming lack of direction." He also criticized Bachmann for claiming to represent the Tea Party, saying, "An individual personality or organization purporting to be a 'leader' of what is truly a grassroots movement can hurt the Tea Party brand by creating false impressions about its core beliefs."
>
> Ryun also stated, "In Bachmann's case, it is clear that the campaign has become less about reform and more about her personal effort to stay relevant and sell books; a harsh commentary, but true."[34]

This was surprising, as many Republican presidential candidates claimed various levels of Tea Party allegiance. Much of the initial funding for American Majority came from a grant from the Sam Adams Alliance in Chicago.

They claim as of February 2013 to have conducted over 720 training events in 45 different states.[35]

FREEDOMWORKS

Like AFP, FreedomWorks was created in 2004 after the split of the decades-old organization, Citizens for a Sound Economy. Former Republican Congressman and House majority leader Dick Armey has

---

[33] "I Stand with Walker Rally in Madison, WI," Fox News (February 11th 2009), available on YouTube.

[34] "American Majority, Tea Party Group, Urges Michele Bachmann to Quit Presidential Race," *Huffington Post* (October 28th 2011).

[35] Americanmajority.org.about.

been on the board of directors from the beginning and served as its chairman. He was criticized during this time for getting paid a $500,000 annual salary.[36] He abruptly resigned his position and severed all ties in November 2012, citing a difference of opinion with top management.[37]

FreedomWorks has had to defend itself against charges that it acts largely on behalf of clients of Dick Armey's lobbying firm,[38] and against charges of being astroturf. The prominence and effective fundraising of FreedomWorks greatly raised Dick Armey's political stature.

FreedomWorks pre-dates the Tea Party movement. It promotes conservative activism in tax reform, privatization of Social Security, expanding school vouchers, combating cap-and-trade legislation, and regulatory reform in telecommunications, finance, and medicine. They played an important role in organizing the Washington D.C. Tea Party rallies on April 15th and September 12th 2009.[39]

In 2009, they also encouraged supporters to vocally express their opposition to Obamacare when congressional representatives held town hall meetings.[40]

Some of their funding is rumored to come from corporations including MetLife, Phillip Morris, Verizon, and AT&T.[41]

Their website claims a very large presence: over seven thousand groups and almost a quarter million users.

National Tea Party Federation

The National Tea Party Federation serves as a loose-knit umbrella organization for multiple groups and organizers which formed in 2010. It co-ordinated responses to anti-Tea-Party attacks and

---

[36] Rachael Marcus, "Tea Party Leader Dick Armey Gets First-class Treatment," *Huffington Post* (April 19th 2012).

[37] David Corn and Andy Kroll, "Exclusive: Dick Armey Quits Tea Party Group in Split Over Direction," *Mother Jones* (December 3rd 2012).

[38] "American Majority, Tea Party Group, Urges Michele Bachmann To Quit Presidential Race," Huffington Post, October 28, 2011, http://www.huffingtonpost.com/2011/10/27/american-majority-tea-party-bachmann_n_1062966.html.

[39] Hopkins, Mahanta, and Poulson, "12 Tea Party Players to Watch."

[40] "CBS, Fox Reports on Town Hall Disruptions Ignore Conservative Strategy," Media Matters for America, August 5, 2009, http://mediamatters.org/research/200908050017.

[41] Dan Eggen and Philip Rucker, "Conservative Mainstays and Fledgling Advocacy Groups Drive Health-Reform Opposition," *Washington Post* (August 16th 2009).

hosted online discussions between its participating groups,[42] but appears to be no longer active.

PATRIOT ACTION NETWORK

Perhaps following in the spirit of Meetup.com, which played a big role in Ron Paul's meteoric rise from obscurity in 2008, the Patriot Action Network is an online social network for conservatives. They claim 1.8 million member and described themselves as "a family of dozens of websites designed to help patriotic citizens get informed, engaged and networked with like-minded citizens. At the heart of PAN is our social network—a Facebook-like platform that allows you to get connected in real ways with other patriots by geography or issue."[43]

They provide a platform for discussion, networking, and online petitions. As is characteristic of online forums, their discussions sometimes degenerate into angry, unproductive claims and counter-claims. Nevertheless, by most accounts it is a valuable tool for dissemination of ideas and plans.

Patriot Action Network caters specifically to the Tea Party movement, while their parent organization, Grassfire Nation (itself a division of Grassroots Action), caters to a broader conservative audience.

TEA PARTY CAUCUS

The Tea Party Congressional Caucus is a caucus of U.S. House of Representatives which was organized in the summer of 2010 by Congresswoman Michele Bachmann.

Looking strictly at the national stage and the number of professional Republican consultants involved in Tea Party groups like Tea Party Express and FreedomWorks, we might conclude that the Tea Party movement has melded with the GOP. Tune in to the right local Tea Party group, and you'll get a very different picture. As Kenneth Vogel expressed in *Politico*:

> To anxious Republicans trying to channel grass-roots conservatism, the Congressional Tea Party Caucus is part of the solution. To many in the tea party, the caucus seems like part of the problem.

---

[42] Chris Good, "A Guide to the Six Major Tea Party Groups," *National Journal* (September 11th 2010, updated January 30th 2011).

[43] http://www.patriotactionnetwork.com/.

Instead of embracing the caucus and its 49 House members, many tea party activists see it as yet another effort by the GOP to hijack their movement—and symptomatic of a party establishment that, they say, is condescending and out of step with their brand of conservatism.

At a news conference after the caucus's first weekly meeting July 21, Rep. Michele Bachmann (R-Minn.), flanked by about a dozen tea party activists, stressed that it was not an effort to control or speak for the movement but, rather, to be "a listening ear to the tea party and nothing more."[44]

Rep. Jason Chaffetz (R-Utah) and Ron Paul both declined to join the caucus, citing a concern about top-down control over the Tea Party movement. A majority of the Members of the House Tea Party Caucus voted to raise the debt ceiling with the Budget Control Act of 2011.

Three Senators also met in January 2011 in what they called the first meeting of the Senate Tea Party Caucus: Senator Jim DeMint (R-SC), Rand Paul (R-KY), and Mike Lee (R-UT).

During the 2012 election, the Tea Party Caucus lost only five members, though they included the influential Allen West of Florida and Richard Mourdock of Indiana. The Senate Tea Party Caucus picked up Ted Cruz of Texas and Jeff Flake of Arizona.

After the election, there was a period of complete inactivity, leading to speculation that the Caucus was defunct.[45] However, a meeting was held in April 2013, reinvigorating the Caucus and focusing it on the 2014 elections.[46]

TEA PARTY EXPRESS

The influential, for-profit Tea Party Express was launched in the summer of 2009 by the political action committee Our Country Deserves Better. Long-time Republican consultants and operatives founded Tea Party Express, which has been accused by other Tea Party organizations, most notably Tea Party Patriots, of representing a Republican hi-jacking of the movement.

---

[44] Kenneth P. Vogel, "Tea Party vs. Tea Party Caucus," *Politico* (August 2nd 2010).

[45] David Weigel, "The Tea Party Caucus Is Dead and That's OK," slate.com (March 20th 2013).

[46] Matthew Boyle, "Tea Party Caucus Reloads for 2014," breitbart.com (April 25th 2013).

An argument has broken out, perhaps inevitably, between Tea Party activists and one of the groups that has laid claim to the Tea Party mantle. The self-described grassroots activists in Tea Party Patriots and the American Liberty Alliance see the Tea Party Express as a sham organization, using the political heft of the movement to push a bland, partisan Republican agenda. Privately and publicly, they accuse the Tea Party Express of being an "astroturf" outfit, a scheme for Republican strategists and candidates to take advantage of a movement that was chugging along fine without them.[47]

Among the leadership of Tea Party Express is Howard Kaloogian, a one-time Republican congressional candidate who, in an attempt to show U.S. military success in Iraq, posted a photograph of a placid Turkish suburban neighborhood and claimed it was Iraq. He blamed the error on a staffer.[48] Sal Russo, their chief strategist has worked on Republican campaigns for thirty years and runs a campaign consultancy. Joe Wierzbicki co-ordinates the Our Country Deserves Better Pac which launched Tea Party Express. He also worked to fight lagging support for the war in Iraq with a "Truth Tour" of conservative radio shows.[49]

They had the privilege of partnering with CNN to host the "Tea Party Debate" on September 12th 2011 for Republican Presidential Primary Candidates.

Tea Party Express made headlines in July 2010, when their Mark Williams wrote a satiric letter from "the Colored People" to President Lincoln. Mark Williams had also worked in 2005 to promote the image of the Iraq war, and battled against building the "Ground Zero mosque" in New York City. The National Tea Party Federation expelled Tea Party Express because of what they considered his racist letter.

Some Tea Party activists went so far as to suggest that this was a deliberate smear against the Tea Party.

Tea Party Express supported numerous political candidates including Scott Brown of Massachusettes, Christine O'Donnell, Joe

---

[47] David Weigel, "Tea Party Activists Reject PAC-Backed 'Tea Party Express'," *Washington Independent* (October 9th 2009).

[48] Justin Rood, "Kaloogian Blames Iraq Photo Error on Staffer," TPM, March 29, 2006, http://tpmmuckraker.talkingpointsmemo.com/2006/03/kaloogian_blames_iraq_photo_er.php.

[49] Justin Elliott, "What you need to know about the Tea Party Express," *Salon* (September 15th 2010).

Miller, Marco Rubio, and Sharron Angle. Their bus tours have generated much publicity.

They seem to have been less active in 2012 as compared with 2010. They continue to provide news over their website and host local events, sometimes jointly with 9/12 groups.[50]

TEA PARTY NATION

Also operating for-profit, Tea Party Nation rose to prominence by hosting a convention in 2010 in Nashville that was criticized by Tea Party Patriots because of its cost. Some of the attendees paid $549 for full access, and tickets to the banquet alone were $349, causing some critics to charge that founder Judson Phillips was more interested in profit than advocacy.[51]

Sarah Palin was the keynote speaker, reportedly, for a fee of $100,000. Mr. Phillips has also drawn fire for expressing his opinions on religion and voting rights through the site.[52] The funding for this PAC appears to come from donations and from events. They have clashed with other organizations over the authenticity of their grassroots credentials.

In December 2011, they condemned the Navy for allowing a "sexual aberration' after a photograph circulated of a lesbian female sailor who won a raffle to be the first off her ship and greeted by a loved one, a Navy tradition.[53]

Mr. Phillips has said that Tea Party Nation is "barely breaking even," and profits from the convention are "going to get plowed back into some form of activism, whether we do it in a 527 or chose some other form, we'll have to wait and see."[54]

TEA PARTY PATRIOTS

Tea Party Patriots formed in 2009. They have always been the most fiercely grass-roots of the various Tea Party organizations.

---

[50] http://www.teapartyexpress.org.

[51] Steven Portinoy, "Whose Tea Party Is It? Nashville Convention Stirs Debate," ABC News (February 4th 2010).

[52] http://en.wikipedia.org/wiki/Tea_Party_Nation.

[53] Brian Tashman, "Tea Party Nation Condemns Navy Kiss for Sanctioning a 'Sexual Aberration," *Right Wing Watch* (December 23rd 2011).

[54] Hopkins, Mahanta and Poulson, "12 Tea Party Players to Watch."

Their website claims, "Tea Party Patriots is 100% grassroots, 100% of the time." They are often the first and loudest voices accusing other national organization of being astroturf.

At one point, they claimed fifteen million members. They pride themselves on being leaderless, though two figures, the founder, Mark Meckler, and Jenny Beth Martin, work as co-ordinators. They decided not to join the National Tea Party Federation for fear of it being a "top-down power-grab."[55]

They promote fiscal responsibility, constitutionally limited government and free market economics, by providing logistical, education and networking support to local groups.[56] They've supported the Tax Day Tea Party on April 15th, Glenn Beck's September 12th 2009 rally, and the town hall protests against President Obama's healthcare plan.[57]

In July, 2012, their Atlanta chapter joined the local NAACP to protest and ultimately defeat a proposed transit tax.[58] They remain very active on social media and locally.

OTHER GROUPS

Other Groups include the political action committee Liberty First, which ran the website taxdayteaparty.com, a hub for the April 15th demonstrations, Smart Girl Politics, Inc. which provides leadership training to conservative female candidates, and the Patriot Caucus, which has sought to mediate infighting between various tea party groups.

On one hand, the infighting and maneuvering of these groups may fracture solidarity and weaken particular causes. It has also provided a ripe target for criticism of the movement as a whole. On the other, the ideological and practical disagreements between groups forces them to examine and justify their positions and policies. This helps keeps their message honest and relevant.

---

[55] Chris Good, "A Guide to Tea Party Infighting," *The Atlantic* (September 22nd 2010).

[56] Group website: https://www.teapartypatriots.org/about.

[57] Hopkins, Mahanta, and Poulson, "12 Tea Party Players to Watch"; Ian Urbina, "Beyond Beltway, Health Debate Turns Hostile," *New York Times* (August 7th 2009).

[58] Patrik Jonsson, "How Tea Party and Its Unlikely Allies Nixed Atlanta's Transit Tax," *Christian Science Monitor* (August 1st 2012).

Corporate Influence and the Koch Brothers

The Koch brothers have been at the center of attacks charging the Tea Party movement with being astroturf—a fake movement of unwitting dupes and corporate agents promoting not their self-interest, but that of their corporate masters. In his *New York Times* column, "The Billionaires Bankrolling the Tea Party," Frank Rich writes:

> There's just one element missing from these snapshots of America's ostensibly spontaneous and leaderless populist uprising: the sugar daddies who are bankrolling it, and have been doing so since well before the "death panel" warm-up acts of last summer. . . . You've heard of one of them, Rupert Murdoch. The other two, the brothers David and Charles Koch, are even richer, ... But even those carrying the Kochs' banner may not know who these brothers are.
>
> Their self-interested and at times radical agendas. . . . The country will be in for quite a ride should these potentates gain power. . . .
>
> Only the fat cats change—not their methods and not their pet bugaboos (taxes, corporate regulation, organized labor, and government "handouts" to the poor, unemployed, ill and elderly).[59]

Any ideological movement which achieves more than a few hundred supporters gets a few comparatively wealthy sympathizers as well, who then provide donations. This was true of the socialist movement from its beginnings in the nineteenth century and is true of the Environmentalist or Green movement today. The Tea Party is no more dominated by its few rich supporters than these leftist movements—perhaps much less so, given the enormous support for the Tea Party among many thousands of middle-income people.

Like many opponents of the Tea Party, Frank Rich ignores the myriad Tea Parties which are self-funded or not funded, and many others which have very extensive donor bases, often relying on modest individual contributions from thousands of people.

Another *New York Times* criticism against the Koch brothers, suggests it was their nefarious dealings which led to Wisconsin governor Scott Walker's scaling back of public sector union privileges:

---

[59] Frank Rich, "The Billionaires Bankrolling the Tea Party," *New York Times* (August 28th 2010).

State records also show that Koch Industries, their energy and consumer products conglomerate based in Wichita, Kan., was one of the biggest contributors to the election campaign of Gov. Scott Walker of Wisconsin, a Republican who has championed the proposed cuts."[60]

Blogger Chris Adamson responded to the *New York Times* article with a post entitled "Follow the Money, unlike the NY Times." While it's true that Walker's gubernatorial campaign received $43,000 from the Koch Industries PAC, and as much as $65,000 from the Republican Governor's Association which also received a donation from the Koch PAC, both of these contributions together amount to one tenth of one percent of the $37.4 million spent on the 2010 Wisconsin Gubernatorial race. This fact was omitted in the article.

Chris Adamson also addressed the *New York Times*'s report that "donations by Koch Industries and its employees climbed to a total of $2 million in the last election cycle, twice as much as a decade ago, with 92 percent of that money going to Republicans":

> Sounds horrible, huh? What are the facts that the *Times* does not enlighten its readers with? . . . Koch Industries is #84 on the list [of biggest campaign donors]. Guess what, of the top 20 donors only 1 leaned Republican.
>
> 12 of the top 20 are unions, all of which gave a huge majority to Democrats. . . . Only in the mind of the *Times* could the Koch donations be considered suspect of influencing the Wisconsin/Public Sector Union debate, while the union donations themselves, at many times the amount of the Koch donations, be considered not the more important story worthy of investigation.[61]

The Koch brothers have financial connections to only one, albeit prominent, Tea Party organization: Americans for Prosperity. They helped fund its predecessor organization, Citizens for a Sound Economy before there was a Tea Party movement.

They have a long history of interest and involvement in politics, very much on the conservative and libertarian side. David Koch

---

[60] Eric Lipton, "Billionaire Brothers' Money Plays Role in Wisconsin Dispute," *New York Times* (February 21st 2011).

[61] Chris T. Adamson, "Follow the Money, unlike the NY Times," *The Right Answer* (February 23rd 2011).

was the Libertarian Party's vice-presidential candidate in 1980. Not all Libertarians support the Kochs. Around the time of David Koch's Libertarian Party candidacy, they had a falling out with radical libertarian icon and philosopher Murray Rothbard over what Rothbard perceived as too much compromise on libertarian principles, including a lack of condemnation of the nuclear weapons industry.[62]

Though it is certainly their right, the Kochs claim no active role in the operations of Americans for Prosperity (which formed before the Tea Party movement in 2004) or any other Tea Party organizations. The *New Yorker* examined the truth of this claim:

> In April, 2009, Melissa Cohlmia, a company spokesperson, denied that the Kochs had direct links to the Tea Party, saying that Americans for Prosperity is "an independent organization and Koch companies do not in any way direct their activities." Later, she issued a statement: "No funding has been provided by Koch companies, the Koch foundations, or Charles Koch or David Koch specifically to support the tea parties." David Koch told the *New Yorker*, "I've never been to a tea-party event. No one representing the tea party has ever even approached me."
>
> At the lectern in Austin, however, Venable—a longtime political operative who draws a salary from Americans for Prosperity, and who has worked for Koch-funded political groups since 1994—spoke less warily. "We love what the Tea Parties are doing, because that's how we're going to take back America!" she declared, as the crowd cheered. In a subsequent interview, she described herself as an early member of the movement, joking, "I was part of the Tea Party before it was cool!" She explained that the role of Americans for Prosperity was to help "educate" Tea Party activists on policy details, and to give them "next-step training" after their rallies, so that their political energy could be channelled "more effectively." And she noted that Americans for Prosperity had provided Tea Party activists with lists of elected officials to target. She said of the Kochs, "They're certainly our people. David's the chairman of our board. I've certainly met with them, and I'm very appreciative of what they do."[63]

It seems that at worst, the Kochs are sincere but distant support-

---

[62] David Gordon, "Murray Rothbard on the Kochtopus," LewRockwell.com (March 10th 2011).

ers of the movement—hardly the puppet masters they are accused by the left of being. Nor do they represent the Republican establishment. In the 2010 election cycle, the Kochs gave $196,000 to Democrats.[64] Looking at Wisconsin alone, where so many accusations surrounded Governor Walker's dispute with public sector unions, Common Cause reported that since 2003, 16.2 percent of political donations by the Koch Brothers went to Democrats.[65]

In addition to promoting free markets and small government, the Kochs have opposed the Iraq War, supported gay marriage,[66] donated $20 million to the ACLU to fight the Patriot Act and $600 million to non-political charities like medical research and the arts[67] (including PBS's *Nova*, the American Museum of Natural History, and the New York State Theater). They also support drug legalization and reduced defense spending.[68]

The other occasional charges of corporate influence best apply to national organizations who receive large contributions from companies, or FreedomWorks, whose leader also runs a lobbying firm on behalf of corporate clients. These charges, like those leveled at the Koch brothers, only describe a minority of the Tea Party movement. This addresses the most important part of the accusation of being astroturf: the authenticity of the sentiment and message. We can also point out a double standard between how Tea Party financing is perceived versus how the financing of left-leading institutions is perceived.

George Soros is probably the left equivalent of the Koch brothers. Soros is ranked as the forty-sixth richest person in the world and has given an estimated $8 billion dollars to humanitarian and political causes.[69] He has personally funded Media Matters in an effort to counter what he perceives to be the "incendiary rhetoric of Fox News."[70] Soros has complained that the right is undermin-

---

[63] Jane Mayer, "Covert Operation," *New Yorker* (August 30th 2010).

[64] Ben Smith, "Kochs gave $196,000 to Democrats in 2010 cycle," *Politico* (September 9th 2010).

[65] Ashland Current, "Rundown of Koch Donations In Wisconsin Since 2003," *Ashland Current* (March 15th 2011).

[66] Ben Smith, "No Koch-Liberal Alliance?" *Politico* (February 25th 2011).

[67] Hans Bader, "The Koch Brothers Unwittingly Subsidized Their Enemies," *Washington Examiner* (March 2011).

[68] Nick Gillespie, "Why the Evil Koch Brothers Must Be Stopped," reason.com (February 24th 2011).

ing democracy and poses a threat to world peace. However he shares the Kochs' interest in decriminalization of drugs,[71] and their opposition to the Patriot Act.[72]

Yet the activities of Soros and other left-of-center philanthropists are widely accepted as patriotic and altruistic while similar activity by the right is automatically decried as a subversion of democracy. If Soros is considered a philanthropic benefactor of the left and Democrats, then the Kochs should be viewed simply as inspired benefactors of the right. There is little difference between their methods and even some overlap in their objectives.

GOP Influence

There seems to be much more merit to the charge of Tea Party activists being servants of the GOP. Unlike the charge of being corporate shills, however, the people accusing various Tea Party groups of GOP influence are usually other Tea Partiers.

Some level of relationship between the Tea Party and the GOP is inevitable, since there is a clear ideological overlap. Though it seldom translates to implementation, Republican talking points generally include limited government, low taxes, and low regulation. Many within the Tea Party see it as their mission to bring the Republican Party back to its small government roots, and are eager to work with and within the party for this reason.

Despite the close relationship, there can be little doubt that the Tea Party has been both willing and able to upend the establishment Republican candidates, party positions, and dialogue. The 2013 gathering of the influential Conservative Political Action Committee (CPAC) was overwhelmingly fiscally conservative and libertarian.[73]

We have seen how Tea Party–supported political candidates upset many establishment favorites in the 2010 elections: Rand

---

[69] "George Soros," *Forbes* (September 21st 2011).

[70] Frank Rich, "The Billionaires Bankrolling the Tea Party."

[71] Dan Gainor, "George Soros, Godfather of the Left Gives $550 Million to Liberal Causes," Fox News (December 14th 2011).

[72] "Transcript: David Brancaccio interviews George Soros," PBS (December 12th 2003).

Paul defeated Trey Grayson in Kentucky's U.S. Senate race; in South Carolina, Nikki Haley defeated several Republican insiders in the primary; Marco Rubio defeated one-time GOP star, Charlie Crist, for U.S. Senate in Florida; Christine O'Donnell defeated Michael Castle in Delaware's Senate race to the disappointment of President Bush's advisor, Karl Rove; in Alaska's U.S. Senate race Joe Miller defeated Lisa Murkowski in the primary, but lost to her in the general election.

In the 2012 Congressional elections, Tea Party–affiliated candidates suffered minor losses in the House, but major gains in the Senate. Tea Party impact on the Presidential election was muted due to a lukewarm or hostile perception of Republican candidate Mitt Romney by most Tea Parties.

There were statements demonstrative of Tea Party versus Republican animosity. For example, after the 2010 election, Senator Trent Lott said, "We don't need a lot of Jim DeMint disciples. As soon as they get here, we need to co-opt them,"[74] as well as other strong signs of animosity: an October 2010 survey by the *Washington Post* found that 87 percent of local Tea Party organizers expressed dissatisfaction of mainstream Republican Party leader.[75]

Since the Tea Party's emergence, the Republicans seem to have grudgingly adjusted to the new reality and relations are less tense.

As we noted earlier, Tea Party Patriots famously accused Tea Party Express of being a Republican Party hijack operation. "We do not want it to be a GOP movement. There are many organizations that are trying to hijack the movement," said TPP organizer Amy Kremer.[76] They also withdrew from the National Tea Party Federation, citing concerns about an attempt at top-down control. Many people, including Congressmen Jason Chaffetz (R-Utah) and Ron Paul have criticized the Congressional Tea Party Caucus for similar reasons. Ron Paul has said:

> As one who is opposed to centralization, I am wary of attempts to
> turn a grassroots movement against big government like the Tea Party

---

[73] Zeke J. Miller, "At CPAC, the Future Looks Libertarian," *Time Swampland* (March 15th 2013).

[74] "Obama Has Turned Out to Be an Utter Disaster," *Spiegel* (October 19th 2011).

[75] "An Up-Close Look at the Tea Party and its Role in the Midterm Elections," *Washington Post* (December 19th 2011).

into an adjunct of the Republican Party. I find it even more worrisome when I see those who willingly participated in the most egregious excesses of the most recent Republican Congress push their way into leadership roles of this movement without batting an eye—or changing their policies![77]

The relationship with the Republican party is one of the Tea Party's most interesting features. It has featured both animosity and co-operation. In an article entitled "Is the GOP Absorbing the Tea Party or Is the Establishment Toppling?" journalist Kenric Ward writes:

> Bill Kristol, the neoconservative editor of the *Weekly Standard* and a Fox News contributor, said the tea party peddles "an infantile form of conservatism." Veteran Republican strategist Scott Reed took the disdain one step further, saying the GOP is steadily co-opting the grassroots movement. "That's the secret to politics: trying to control a segment of people without those people recognizing that you're trying to control them," Reed said of the GOP's assimilation strategy. This may sound like good news for Barack Obama's beleaguered Democrats, but . . . tea partiers in Florida and nationally say the establishment types have it exactly backward. "I would just say that we are busy taking over the GOP," said Brendan Steinhauser, director of federal and state campaigns for the national Tea Party network . . . FreedomWorks.
>
> "It will take us years to do, but we are on track. We are starting with taking over as precinct captains and county GOP chairmen. We are also electing true fiscal conservatives to local, state and national office."[78]

A Florida Tea Party leader, Patricia Sullivan, who heads the North Lake County Tea Party, said at a county Republican executive committee meeting, "there are some establishment folks who didn't like the Tea Party initially. But new leadership has come in that appreciates the energy the movement brings."

[76] Staul, "Tea Party Group Accused of Astroturf Lobbying."
[77] Ron Paul, "A Tea Party Foreign Policy. Why the Growing Grassroots Movement Can't Fight Big Government at Home while Supporting It Abroad," *Foreign Policy* (August 27th 2010).
[78] Kenric Ward, "Is GOP Absorbing the Tea Party, or Is the Establishment Toppling?" *Sunshine State News* (October 20th 2011).

The Relevance of Influence

The Tea Party is a huge constellation of many overlapping organizations. Parts of the Tea Party have been created by, or come under the control of, various pre-existing rightwing organizations. But this does not characterize the movement as a whole, and the precise situation is in continual flux.

It is impossible to accurately gauge how much of the Tea Party exists locally versus on the national scale, or how much exists within the Republican Party versus in opposition to it. Alliances are tenuous and often shifting.

Furthermore, when the accusations take the form of outright condemning the Tea Party, they often apply a double standard. Groups which advocate leftist policies have similar practices and institutions. The Tea Party influence is no different than the sort exerted among left leaning organizations. They have their wealthy patrons too, and are probably more dependent on them.

We think that all such matters of funding should be discussed without inhibition and also without morbidly dwelling on the subject. After all, a wealthy individual or self-interested cabal could invent and fund an organization with entirely flawless and beneficial analyses and arguments, while a popular movement that for some strange reason had no wealthy sympathizers could propagate a thoroughly fallacious and pernicious system of beliefs. In any free society, some wealthy individuals are going to attach themselves to any popular movement, and that fact has absolutely no bearing on whether that movement's arguments are right or wrong.

5

God and War

The original, relatively obscure Tea Party protests were orchestrated by supporters of Ron Paul. They shared his beliefs, including his opposition to war and his belief that government, for practical, ethical, and constitutional reasons, should not legislate morality.

The movement gained prominence after being energized by economic concerns as expressed, most famously, by CNBC commentator Rick Santelli's diatribe on February 19th 2009. People's frustration over economic issues brought them out to protest, and they brought with them a wide variety of other beliefs. Other political organizations and power brokers also made deliberate attempts to harness the energy of the Tea Party movement.

While the 2009 Tax Day protests were narrowly focused on profligate spending, expanding government, healthcare reform, and other fiscal issues such as bailouts and over-regulation, the message quickly became more mixed.

Much like the Occupy Wall Street protests which began in 2011, the Tea Party movement was a spontaneous one with no formal membership or official spokesperson. Anyone who made their beliefs heard at a Tea Party protest was, in fact, a Tea Party protester, with as much or as little right to speak for the movement as anyone else. The divergence on issues related to foreign policy and social conservatism was evident as soon as the movement gained prominence.

Tea Party rhetoric in 2011 and 2012 generally hit all the small-government talking points, but often included the importance of a strong military, recognition of the threat of Islamic terrorism, Biblical quotations, and Christian values. This seems to be the case on the national stage much more so than at the local level. Many Tea Party groups remain narrowly focused on fiscal issues, and some explicitly oppose America's military interventions in the Muslim world.

When the schisms began, many Tea Party organizations, though not all, feared diluting or destroying the image of their movement and jeopardizing its future. A tenuous alliance formed between those who were strict fiscal conservative and small government advocates (and little else) and the late comers more inclined to social conservativism and the expression of American greatness through military strength. As time passed, alliances between disparate groups would form and then dissolve, based on single issues, or single political rallies.

Fiscal Versus Social Conservatives

Tea Party members who opposed inclusion of a social conservative message claimed a contradiction between the Tea Party's small-government message and such social conservative goals as passing a constitutional amendment defining marriage, banning abortion at the federal level, or continuing with the criminalization of drugs, alcohol, prostitution, and pornography. Though many Tea Partiers support all these goals on a moral level, calling for more government laws, agencies, and bureaucracies as a means of achieving them looks like a fundamental contradiction with the message of limited government and reduced spending. Some fiscal conservatives also simply feared that a larger Tea Party role for the religious right would scare away moderates they hoped to attract.

As one of the state co-ordinators of the Tea Party Patriots from Maine, Andrew Ian Dodge, put it:

> That ilk want government to regulate marriage and abortion. . . . The Tea Party movement wants government to get off our backs. Government is big enough already, thank you very much.

He went on to explain how social conservatives, and the religious right in particular might weaken the movement:

We're trying to attract as many people as possible, not say: oh, if you're not a Christian, you can't be a member. We don't want to be seen as a bunch of fanatical, evangelical Christians.[1]

Many newspapers reported on the committed secularism of most of the early Tea Party members:

For decades, faith and family have been at the center of the conservative movement. But as the Tea Party infuses conservatism with new energy, its leaders deliberately avoid discussion of issues like gay marriage or abortion. . . . As the Tea Party pushes to change the Republican Party, the purity they demand of candidates may have more to do with economic conservatism than social conservatism. . . . Jenny Beth Martin, the leader of the Tea Party Patriots, complained that she spent days after the convention answering questions about social issues. "When people ask about them, we say, 'Go get involved in other organizations that already deal with social issues very well,'" she said. "We have to be diligent and stay on message."[2]

When Amy Kremer of Tea Party Express was interviewed on the radio show of American Family Association's Bryan Fischer, Fischer asked Kremer for a sign that the Tea Party would support the social conservatives' views on social issues such as abortion and gay marriage.

"Can we hear that message from the Tea Party leadership?" Fischer asked.

"You're not going to hear that from me. I'm sorry; I'm going to disappoint you," Kremer responded. "As long as we stay focused on the fiscal issues, that's the glue that holds us together. If we start delving into the religious aspect or the social aspect, that's when we're going to become divided and when people are going to disagree."

Fischer warned that the strategy might drive social conservatives out of the movement:

"And if they begin to discover that the leadership of the Tea Party movement isn't going to fight for them on those issues, then

---

[1] Tim Mak, "The Tea Party's Growing Religious Divide," *Frum Forum* (October 5th 2010).

[2] Kate Zernike, "Tea Party Avoids Divisive Social Issues," *New York Times* (March 12th 2010).

I think they're going to lose their enthusiasm for the movement. And they'll go back to being disengaged or they'll invest that energy in some other direction."[3]

The fear of the religious right or the GOP hijacking the movement weighed heavily on the movement. The possibility was often explicitly discussed.

An article titled "Will Religious Conservatives Hijack the Tea Party Movement?" appeared in *Capitalism Magazine* in April 2010, shortly after the first anniversary of Rick Santelli's rant.[4] It surveys other accounts of social conservative reaction to Tea Party secularism.

There are various reasons why social conservatives have come to play an increasing role in the movement. Many people who joined the Tea Party movement simply brought their social beliefs with them. In some areas, particularly Texas and the Bible Belt, Tea Parties were united with the religious right from the beginning. Many of them formed around church groups.

Other social conservatives simply welcomed a new opportunity to express frustration and attack President Obama whom they considered their greatest political and ideological opponent.[5] Outrage and dissent were more important than any carefully defined ideology on which the outrage might be based. Many social conservatives were happy to embrace the fiscal message of their fellow malcontents.

There was also conscious political maneuvering to win influence by joining the Tea Party movement, or to re-brand existing organizations with the Tea Party label. The religious right did not fare well in the 2008 election. Their influence had been in steady decline since the election of George W. Bush, if not before. The energy behind their agenda remained second to that of fiscal conservatives.[6] Partnering with the Tea Party movement created new momentum and reinvigorated the religious right. Much of the

---

[3] Barbara Bradley Hagerty, "The Tea Party's Tension: Religion's Role In Politics," NPR (September 30th 2010).

[4] Harry Binswanger, "Will Religious Conservatives Hijack the Tea Party Movement?" *Capitalism Magazine* (April 1st 2010).

[5] "To Hell with Health Care Reform: Religious Right Leaders Attack Obama, Spout GOP Dogma about 'Socialism' While Fanning Flames on Abortion," pfaw.org.

[6] Nicole Russell, "Social Conservatives in the Age of Red Ink," *American Spectator* (February 17th 2011); Dana Milbank, "For the Religious Right, Faith Without Works," *Washington Post* (January 20th 2011).

appeal for the religious right lay in an alternative strategy for achieving their social agenda.

Blogger and separation of Church and State advocate, Rob Boston, offered this observation:

> The tea partiers have all of the energy in the conservative movement right now. Religious right leaders like Perkins and the gang at the AFA are savvy enough to see that. They're not going to let that activism, enthusiasm, and money slip through their fingers.[7]

Regardless of the reason for the shift toward social conservatism within the Tea Party, the shift has occurred. It's now not uncommon at tea party rallies to hear people speak of the nation as having been founded by religious men on biblical principles, or that the United States is a Christian nation. Social conservatives have called themselves the "sleeping giant in the Tea Party."[8]

The ideological overlap between the Tea Party and social conservatives exists most naturally where and when social conservatives perceive government laws and agencies as promoting anti-family and anti-Christian ideas. As expressed by a 2012 CPAC attendee, "The parents, the churches, the communities, that's where they lose the power . . . when the funds come from the government . . . sex ed. in schools—that was all funded by the federal government."[9] In such instances, the Tea Party's limited-government rhetoric meshes well with the social conservative criticism of programs they find offensive.

The religious right also finds some common ground by linking the basis of the Tea Party's economic philosophy to a religious moral underpinning. Jay Richards, the editor of a collection of essay entitled *Indivisible: Social and Economic Foundations of American Liberty*, wrote:

> In the long run, economic prosperity and limited government depend on moral principles like respect for the property right of others and social institutions such as marriage.[10]

---

[7] Rob Boston, "Having a Party: Religious Right Gets an Invitation to Tea," au.org (February 18th 2010).

[8] Hagerty, "The Tea Party's Tension: Religion's Role In Politics."

[9] "Ron Paul: The Buzz at CPAC 2012," Youtube (February 11th 2012).

[10] Jay Richards, "Indivisible: Social and Economic Conservatism," *The American* (February 5th 2010).

Congresswoman, Republican Presidential candidate, and frequent Tea Party keynote speaker Michele Bachmann has gone as far as to claim that "social conservatism is fiscal conservatism."[11]

The individuals and organizations which sought to limit the role of the social conservatives in the Tea Party's early days had limited success. Since the Tea Party has no formal organization, there is no barrier to entry for Tea Party protesters with divergent messages, nor is there anything stopping social conservative groups from rebranding themselves as 'Tea Party'.

Some fiscal-minded Tea Partiers welcomed the inclusion of the religious right, hoping it would give them larger numbers and more clout. This was particularly true for those national organizations which depend on newcomers for monetary support, membership, ideas, and political influence.

Danielle Bean writes in the *Washington Post*, "Frustration always looks a little bit crazy. And today's tea party participants surely are frustrated. They are frustrated with a President and a Congress that do not represent their values, but also (and perhaps most especially) with a Republican Party that has largely abandoned the principles of small government and fiscal conservatism."[12] The religious right shares similar frustrations.

Grover Norquist, head of Americans for Tax Reform, explained the potential for co-operation in the *Los Angeles Times*:

> The reason why social conservatives and economic conservatives can play well together . . . is, the guy who wants to go to church all day just wants to be left alone. So does the guy who wants to play with his gun all day, and the guy who wants to make money all day. They don't agree on how to spend their time, but they do agree on their central issue: They want to be left alone.[13]

Glenn Beck's Restoring Honor Rally was considered a watershed moment when the Tea Party officially merged with the religious right. The event wasn't universally welcomed:

---

[11] Brian Lambert, "'Social Conservatism Is Fiscal Conservatism,' Says Bachmann," minnpost.com (March 28th 2011).

[12] Danielle Bean, "Conservative Conflicts Are Brewing," *Washington Post* (September 22nd 2010).

[13] Binswanger, "Will Religious Conservatives Hijack the Tea Party Movement?"

Beckapalooza was the embodiment of emotion over reason and religious right fanaticism. It is representative of what has turned millions of Americans away from the Republican Party and into political independents. To Americans who believe that religion and politics should not mix, the event was one big travesty.[14]

The estimates of attendees at the August 28th 2010 event range from eighty thousand to a quarter of a million. The distance which many participants traveled demonstrated their commitment. Some observers claimed after the event that the Tea Party had taken the place of the old Christian Coalition as the leader of social conservative activism.[15]

Southern Baptist pastor Rick Scarborough, who has gone from leading a Southern Baptist congregation to leading Vision America, has been a keynote speaker at various Tea Party events. He represents exactly the sort of social conservatives whom the fiscally focused Tea Partiers fear. He once famously stated "I'm not a Republican; I'm not a Democrat; I am a Christocrat."[16]

The true distinction for a group lies in what legislation and activism it engages in. In Texas, the Tea Party agenda focused initially on anti-abortion legislation rather than the state's budget deficit in early 2011, following massive wins by conservatives that brought large majorities to the Texas Statehouse. South Dakota and Oklahoma Tea Party lawmakers also sought passage of legislation on abortion. Indiana prohibited same sex marriage while Montana worked to limit gay rights.

Although these states have incorporated the religious right into their respective movements, there are still Tea Party factions in all parts of the country striving to keep the social conservatives out and to preserve the identity of the Tea Party movement as a fiscal conservative movement focused on financial responsibility. These counter-social conservatives consider the social conservative agenda a threat to the true Tea Party message.

According to Steven Schier, a political scientist at Carleton College, "Social issues have created a potential for internal schism

---

[14] Mak, "The Tea Party's Growing Religious Divide."

[15] Hagerty, "The Tea Party's Tension: Religion's Role In Politics."

[16] Michael Stone, "Religion: Tea Party Politics and the New Christocrats," Examiner.com (February 7th 2010).

within the Tea Party. They have consensus against big government, but the libertarian wing is against introducing social issues." [17]

Andrew Ian Dodge of Maine's Tea Party Patriots adds this libertarian viewpoint: "I want to build on our success, not ruin the coalition by bringing 'God's will' into it."[18]

One Texas observer describes the decision to pursue social legislation as a pragmatic one. Sean Theriault, political scientist at the University of Texas at Austin writes: "Social issues are coming up because they're easier to pass, and there are huge [Republican] margins in the Texas House, so if there was ever a time to pass this kind of legislation, it's now.'" He warned, however, "It's clear that there's more consensus on fiscal issues within the movement. So the more the movement focuses on social ones, the less power it will have." [19]

The Texas libertarian contingent has begun to reassert itself by pushing for more austerity ahead of social legislation. Yet Tea Party favorite, Indiana Governor Mitch Daniels, asked for a truce on discussing social issues among the conservatives in order to prevent a fracture and maintain political power.

Neocons in Tea Bags

The other great split within the Tea Party movement, namely over foreign policy, occurred at the same time as the split on social issues, just as soon as the movement asserted itself as a political force. As Peter Baker detailed in *Foreign Policy*:

> [The Tea Party movement] very decidedly owes its campaign appeal to domestic politics, tapping into economic anxiety and visceral antipathy to what it considers President Barack Obama's big-government program. When it comes to foreign policy, the unity of the Tea Party stops at the water's edge.
>
> Its leaders are hopelessly divided over everything from the war in Afghanistan and counterterrorism policies to free trade and the promotion of democracy abroad. And with the Tea Party increasingly

---

[17] Jon Brand, "Tea Party: Libertarian Revolt or Religious Right in Disguise?" *Christian Science Monitor* (April 21st 2011).

[18] Colin Woodard, "The Soul of the Tea Party," *Daily Beast* (December 1st 2010).

[19] Brand, "Tea Party: Libertarian Revolt or Religious Right in Disguise?"

serving as the Republican Party's driving force, the schism underscores the emerging foreign-policy debate on the American right. . . .

The Tea Party, in other words, is stumbling over a familiar divide on the American right.

When Ron Paul appeared on her MSNBC show, Rachel Maddow discussed the Republican Party's marginalization of Ron Paul, noting that all three Republican challengers to Paul's Congressional seat in the 2010 election claimed Tea Party allegiance.

His opponents cited Ron Paul's "dangerous isolationism and blame-America-first tendencies."[20] Ron Paul later won his district's Republican primary with over 80 percent of the vote, and the general election with 76 percent.

During the interview, Ron Paul spoke about his already tenuous relationship with the Tea Party movement. He never claimed any ownership over the movement and spoke of it as its own entity. With regard to non-interventionist foreign policy and civil liberties, he remarked, "Sometimes the Tea Party accepts these ideas and sometimes they don't." He also said, "The Republican Party wants to make sure there's a neo-con type of influence."[21]

Former George W. Bush speech writer Michael Gerson also acknowledged that the Tea Party had no foreign policy: "There is no clear Tea Party foreign policy ideology—Senator-elect Rand Paul's isolationist tendencies could hardly be more different from Senator Jim DeMint's internationalism." But Gerson predicted that a "Jacksonian" militarism will prevail on Capitol Hill. "Jacksonians like to win wars," he wrote.[22]

Sarah Palin ratcheted up her aggressive foreign policy language when she spoke at the National Tea Party Convention in Nashville in February 2009. Neoconservative and perpetual hawk David Frum praised her hawkish speech, but lamented in his live commentary: "Interesting—no applause for sanctions on Iran. No

---

[20] Daria DiGiovanni, "Conservative Tim Graney Challenges 20-Year Incumbent Congressman Ron Paul in Texas District 14," parcbench.com (February 16th 2010).

[21] *The Rachel Maddow Show*, MSNBC (February 9th 2010).

[22] Michael Gerson, "Will the Tea Party Shift American Foreign Policy?" *Washington Post* (November 9th 2010).

applause for Palin's speculations that democracies keep the peace."[23]

Over time, the perception of the Tea Party movement seemed to shift toward militarism. During a Tax Day protest organized by FreedomWorks in April 2010, under the Washington Monument, Ron Paul spoke about the perils of attempting to police the world, and ending the military presence in Korea and Japan. He was heckled by people toward the back of the crowd who shouted: "God bless the military!"[24]

The contradiction between, on the one hand, small government and low taxes, and, on the other, an aggressive foreign policy and a security state, was widely noted.

James Bovard wrote in the *Christian Science Monitor*: "Many 'Tea Party' activists staunchly oppose big government, except when it is warring, wiretapping, or waterboarding. A movement that started out denouncing government power apparently has no beef with some of the worst abuses of modern times."[25]

Libertarians were alarmed by this trend. The alternative news websites and forums which characterize the suspicious libertarian movement buzzed with anger at what they perceived as a neoconservative takeover of "their" movement. Though libertarians may have a strong case for having originated the Tea Party movement, it was, by this time, no longer theirs.

An October 2010 *Washington Post* survey of 647 local Tea Party organizers asked "Which national figure best represents your groups?" "No one" led with 34 percent of the vote, reflecting the Tea Party movement's tendency toward individualism and independence. Sarah Palin received 14 percent, Glenn Beck 7, Jim DeMint 6, Ron Paul 6, Michele Bachmann 4 percent.[26]

About the split on the issue of foreign policy, longtime conservative strategist Richard Viguerie told the *New York Times*, "We're all on the same page until the polls close November 2nd. . . . Then

---

[23] David Frum, "YouTube Blogging Palin's Speech," FrumForum.com (February 8th 2010).

[24] Kate Zernike, *Boiling Mad: Inside Tea Party America* (Times Books, 2010), 158.

[25] James Bovard, "'Tea Party' Activists: Do They Hate Liberals More than They Love Liberty?" *Christian Science Monitor* (April 23rd 2010).

[26] "Gauging the Scope of the Tea Party Movement in America," *Washington Post* (October 24th 2010).

a massive, almost historic battle for the heart and soul of the Republican Party begins."[27]

One-time presidential candidate and paleoconservative commentator Pat Buchanan put the foreign policy debate front and center in an article entitled, "Tea Party vs. War Party?" Referring to Viguerie's quote, he wrote that "such a battle seems unavoidable." He argued that the military and empire spending are the most feasible place to build a consensus on budget cuts, but, "here is where the Tea Party and War Party split the blanket. . . . If Obama refuses to go to war against Iran, a war that would send oil prices soaring, close the Persian Gulf and be a disaster for the global economy, will the Tea Party join the War Party in denouncing Obama for not launching a third war in the Near East?"[28]

The answer, at least on the national stage, seems to be a resounding "Yes," as exemplified by Freshman Congressman and 2010 Tea Party darling Allen West, who gave an impassioned speech at the 2012 Conservative Political Action Committee (CPAC) Conference.

The CPAC conference is considered an important rally for conservatives, except when Ron Paul wins its straw poll, as he did in 2010 and 2011. Then, the conference is considered to be "hijacked" by "fringe" elements.[29]

At the 2012 conference, Congressman West rang all the fiscal conservative talking points—limited government, individualism, the perils of big government, fiscal conservativism, Constitutionalism. The audience went wild with enthusiasm. He even mentioned "legalized plunder" and the inventor of the term, nineteenth-century anarchist Frédéric Bastiat whose classic essay *The Law* is often cited as an inspiration to modern libertarianism. West told the audience, "We believe . . . in a strong national security posture." He finished by quoting the Book of Joshua and saying that he and his family, like Joshua, "will serve God and we serve this constitutional republic, and we will serve America."

---

[27] Jim Rutenberg, "Rove Returns, with Team, Planning G.O.P. Push," *New York Times* (September 25th 2010).

[28] Patrick J. Buchanan, "Tea Party vs. War Party," *American Conservative* (September 10th 2010).

[29] Jack Hunter, "Conservatives Hijack CPAC," *American Conservative* (February 15th 2011).

West said that the founders "laid out in no uncertain terms the types of things government would have the right to do, and the types of things it wouldn't." Someone who's read the Constitution might speculate whether Congressman West recognizes that only Congress has constitutional authority to declare war. Since entering office, West's comments on foreign policy have been extremely interventionist. He has discussed "a Chamberlin-Churchill moment," "kinetic solutions" to Iran's nuclear research, and "the precipice of World War Three."[30] Perhaps when it comes to threats of war, political posturing is more justified than in other topics.

He also said, "The founders knew that if government were allowed to restrict the freedom of the people . . . freedom would not long survive." Earlier, Congressman West had to defend his vote in favor of renewing provisions of the Patriot Act, widely considered to be violations of the Fourth Amendment.[31] This is also difficult to reconcile with his apparent support for the Constitution.

He decried reckless spending: "We've allowed the federal bureaucracy to balloon out of control," yet, prior to the conference, he voted to raise the debt ceiling. When questioned by Young America's Foundation's Ron Meyer about the vote, he asked for the thing all politicians have always requested: unity and support.[32] He explained that major changes would take time.

Allen West asked the CPAC audience, "Will we re-dedicate ourselves to the values upon which the United States was founded?" Yet he voted in favor of the 2012 National Defense Authorization Act, which authorizes military arrest and detention "without trial until the end of the hostilities" of American citizens.[33]

His earlier attempt at explaining how the bill was not as dangerous as perceived[34] didn't address its most damning part. As

---

[30] "Florida Congressman Allen West Talks about Israel, Iran, Politics and More: Video," allenwestrepublic.wordpress.com (January 20th 2012).

[31] Anthony Man, "Allen West Catches Some Flak for Supporting Patriot Act Provisions," *Sun-Sentinel* (February 15th 2011).

[32] Katie Pavlich, "Allen West Explains Debt Ceiling Vote," townhall.com (August 3rd 2011).

[33] Andrew Nappi, "Allen West and NDAA: Failing Liberty 101," florida.tenthamendmentcenter.com.

[34] "Allen West Finally Sets Record Straight about National Defense Authorization Act," http://www.youtube.com/watch?v=w5KJPm2b-v8#!.

detailed by *Salon*'s Glenn Greenwald,[35] NDAA explicitly "'affirms that the authority of the President' under the AUMF 'includes the authority for the Armed Forces of the United States to detain covered persons.'" Also, "It expressly empowers the President—with regard to anyone accused of the acts in section (b)—to detain them '*without trial* until the end of the hostilities.'"

Originally the antithesis of the Tea Party movement, neoconservativism has, as of the 2012 primary election season, become, at times, indistinguishable from it, especially on the national stage. This isn't unanimous, however. Some politicians elected with Tea Party support have called for cuts to defense spending.[36] Jenny Beth Martin, co-founder of Tea Party Patriots, and other activists have called for consideration of defense cuts.[37]

Local groups hold a wide variety of views, from staunchly anti-war, to indifferent, to resolutely supportive of American exceptionalism. Based on the observation of the authors, most independent Tea Party groups keep their focus away from foreign policy issues and some are explicitly anti-war. In the 2012 Republican presidential primary, Ron Paul enjoyed some local Tea Party support specifically because of his anti-war views.[38]

Glenn Beck

Radio personality, and one-time Fox News icon Glenn Beck seemed to be at the center of both shifts. He also became identified with the Tea Party movement once it achieved prominence, often making provocative statements and providing a ripe target for critics of the movement.

The October 2010 *Washington Post* survey of Tea Party organizers found that while 34 percent considered the groups leaderless, 14 percent considered Sarah Palin their best representative, and

---

[35] Glenn Greenwald, "Three Myths about the Detention Bill," Salon.com (December 16th 2011).

[36] "Tea Party: Defense Spending Not Exempt From Cuts," CBS News (January 24th 2011).

[37] Cristina Marcos, "Tea Party Activists: Bring on Defense Cuts," *The Hill* (August 10th 2011).

[38] Catalina Camia, "S.C. Tea Party Fave: Paul's Anti-War Views Play Well," *USA Today* (January 12th 2012).

Glenn Beck came next with 7 percent.[39] Sarah Palin faded in prominence following her decision not to run for President, and Glenn Beck's name came to represent the Tea Party movement.

Beck wasn't always a Tea Party supporter. While still working for CNN, he ran a political poll on his show asking "Who will win the Republican nomination?" As was common at the time, Glenn Beck's poll excluded the most ardent advocate of small government, Ron Paul.[40]

In a show that took place in November 2007, just a month before the first modern Tea Party event, a Ron Paul fundraiser, Beck accused Ron Paul supporters of sympathizing with terrorism. Glenn Beck began the eight-minute segment by stating he wanted to discuss not foreign but domestic threats to the Constitution: "While our foreign enemies are the obvious ones, the physical threat may be developing domestically as well." Throughout his rant, the words "Divided We Fall" appeared over a picture of American soldiers.

Beck seized upon the fact that Ron Paul had just raised four million dollars on November 5th, Guy Fawkes Day. "Paul's supporters called donation, and I'm quoting, 'a money bomb.'" Beck said he would not "tie [his] movement in with a historical terrorist attack." Then he throws up his hands and says, "you raise money however you want, as long as you're not blowing people up."

Two guests appeared on the show, David Horowitz and Jonathan Sandys. After establishing that Guy Fawkes was a terrorist, they talked about the anti-war movement being joined by a "constituency of Muslim radicals," and disenfranchisement being fueled by Democratic Party leaders defecting from a war they once supported. David Horowitz accused libertarian writer Lew Rockwell of being "totally in bed with the Islamo-fascists," and Jonathan Sandys decries a "total loss of traditional values," which is causing people to advocate a withdrawal from Iraq and preventing them from considering military action in Iran.

After the Tea Party movement began making national headlines, Glenn Beck, now with Fox News, further promoted the cause of military interventionism by launching the 9/12 Project on March 13th 2009, during an episode of his show. On

---

[39] "Gauging the Scope of the Tea Party Movement in America," *Washington Post* (October 24th 2010).

[40] "Glenn Beck at It Again," dailypaul.com (November 16th 2007).

September 12th 2009, 9/12 joined the Taxpayer March on Washington. The following year, in August, the 9/12 Project held a large "Restoring Honor" rally in Washington, D.C.

In both his speaking engagement at the events, and in choosing the organization's principles, Glenn Beck incorporated enough limited-government and fiscal-conservative rhetoric to blur the distinction between 9/12 and the Tea Party movement. The Restoring Honor Rally was covered without distinguishing it from the Tea Party movement, and indeed, many Tea Party supporters attended the rally, and both FreedomWorks and Americans for Prosperity promoted it. It gave new prominence to social conservative issues and to the idea of American greatness through military strength, a tendency evident even in the name of the group, which invokes the attacks of September 11th 2001. Lew Rockwell called the event "Glen Beck's Religio-Death Rally."[41]

Two weeks after the rally, Beck's status as a major Tea Party figure was cemented with his appearance on the cover of *Time*. The cover story, written by David Von Drehle, did not specifically name the Tea Party, but discussed Beck as a representative of contemporary protests and discontent, and except for the anomalous 9/12 rally, the Tea Parties were the only major protests at the time.

Sarah Palin also appeared on *Time*'s cover (three times, from December 20th 2008 to September 15th 2009), but she was always scrutinized and discussed in terms of her viability as a presidential candidate, not as an icon of the popular protests under way.

Two months prior to the rally, Glenn Beck also achieved for the Tea Party movement a strong association with issues of race. He accused President Obama of having "a deep seeded [*sic*] hatred for white people or the white culture."[42]

Glenn Beck also repeatedly identified himself as libertarian. He has invited many libertarian figures to be guests on his show, including one of this book's author's, Yuri Maltsev. Occasionally, he entertained limited anti-war positions.[43] During the 2012

---

[41] Lew Rockwell, "Glenn Beck's Religio-Death Rally," lewrockwell.com (August 28th 2010).

[42] "Glenn Beck Calls Pres. Obama 'Racist,' Accuses Him of 'Deep-Seeded Hatred for White People'," democraticunderground.com (July 28th 2009).

[43] David Swanson, "Is Best Antiwar Voice on TV Glenn Beck?" opednews.com (April 17th 2010).

Republican Presidential Primary, before his show was cancelled by Fox, Beck also passionately endorsed the only anti-war candidate, Ron Paul.

On the one hand, Beck gave a national voice to many important Tea Party and free market ideas. On the other, he seemed to confuse the Tea Party movement, distort its message, and damage its reputation by his often bizarre assertions. Glenn Beck may have been conducting his political education in public, moving from a neoconservative interventionist position to a Ron Paul anti-war position, but as it turned out, he was a key figure in transforming the Tea Party's message from one of fiscal conservatism and limited government, to one of social conservatism and American military assertiveness. And then Fox News pulled the plug on his show, and he lost his effective voice.

Tea Party Baggage

The original Boston Tea Party was, of course, a tax protest, thus the title of 'Tea Party' fits fiscal conservatives much more than social conservatives or foreign policy hawks. The roots of the Tea Party were libertarian. Fiscal conservatives quickly joined the libertarians in 2009, and social conservatives, together with neoconservatives followed once the movement achieved prominence.

Today, all these groups protest and organize under the Tea Party banner. It isn't always clear whether they are allies, opponents, or something in between. Separate ideas use the same name. In some places, social conservatives and neoconservatives are indistinguishable from the Tea Party movement. In others, they are latecomers attempting to harness the energy of popular protests for their own contradictory goals.

The movement as a whole defies categorization. Locally, disparate groups can be seen coming together on specific issues, or for specific events, and then separating.

All the advocacy trends under the Tea Party banner existed before the Tea Party, and all of them will continue into the future. The struggle is largely over the moniker 'Tea Party'. Given the nature of the original Boston Tea Party, the Tea Party movement is unlikely ever to stray completely from the idea of fiscal conservativism, but it remains to be seen where the balance will be struck.

Mitt Romney, generally perceived as a liberal Republican, received several Tea party endorsements, perhaps on the 'lesser evil' principle, including one from Tea Party star Nikki Haley who became governor of South Carolina in 2010. She has received Tea Party criticism for her endorsement. The three other Republican candidates who made it past the beginning of the primary season, Newt Gingrich, Ron Paul, and Rick Santorum, also received Tea Party endorsements. Among active local Tea Party members, we have heard speculation that some Tea Party organizations are hollow shells, created for the express purpose of endorsing a particular candidate.

One telling sign of the shifting perception of the Tea Party is manifest in the actions of the Cedar Rapids Tea Party. It was organized in November 2008, for the specific purpose of opposing a "flood recovery" tax hike, which seemed to have little to do with flood recovery (it included spending for a library and an amphitheater). The Tea Party failed to block the tax increase, and took up a number of other fiscal issues. When the municipal government sought an extension to the tax hike in May 2011, the Cedar Rapids Tea Party organized to block it. Ultimately they succeeded. What's most telling is that they decided not to use the name 'Tea Party' in association with their later efforts, "because of too much confusion and negative association with the term," said the group's leader, Tim Pugh. "It has too much baggage."[44]

---

[44] Interview with Tim Pugh (February 11th 2012).

6

The Tenth Amendment Movement

There's a reason Tea Party protests often include people in tri-corne hats—the hats worn during the time of the revolution, the era in which the U.S. Constitution was drafted. The hats symbolize both the opposition to authority which existed during those years, and the desire for government to observe constitutional restraints.

The Tea Party movement and ideology overlaps considerably with another movement that officially started the year before Ron Paul's "Tea Party" fundraiser. It was called "The Tenth Amendment Movement." Unlike the Tea Party, its goal was very focused: to revive the Tenth Amendment to the U.S. Constitution and thereby limit the federal government's power.

This movement embraces a largely forgotten historic precedent of state-level nullification and challenges what it considers a multitude of federal intrusions, ideas which are now prominent is some (but not all) Tea Party organizations.

The Tenth Amendment to the United States Constitution reads: "The powers not delegated to the United States by the Constitution, nor prohibited by it to the States, are reserved to the States respectively, or to the people."

To understand how both movements might use the Tenth Amendment to further their smaller-government goals, we have to consider the nature of the government specified in the Constitution.

The Constitution was ostensibly designed to define and there-fore limit the powers of the federal government.[1] Article I of the

---

[1] This is the common view; not everyone agrees. Some libertarians have argued that the Constitution's primary purpose was to centralize power in a

Constitution lists the powers of Congress. There are only seventeen of them. Article II confers limited powers on the President, such as the power to make treaties. Article III gives certain powers to the judicial branch. The powers identified in these three parts of the Constitution are the only powers the federal government is supposed to have, and they are only supposed to be exercised by the particular branch of government to which they have been assigned.

Even these powers were hotly contested before ratification of the Constitution by writers and speakers who became known as the "Anti-Federalists." This is a misnomer, as the word federal refers to decentralization, but during the debates, those arguing for the stronger centralization of the Constitution came to be known as "Federalists," and those arguing to sustain the relative decentralization of the Articles of Confederation were labeled "Anti-Federalists." One Anti-Federalist writing under the pseudonym "Brutus" wrote in the *New York Journal* in 1787, "although the government reported by the convention does not go to a perfect and entire consolidation, yet it approaches so near to it, that it must, if executed, certainly and infallibly terminate in it."

"Federal Farmer" wrote for the *Poughkeepsie Country Journal* in 1787, "The plan of government now proposed is evidently calculated totally to change, in time, our condition as a people. . . . it is clearly designed to make us one consolidated government. . . . whether it can be effected without convulsions and civil wars; whether such a change will not totally destroy the liberties of this country—time only can determine."

"Old Whig" wrote in Philadelphia's *Independent Gazetteer* in late 1787, "The new constitution vests Congress with such unlimited powers as ought never to be entrusted to any men or body of men."[2]

James Madison, widely considered the father of the U.S. Constitution reassured dissenters, "The powers delegated by the

---

strong federal government. See Albert Jay Nock, *Our Enemy, the State* (Caxton, 1950 [1935]), 152–183, http://mises.org/books/Our_Enemy_The_State _Nock.pdf; Gary North, "The U.S. Constitution: Tool of Centralization and Debt, 1788–Today," Gary North's Specific Answers, April 4th 2011; Sheldon Richman, "That Mercantilist Commerce Clause," FEE.org (May 11th 2007).

[2] Laurence M. Vance, "The Anti-Federalists Were Right Again," LewRockwell.com (March 13th 2007).

proposed Constitution to the federal government are few and defined. Those which are to remain in the State governments are numerous and indefinite."[3]

Many of the powers that Article I gives to Congress are easy to understand, leave relatively little room for abuse, and haven't caused many disputes: for example, the power to establish post offices and post roads, the power to establish uniform laws on naturalization of immigrants and on bankruptcy, and the power to provide and maintain a navy. Others, however, have been the subject of vigorous debate.

Constitutional Backdoors

Of the three constitutional clauses frequently cited on behalf of expansions of federal government power, the general welfare clause, the commerce clause, and the "necessary and proper" clause,[4] it is arguably the commerce clause which has been the greatest and most audacious legal lever used to expand federal government beyond the specified powers. The clause allows Congress to "regulate Commerce with foreign Nations, and among the several States, and with the Indian Tribes." What exactly this entitles Congress to do depends on how you define "Commerce" and "regulate."

Some conservative and libertarian legal scholars have argued that at the time of the founding, "commerce" was understood to refer only to trade and shipping of merchandise, not to all manner of economic activity.[5] Those scholars have also argued that "regulate" as it used in the Commerce Clause meant only to "make regular"—that is, it empowered Congress to keep trade free between the states and to keep trade free (or unfree) with foreign nations.[6]

However, that's not how the federal government has interpreted the Commerce Clause since the time of President Franklin

---

[3] *Federalist* No. 45

[4] For more detailed information, see Thomas E. Woods, Jr., *Nullification: How to Resist Federal Tyranny in the 21st Century* (Washington: Regnery, 2010), 21–30.

[5] See Randy E. Barnett, *Restoring the Lost Constitution* (Princeton: Princeton University Press, 2004), 281.

[6] See for instance Barnett, 303; Richard A. Epstein, "The Proper Scope of the Commerce Clause," *Virginia Law Review* 73 (1987).

Delano Roosevelt's New Deal. In the modern era, Congress has treated the Commerce Clause as a license to regulate virtually any sphere of human activity on the ground that anything a person does indirectly "affects" Commerce in some way. Thus, for example, in the landmark case of *Wickard v. Filburn* (1942) the U.S. Supreme Court held that the federal government could regulate a farmer's cultivation of wheat on his own property for his own consumption under its power to regulate interstate commerce, even when the farmer has no intention of selling it.[7] The Court concluded that the farmer's wheat-growing "affected" interstate commerce because, if he hadn't grown his own wheat, he would have had to buy wheat on the market, and the market for wheat is a national market.

Since *Wickard*, the Supreme Court has recognized very few limits on Congress's power. In fact, from 1937 until 1995, the Supreme Court didn't strike down a single federal law for exceeding Congress powers under the Commerce Clause. Since 1995, it has struck down only two laws for this reason.

This brings us to the relationship between these three clauses and the Tenth Amendment. The Tenth Amendment states very clearly that any power the U.S. Constitution does not give to the federal government belongs to the states. People who reject the modern broad reading of the Commerce, General Welfare, and Necessary and Proper Clauses believe Congress acts outside of its constitutional powers, exercising powers that were—as the Tenth Amendment says—reserved to the states.

As some legal scholars have put it, the Tenth Amendment really just "made explicit what was already implicit in Article I of the Constitution—the federal government would exercise delegated powers, and all other powers were reserved to the people and the states."[8] State governments have always had a general "police power" over their citizens, which is legally limited only by the provisions of the states' respective state constitutions and by the powers the states have given to the federal government through the U.S. Constitution. Thus, whatever powers the states didn't give up, they still have.

---

[7] 317 U.S. 111 (1942).

[8] Thomas B. McAffee, Jay S. Bybee, and A. Christopher Bryant, *Powers Reserved for the People and the States: A History of the Ninth and Tenth Amendments* (Westport: Praeger, 2006), 44.

So if the Tenth Amendment is redundant, as this suggests, why have it at all? For the same reason that we have the other provisions in the Bill of Rights. The Bill of Rights, which included the first ten amendments to the Constitution, was intended to reassure the Anti-Federalists. As Yale law professor Akhil Reed Amar has put it, one major reason for the Tenth Amendment in particular is "emphasis." The Tenth Amendment is "a kind of exclamation point, an italicization of the Constitution's basic themes of federalism and popular sovereignty."[9]

The Nullification Remedy

How is the Tenth Amendment enforced?

Typically when someone believes that a federal law is outside the proper scope of Congress's powers, he or she tries to get a federal court to strike the law down. Then ultimately the Supreme Court has the final say as to whether the law passes constitutional muster. When federal courts have struck down federal laws, they have usually not relied on the Tenth Amendment specifically because, as we just saw, there is no real need to mention the Tenth Amendment; either Article I grants Congress a particular power or it doesn't.

Although judicial challenges are the most common way to attempt to overturn unconstitutional laws, they may not be the only way or even the best way. In America's early history, some people, including Thomas Jefferson, believed there was another appropriate method: state nullification—the idea that any state should be able to declare a federal law unconstitutional and protect its citizens from its enforcement.

This concept is not mentioned specifically in the text of the Constitution, but nullification advocates believe it is implicit in the Constitution's nature and some say it was a part of the agreement between the states when they originally accepted the Constitution.[10] Additionally, if a law isn't authorized by the Constitution, many

---

[9] Akhil Reed Amar, "Constitutional Redundancies and Clarifying Clauses," *Valparaiso University Law Review* 33 (1998), 12 (quoted in McAffee et al. at 44).

[10] Historian Thomas Woods's case for nullification is premised on the idea that the Constitution was a "compact" among the states, and nullification was part of the deal the states agreed to. See Woods, *Nullification*, 87–113.

will argue that as a constitutional matter, it is null and void, and the states aren't obligated to respect it, whether they have an explicit right of nullification or not.

Nullification advocates also argue that nullification is the only way that the Constitution can have any chance of limiting federal power. If the federal government can decide the extent of its own powers—as it does through the federal courts—then it will of course decide that its powers are very broad. As historian and nullification advocate Thomas E. Woods, Jr., has put it, "If the federal government has the exclusive right to judge the extent of its own powers . . . it will continue to grow—regardless of elections, the separation of powers, and other much-touted limits on government power."[11] Nullification lets people outside the federal government have say.

Nullification has been invoked numerous times in America's history, especially its early history. In 1798, Jefferson anonymously wrote the Kentucky Resolutions, in which the Kentucky legislature declared that the federal Alien and Sedition Acts—which prohibited speech criticizing the federal government—were unconstitutional and that nullification would be the appropriate remedy. That same year, James Madison wrote the Virginia Resolutions, in which the Virginia legislature made the same argument. In 1832 and 1833, South Carolina nullified a tariff imposed by the federal government and almost faced a federal invasion as a result. Later, some Northern states refused to enforce—and therefore effectively nullified—fugitive slave laws, which required the return of runaway slaves.

After the Civil War, nullification mostly went by the wayside as the federal government asserted unprecedented authority over the states and the states mostly accepted it. The idea resurfaced in the mid-twentieth century when Southern supporters of segregation invoked "states' rights" and nullification in support of their battle against federal civil-rights legislation. Of course there is nothing inherently segregationist or otherwise racist about the concept of nullification, and segregationists' invocation of states' rights does not discredit nullification or the Tenth Amendment any more than Ku Klux Klan members' invocation of their right to free speech discredits the First Amendment. Despite nullification also being

---

[11] See Thomas E. Woods, Jr., "The States' Rights Tradition Nobody Knows," LewRockwell.com (June 29th 2005), http://www.lewrockwell.com/woods/woods44.html.

used to fight fugitive slave laws, some legal scholars and journalists claim that the Tenth Amendment and nullification have, as one writer put it, "repellent associations" and an "unsavory legacy" that they are unlikely to shake.[12]

Still, states *have* essentially nullified federal laws in recent years, even if they haven't explicitly invoked the term "nullification."

For example, through a ballot initiative, California legalized marijuana for medicinal use in 1996 despite federal laws that make the sale and possession of marijuana a crime. When the U.S. Supreme Court declared in *Gonzalez v. Raich* (2005)[13] that federal drug laws trumped the California law—even in situations where the marijuana was grown and used entirely within California and was never part of any commercial transaction—California paid it no mind. In other words, the United States Supreme Court did not have the final say for a change.

Hundreds of medical marijuana facilities continue to operate in California despite occasional threats from federal officials.[14] Since Proposition 215's passage in California, sixteen other states and the District of Columbia have adopted their own laws allowing at least some medical-marijuana use.

Another modern example of nullification involves the 2005 federal Real ID Act, which included a requirement that states meet national standards for driver's licenses and would have created a de facto national identification card. Many activists objected to the law because of privacy concerns and state governments didn't like the costs that compliance with the law would impose on them—so many states have simply refused to comply with the law. Without co-operation from every state, the system can't serve its purpose of creating a national ID system, and the federal law therefore has essentially been nullified.[15]

---

[12] William E. Leuchtenberg, "The Tenth Amendment Over the Centuries: More Than a Truism," in Mark R. Killenbeck, ed., *The Tenth Amendment and State Sovereignty: Constitutional History and Contemporary Issues* (Lanham: Rowman and Littlefield, 2002), 103; see also Sean Wilentz, "States of Anarchy," *The New Republic* (April 29th 2010), 5 (calling nullification "harebrained," "discredited," and the product of "mendacity" on the part of its advocates).

[13] 545 U.S. 1 (2005).

[14] "Feds Cracking Down on California Medical Marijuana Dispensaries," *Los Angeles Times* (October 6th 2011).

[15] See Tenth Amendment Center, "Real ID Nullification Legislation."

The Comeback Begins

Encouraged by these examples of de facto nullification, some activists began trying to get people talking explicitly about the Tenth Amendment and nullification once again.

One major force behind this revival is the Tenth Amendment Center, based in Los Angeles. It was founded in 2006 by Michael Boldin, a web marketer who was involved in various types of political activism, particularly anti-war activism, in the first part of the decade.

What prompted Boldin to start focusing on the Tenth Amendment? "Two words," he said, "George Bush."[16] Like many Ron Paul supporters and early tea party activists, Boldin (who supported Paul but does not identify with the Tea Party) was dismayed to see conservatives who had claimed to support limited government during the Clinton Administration embrace George W. Bush's centralizing big-government policies, such as the wars, the Patriot Act, Medicare Part D, and the No Child Left Behind Act. Boldin thought he might be able to use the Tenth Amendment to wake conservatives up to this betrayal of their past professed principles.

The Tenth Amendment had, after all, briefly gotten some respect from conservatives during the height of the anti-Clinton (and supposedly anti-big-government) "Republican Revolution" of the mid-1990s. During that time, the legislatures of at least fifteen states passed non-binding "state sovereignty resolutions," which affirmed the states' rights under the Tenth Amendment and, as Colorado's resolution put it, served as "a Notice and Demand to the Federal Government . . . to cease and desist, effective immediately, mandates that are beyond the scope of its constitutionally delegated powers."[17]

The idea probably caught on as much as it did at that time because it was an easy way for state Republican state legislators to please angry Republican voters at virtually no cost because the resolutions were simply declarations; they didn't actually require any-

---

[16] Except where otherwise noted, quotes from Michael Boldin and details on the Tenth Amendment Center's history are derived from an interview conducted on July 27th 2011.

[17] Dirk Johnson, "Conspiracy Theories' Impact Reverberates in Legislatures," *New York Times* (July 6th 1996), A1.

one to *do* anything. The Tenth Amendment even became enough of a theme among conservatives around this time that the 1996 Republican presidential candidate, Bob Dole, claimed—not too credibly, in light of his voting record during his decades in the Senate—to carry a copy of the Tenth Amendment in his pocket.[18]

Like so much other libertarian-leaning Republican rhetoric of the 1990s, the resurgent interest in the Tenth Amendment was forgotten by most conservatives the instant George W. Bush took office. Thus, when Boldin founded the Tenth Amendment Center, he had to introduce the ideas all over again. This time, though, he wanted the public to receive the message in a deliberate, consistent, uncompromising manner.

As he began blogging on the TAC's website in 2007, Boldin found that much of the interest he received was not from the right but from the left. This made some sense: Medical marijuana legalization, after all, tends to be favored by leftists. People on the left (if not many Democrat politicians in Washington) also tended to be concerned about civil liberties and government invasions of privacy, so he found allies on the left regarding the Real ID Act as well. Boldin also wrote against the wars and the growing domestic police state arising in connection with the war on terror, which also appealed to the left. (What does foreign policy have to do with the Tenth Amendment? Maybe nothing directly, but, Boldin says, it certainly relates to the federal government, particularly the executive branch, acting outside of its constitutional powers by starting wars without Congressional declarations.)

Many conservatives were not so receptive to the message at that time. Hate mail from rightwingers included suggestions that Boldin was a communist, that he should move to Cuba, and that he sided with "the terrorists."

Still, not everyone on the right had forgotten. In 2008, while George W. Bush was still president, Oklahoma state legislator Charles Key, a Republican who helped instigate the wave of state Tenth Amendment resolutions in the 1990s, introduced a new Tenth Amendment (or "state sovereignty") resolution in response to the No Child Left Behind Act, which forced states to conform their educational systems to federal requirements, and the Real ID

---

[18] See for example "Debating Our Destiny: The First 1996 Presidential Debate," PBS (October 6th 1996).

Act, which Oklahoma's legislature had already rejected in 2007.[19] Key's measure failed in 2008, but passed in 2009, and it touched off a new wave of resolutions across the country.

As of December 2011, fourteen states have passed similar resolutions (Alabama, Alaska, Arizona, Idaho, Kansas, Louisiana, Nebraska, North Dakota, Oklahoma, South Carolina, South Dakota, Tennessee, Utah, and Wyoming).[20] Tennessee's, passed in February 2009, declares:

> [W]e hereby affirm Tennessee's sovereignty under the Tenth Amendment to the Constitution of the United States over all powers not otherwise enumerated and granted to the federal government by the Constitution of the United States. We also demand the federal government to halt and reverse its practice of assuming powers and of imposing mandates on the states for purposes not enumerated by the Constitution of the United States.[21]

What's the point in passing such a resolution when it has no "teeth"? Boldin—who has not been directly involved in the resolutions, apart from tracking their progress and celebrating their passage on the TAC's website—compares the situation to a landlord threatening to evict a tenant:

If you owned an apartment building and had a tenant not paying rent, you wouldn't show up with an empty truck to kick them out without first serving notice. That's how we view these Resolutions—as serving "notice and demand" to the Federal Government to "cease and desist any and all activities outside the scope of their constitutionally-delegated powers." Follow-up, of course, is a must.[22]

Partisan allegiance remains a powerful force. While the centralizing policies of the Bush Administration motivated some principled conservatives, as they did Mr. Key, the election of Barack Obama was undoubtedly the greatest factor among conservatives.

---

[19] Michael McNutt, "House Member Says Resolution on 10th Amendment Isn't About Partisanship," *The Oklahoman* (January 4th 2009), 6A.

[20] "10th Amendment Resolutions," Tenth Amendment Center; Kathy Kiely, "Some States Pass Sovereignty Measures," *USA Today* (May 15th 2009), 5A.

[21] HJR 0108 (2009).

[22] Michael Boldin, "The 10th Amendment Movement," LewRockwell.com (March 15th 2010).

Just as many right-leaning Tea Party supporters quickly rediscovered the Constitution as a whole after Obama took office, many nullification supporters rediscovered the Tenth Amendment.

Meanwhile, many on the left quickly changed their priorities. With Democrats controlling the White House and Congress, liberals became less interested in challenging the wars and the police state and more interested in defending the Obama Administration's legislation and policies – though Boldin still finds, and believes he will continue to find, principled people of the left who see political decentralization as the best means of addressing issues that are important to them.[23]

Obamacare and the Commerce Clause

Tea partiers, "Tenthers" and other conservatives and libertarians object to the Patient Protection and Affordable Care Act ("Obamacare") not only as an unjustifiable restriction on individual liberty, but also because they believe it is unconstitutional. One of their main legal objections is that the Act's "individual mandate"—the provision that requires every American above a certain income level to purchase health insurance or pay a monetary penalty—is outside of Congress's Commerce Clause powers.

Its critics point out that insurance contracts were not included in the definition of "commerce" that existed at the time the Constitution was adopted. The original meaning of "commerce" contemplates the trade of *merchandise* among *merchants*. As libertarian Georgetown University law professor Randy E. Barnett argues, insurance contracts are not merchandise; they "are mere promises to pay money upon the occurrence of specified conditions, and do not involve the conveyance of goods or other items from one state to another."[24] The Supreme Court took this view in *Paul v. Virginia* (1869) but then changed its mind seventy-five years later in *United States v. South-Eastern Underwriters* (1944)—without much justification according to critics.[25]

---

[23] See Michael Boldin, "Left Wing Tenther Movement Growing?" Tenth Amendment Center (January 17th 2011).

[24] Randy E. Barnett, "Commandeering the People: Why the Individual Health Insurance Mandate Is Unconstitutional," *NYU Journal of Law and Liberty* 5 (2010), 584.

[25] Barnett, 585–86.

Some conservative and libertarian legal scholars have argued that the Supreme Court should simply overturn the *South-Eastern Underwriters* decision and then strike down Obamacare on the ground that the purchase or non-purchase of health insurance isn't "commerce."[26] This, however, has not been the primary argument Obamacare's opponents in the legal world have made. Their main argument has been that even if we assume that insurance contracts are part of "commerce," and even if we accept all of the Supreme Court's modern case law on the Commerce Clause, forcing someone to buy a product—as Obamacare forces people to buy health insurance—goes too far.

The Supreme Court has approved laws regulating every sort of economic activity, but it has never approved a law regulating economic *inactivity* (such as non-purchase of health insurance). As Barnett argues:

> While Congress has used its taxing power to fund Social Security and Medicare, never before has it used its commerce power to mandate that an individual person engage in an economic transaction with a private company. Regulating the auto industry or paying "cash for clunkers" is one thing; making everyone buy a Chevy is quite another. Even during World War II, the federal government did not mandate that individual citizens purchase war bonds.
>
> If you choose to drive a car on public roads, then maybe you can be made to buy insurance against the possibility of inflicting harm on others. But making you buy insurance merely because you are alive is a claim of power from which many Americans instinctively shrink.[27]

Many Tea Partiers and Tenthers believe there is only one legitimate way to interpret the Constitution, namely, according to its original meaning and not allowing its meaning to change over time. This view, called "originalism," is accepted by a small minority of American legal scholars. The overwhelming majority of scholars are liberal Democrats who favor a flexible, "living" Constitution.[28]

---

[26] See for example Rob Natelson and David Kopel, "Health Insurance Is Not 'Commerce,'" *National Law Journal* (March 28th 2011).

[27] Randy E. Barnett, "Is Health-Care Reform Constitutional?" *Washington Post* (March 21st 2010).

[28] See John O. McGinnis, Matthew A. Schwartz, and Benjamin Tisdell, "The

Most law professors—including even some conservatives, such as Harvard Law School professor Charles Fried—argue that Obamacare should and will receive the Supreme Court's approval on the basis that consumption of, or refusal to buy, health care affects commerce in the sense that modern Supreme Court cases have used the term.[29]

Health Care Freedom Act

One of the most visible fronts on which Tea Partiers and their conservative and libertarian allies have fought against Obamacare is the "Health Care Freedom" legislation introduced and passed in several states. Like many things related to the Tea Party and the Tenth Amendment movements, Health Care Freedom Acts ("HCFAs") have their origin in the years *before* Barack Obama was elected.

Eric Novack, a Phoenix-area orthopedic surgeon, had the idea that led to the HCFA in 2006—not to combat federal healthcare legislation but to prevent Arizona from imposing its own health-insurance mandate like the one Massachusetts had recently enacted under then-Governor Mitt Romney. To implement his idea, Novack got in touch with libertarian lawyer Clint Bolick, director of litigation for the Goldwater Institute, an Arizona-focused public-policy think tank. With help from some additional collaborators, Novack and Bolick got a "Freedom of Choice in Health Care Act" placed on the November 2008 ballot in Arizona as "Proposition 101." If passed, it would have amended the Arizona Constitution to say:

> Because all people should have the right to make decisions about their health care, no law shall be passed that restricts a person's freedom of choice of private health care systems or private plans of any type. No law shall interfere with a person's or entity's right to pay directly for lawful medical services, nor shall any law impose a penalty or fine, of any type, for choosing to obtain or decline health care coverage or for participation in any particular health care system or plan.[30]

Patterns and Implications of Political Contributions by Elite Law School Faculty," *Georgetown Law Journal* 93 (2005), 1167.

[29] See for instance Ruth Marcus, "Health Care Mandate Is Constitutional," *Real Clear Politics* (November 25th 2009); Steve Chapman, "A Conservative Defense of ObamaCare," *Real Clear Politics* (April 17th 2011).

[30] Available at http://www.azsos.gov/election/2008/general/ballotmeasuretext/c-15-2008.pdf.

The measure failed narrowly in the face of opposition from then-Governor Janet Napolitano, insurance companies, the Arizona Chamber of Commerce and Industry, and the Arizona Academy of Family Physicians.[31]

Despite the measure's defeat, it was picked up by the American Legislative Exchange Council ("ALEC"), a right-leaning organization that provides "model" legislation for states to adopt. They encouraged activists and legislators in other states to follow Arizona's example.[32] With the Tea Parties and others up in arms over Obamacare, this effort had rapid success. In 2010, people in forty-two states introduced or announced some version of ALEC's model health care legislation, either as a statute or an amendment to their state's constitution.[33] Two states (Arizona and Oklahoma) passed it as a state constitutional amendment, and six states (Virginia, Idaho, Arizona, Georgia, Louisiana, and Missouri) passed it in the form of a statute. Two more states, Kansas and Tennessee, passed statutes in 2011, with several more states slated to place similar measures before voters in coming elections.[34]

These amendments and laws vary in their wording, but all of them, like the original Arizona proposition, seek to explicitly enshrine two principles into state law: Firstly, that a person should have a right to participate or not participate in any health care system without penalty, and secondly, that individuals should be allowed to purchase, and doctors should be allowed to provide, lawful medical services without penalty.[35]

Without question, the HCFAs should serve the original purpose that Dr. Novack had in mind: they will impose a substantial barrier to future *state-level* universal health care programs, especially in states where they have become constitutional amend-

---

[31] Ken Alltucker, "Health Care Debate Will Rage On," *Arizona Republic* (November 23rd 2008).

[32] "ALEC's Freedom of Choice in Health Care Act," American Legislative Exchange Council, www.alec.org.

[33] Christie Herrera, *The State Legislators' Guide to Repealing Obamacare* (Washington: American Legislative Exchange Council, 2011), 12.

[34] "Health Care Freedom Act," Tenth Amendment Center, www.tenthamendmentcenter.com/nullification/health-care.

[35] See Clint Bolick, "The Health Care Freedom Act: Questions & Answers," Goldwater Institute (February 2nd 2010).

ments which are more difficult to repeal than ordinary statutes. It's not obvious, however, what, if anything, the HCFAs will do to stand in the way of Obamacare. The HCFA does not purport to nullify Obamacare (in fact, its proponents deny that it does so), nor does it suggest any means by which the states will protect their citizens' rights or by which citizens may protect themselves.

It appears that the HCFA's main purpose is to give states that pass it "standing" to sue the federal government. In federal courts, a person or entity must suffer an injury to be able to sue; that is, as the courts put it, a person must suffer injury to have *standing*. Once a state has the HCFA in place, its laws will of course directly conflict with federal law—and it will suffer a legal injury and have standing if the federal law is enforced against its citizens. When the states file their lawsuits, the federal courts will have to decide which will prevail: state HCFAs or Obamacare. To decide these cases, the courts will have to consider where the line is to be drawn between the powers of Congress under the Commerce Clause and the rights of the states under the Tenth Amendment.

In fact, the attorneys general of numerous states (including some that have not passed an HCFA) have been attacking the Obamacare insurance mandate in federal lawsuits. This has been a major issue for many in the Tea Party movement, who have pressured their state attorneys general to bring a lawsuit or to join other states' lawsuits, and who have endorsed candidates who promise to do the same. At this writing, cases are pending in various federal courts. This is likely to lead to conflicting rulings from U.S. Courts of Appeals in different parts of the country. The issue is therefore likely to reach the U.S. Supreme Court.

Stronger Medicine: Nullification

Nullification advocates like the goal of the Health Care Freedom Acts, but they believe that the HCFAs' proponents may be making a critical mistake because their strategy depends on the Supreme Court striking down the federal law—which, if history is any guide, is unlikely. To really stand up to the federal government, nullification advocates say, the states must be willing to stick to their guns not only against Congress but against the federal government as a whole, including the Supreme Court. That is, the states must be willing to protect their citizens' rights even in the face of a Supreme Court decision that declares Obamacare to be lawful and that purports to strike down state laws to the contrary.

The Tenth Amendment Center has therefore proposed its own model legislation—the Health Care Nullification Act—which numerous state legislatures have considered, and which at least one has passed, albeit in a watered-down form.

Whatever else one might say about it, the Center's health freedom law appears to have "teeth." Rather than just make an abstract statement about freedom of choice, it specifically states (among other things) that the Patient Protection and Affordable Care Act is unconstitutional and therefore "null and void," that the purpose of the Nullification Act is to prevent its enforcement, and that any federal agent who attempts to enforce the federal law will be guilty of a felony punishable by a fine of up to $5,000 and a prison term of up to five years.[36]

The Health Care Nullification Act has been introduced in thirteen states' legislatures, and it was passed and signed by the governor—in a watered-down form—in North Dakota.[37] The North Dakota version removed, among other things, the criminal penalties for federal law enforcement officials.[38]

How the Health Care Nullification Act would work in practice, if passed in its pure form, is unclear. Even Thomas Woods, one of nullification's foremost advocates, questions whether enforcement would be feasible. "Will they arrest IRS agents?" Woods asks. "The IRS doesn't even need to send in agents; they can just take the money directly from your bank account." Still, merely proposing the bills and forcing their discussion strikes a blow against the prevailing view of federal law and of the Supreme Court as the ultimate arbiter of what is constitutional. And even the less radical HCFAs, Boldin acknowledges, may still be beneficial to the Tenth Amendment and nullification causes, even if the federal lawsuits based upon them fail, because the laws will help popularize the

---

[36] "Federal Health Care Nullification Act," Tenth Amendment Center, www.tenthamendmentcenter.com/legislation/federal-health-care-nullification-act.

[37] "Health Care Nullification Act," Tenth Amendment Center.

[38] For the text of the version that passed, see Michael Boldin, "Health Care Nullification on Governor's Desk in North Dakota," Tenth Amendment Center (April 22nd 2011); see also "North Dakota Governor Jack Dalrymple Signs Obamacare Nullification Bill," Tenth Amendment Center (April 28th 2011).

idea that the states' and the people's opinion of the constitutionality of a federal law matters.

The Tenth Amendment Versus the TSA

Activists also use the Tenth Amendment to push back against unprecedented federal intrusion in the area of air travel—specifically, to fight back against increasingly burdensome and invasive policies of the Transportation Security Administration ("TSA").

With the passage of the Aviation and Transportation Security Act shortly after September 11th 2001, the TSA took over passenger screening at the nation's airports. Previously, airports or airlines contracted with private firms to screen passengers, who normally just had to pass through a metal detector and allow their carry-on luggage to be x-rayed. With the TSA, however, security measures soon became far more intrusive.

From the early days of the TSA, travelers grumbled—at least when out of earshot of TSA screeners—about apparently senseless rules regarding what one can and cannot bring onto a plane, about having to remove one's shoes and belt when going through security, and about searches of the elderly and small children who are obviously not terrorists. During the Bush years, the TSA received little political pushback and not much attention in the mainstream or conservative media. Only a handful of libertarian writers focused much attention on the TSA's abuses.[39]

Like so much else, this changed once Barack Obama took office. The tea party and conservative media began to highlight TSA abuses and took to calling Secretary of Homeland Security Janet Napolitano "Big Sis."

Of course, there was much to complain about as the TSA rolled out millimeter-wave scanners in airports across the country. Initially introduced at a dozen airports, the millimeter-wave scanners allow TSA screeners to see through passengers' clothes and essentially view their naked bodies, leading some critics to call the machines "pornoscanners."

---

[39] See for example Andrew P. Napolitano, *A Nation of Sheep* (Nashville: Thomas Nelson, 2007), 122–129; James Bovard, *Terrorism and Tyranny: Trampling Freedom, Justice, and Peace to Rid the World of Evil* (New York: Palgrave Macmillan, 2004); Becky Akers, "Big Brother Is Watching as He's Never Watched Before," *The Freeman* (July 2008).

Originally, the TSA scanners were announced as merely an option for people who set off the standard metal detector but didn't want to be subjected to a pat-down search. In 2009, however, the TSA predictably changed its policy; telling everyone to submit to the scans as a matter of course.[40] Passengers may choose to opt out of being scanned, but doing so subjects them to a highly intrusive pat-down search, in which the TSA screener puts his or her hands inside the waistband of the traveler's pants. A policy adopted in 2010 required screeners conducting a pat-down to touch passengers' genitals and female passengers' breasts.[41] Such offensive frisks discouraged some passengers from opting out of the full body scans.

The scanners not only severely compromise privacy and dignity; they also have uncertain health effects. A group of biologists and biochemists from the University of California at San Francisco wrote a letter to Obama science advisor John Holdren expressing concern that the machines' safety had not been independently verified and that their radiation could cause cancer.[42] In November 2011, the European Union banned the body scanners, citing health concerns.[43]

Although Tea Partiers mostly blame Obama and Napolitano for these policies, the scanners were originally introduced under the Bush Administration. Moreover, Michael Chertoff, Secretary of Homeland Security under Bush from 2005 to 2009, owns a consulting firm, the Chertoff Group, which has as its clients the manufacturers of the scanners—a flagrant conflict of interest that went unmentioned when Chertoff appeared on television to defend the scanners' use.[44]

So far, the TSA has endured a parade of bad press and humiliating headlines. In April 2011 the parents of a six-year-old posted

---

[40] See William Saletan, "Deeper Digital Penetration," *Slate* (April 18th 2009).

[41] Gary Stoller, "Airport Screeners Get More Aggressive with Pat-downs," *USA Today Travel* (October 29th 2010).

[42] Letter from John W. Sedat, et al., to John P. Holdren, April 6, 2010, available at http://www.npr.org/assets/news/2010/05/17/concern.pdf.

[43] David DiSalvo, "Europe Bans Airport Body Scanners For "Health and Safety," *Forbes* (November 15th 2011).

[44] Adrian Chen, "Why Is Michael Chertoff So Excited About Full-Body Scanners?" *Gawker* (December 30th 2009).

a video of the TSA frisking their child.[45] Former Miss USA Susie Castillo reported that a TSA agent had touched her genitals four times in the course of a pat-down.[46] The TSA announced it was pleased with a pilot program for new screening procedures after it caused a four-hour delay at Boston's Logan International Airport.[47] TSA agents have been caught stealing or trafficking drugs.[48]

After a failed terror attack aboard a Northwest Airlines Detroit-bound flight on Christmas day, 2009, Homeland Security Secretary Janet Napolitano flip-flopped in her reaction, saying initially, "Once the incident occurred, the system worked," then, "Our system did not work in this instance."[49] TSA agents shut down the entire Bakersfield, California, airport after they mistook jars of honey for explosives. The agents also complained of nausea resulting from what turned out to be the smell of honey, and were taken to a local hospital for treatment.[50]

The Department of Homeland Security reported in 2011 that more than 25,000 breaches of TSA security had occurred since their creation—an average of seven per day. A 2006 test by the TSA showed that screeners at the Los Angeles International Airport and Chicago's O'Hare International Airport failed to find fake bombs in over 60 percent of tests. In 2003, five undercover Department of Homeland Security agents posing as passengers carried weapons through several security checkpoints at Boston's Logan International Airport.[51] These and other pathetic failures have

---

[45] Jenny Wilson, "Six-Year-Old's TSA Pat-Down: Careful or Crossing the Line?," *Time* NewsFeed (April 13th 2011).

[46] David Edwards, "Former Miss USA Winner: TSA Agent 'Touched My Vagina'," *The Raw Story* (April 28th 2011).

[47] "New Security Program Causes Major Logan Jam," WCVBTV (ABC) The Boston Channel (September 16th 2011).

[48] Jennifer Bergen, "TSA Agent Caught Stealing Passenger's iPad, Hides It in His Pants," Geek.com, (July 8th 2011); Andrew Hickey, "TSA Agents Caught Stealing $40,000 Cash from Passenger's Bag at Airport," Cheapoair Travel Blog; "Ex-NY TSA Agent Admits Aiding Accused Drug Dealer," *Wall Street Journal* (August 28th 2011).

[49] "Sorry, Secretary Napolitano, But the System Didn't Work," *The Ostroy Report* (December 28, 2009).

[50] Mike Adams, "Airport Shut Down by Incompetent TSA Authorities after Jars of Honey Flagged as Explosives," *Natural News* (January 9th 2010).

[51] Gary Stoller, "Airport Security Breaches Since 2001 Raise Alarms," *USA Today* (July 13th 2011).

caused many dissenting writers to label the TSA "security theater."

Nevertheless, the TSA has its defenders. On ABC's popular television program *The View*, Whoopi Goldberg accused the founders of a group called "We Won't Fly" which encourage passengers to opt out of full-body scans, of committing an "act of terror" by encouraging interference with official TSA procedures. The show's Elisabeth Hasselbeck suggested their names be put on a list, and Sherri Shepherd explained how the distraction caused by people opting out can help terrorists.[52]

It was against this background that a a newly elected Tea-Party-backed member of the Texas House of Representatives and a University of Texas Ph.D. student and libertarian activist hatched a plan to challenge the TSA's new policies through state laws. In early December 2010, the lawmaker, David Simpson of Longview, Texas, and the student, Norman Horn, convened a group of Tea-Party activists and conservative- and libertarian-leaning legal experts to draft legislation, which Simpson would then introduce.

Initially, they produced three separate pieces of legislation:

- a resolution that declared that the TSA scanners violated Texans' rights under the U.S. and Texas Constitutions

- a bill that would have outlawed the use of millimeter-wave scanners at airports, subjecting offending airports to civil penalties of up to $1,000 per offense per day

- a bill that would have amended Texas's sexual assault law to apply specifically to airline-travel searches

Through Tea Party groups, the Republican Liberty Caucus, and the Campaign for Liberty, the TSA bills' backers were able to spread the word across Texas. Calls and letters poured into Texas legislators' offices.[53]

The first two of the bills died early deaths in the legislature, never making it to the House floor for a vote. The third, however, not only

---

[52] Jennifer Chou, "Whoopi Goldberg and Elisabeth Hasselbeck Are 'Terrorists'," examiner.com (November 29th 2010).

[53] Except where noted, background details on the Texas anti-TSA measures are derived from an interview with Norman Horn on July 29th 2011.

made it to the House floor, but also made national headlines before it too was quashed by Texas Republican political leaders.

The "anti-groping" bill, as supporters called it, would have made it a "state jail felony" if a person, "as part of a search performed to grant access to a publicly accessible building or form of transportation . . . intentionally, knowingly, or recklessly . . . searches another person without probable cause to believe the person committed an offense; and touches the anus, sexual organ, or breasts of the other person, including touching through clothing, or touches the other person in a manner that would be offensive to a reasonable person."[54]

The anti-groping bill was passed in the Texas House by a unanimous voice vote on May 12, 2011, after a near-supermajority of Texas House members signed on to be (nominal) co-authors. This made national news—and drew the attention of the U.S. Department of Justice, which did not like the prospect of Texas law-enforcement officials arresting federal TSA agents. United States Attorney John E. Murphy sent Texas Senate leaders a letter on May 24, 2011, telling them that "Texas has no authority to regulate federal agents and employees in the performance of their federal duties or to pass a statute that conflicts with federal law." Murphy threatened that if the law went into effect, the "TSA would likely be required to cancel any flight or series of flights for which it could not ensure the safety of passengers and crew."[55] In other words, as the bill's advocates put it, the DOJ essentially threatened to turn Texas into a "no-fly zone" if the legislature defied the feds.[56]

After the letter, the bill was taken off the floor and did not receive a vote during the legislature's regular session. Governor Rick Perry, however, called a special session of the legislature to pass various measures, as the Texas Constitution allows, and activists clamored for him to place the anti-groping bill on the agenda.

In a May 31, 2011 conference call with the Waco Tea Party, Perry, who claimed to support the bill, promised to put it on the

---

[54] Texas H.B. No. 1937.

[55] Letter from John E. Murphy to Texas Senate leaders (May 24th 2011).

[56] Bob Unruh, "Feds to Texas: We'll Make You a 'No-Fly' Zone," WorldNetDaily (May 25th 2011).

agenda if there were a majority of votes in the House and Senate to pass it.[57] On June 18, Perry still had not done so, and he told one of the bill's supporters that he didn't "have the votes" on either side.[58] The bill's supporters found this incredible since the House bill had 112 co-sponsors (out of 150 total members) and the bill's main backer in the state Senate, Dan Patrick, had told Perry that the votes were present in the Senate as well.[59]

Under pressure from Tea Partiers and others, Perry put the bill on the agenda for the special session. The bill, however, never came up for a final vote before both houses before the special session was ended. Many of the bill's supporters place the blame for this on Perry; his Lt. Governor David Dewherst, who served as the head of the Senate; and Speaker of the Texas House Joe Strauss. They allege, in sum, that the Republican leadership deliberately delayed proceedings so the bill would not be passed by the time the special session was over, despite overwhelming support from legislators and the public.[60]

Why would Perry or other Republicans want to do that? Probably the politically ambitious Perry did not actually want a showdown with the federal government in which Texas law enforcement agents would attempt to arrest federal agents; it's too uncertain how that would play out as a legal and practical matter, how the national media would treat it, and how it would affect Perry's already-suspected ambition to seek the Republican presidential nomination. By claiming to support the bill while working behind the scenes to kill it, Perry may have hoped to placate the Tea Party without paying any price.

The legislation's backers hope to reintroduce it in the next legislative session. Meanwhile, similar legislation has been introduced in Michigan, New Hampshire, New Jersey, and Pennsylvania.[61]

---

[57] "Gov. Perry Confronted at New Orleans Book Signing for Breaking His Word on TSA Bill," *TSA Tyranny* (June 20th 2011).

[58] Joe Holley, "At Least He Got a Perry Autograph," *Texas Politics* (June 20th 2011).

[59] "Gov. Perry Confronted at New Orleans Books Signing."

[60] See "Who Killed the Texas TSA Bill?" *Lone Star Watch Dog* (July 15th 2011); Glenn Evans, "Simpson Rips State Leadership Over Pat-Down Bill Failure," *News-Journal* (Longview, Texas) (July 10th 2011).

[61] "TSA: Freedom to Travel Legislation," Tenth Amendment Center.

The Tenth Amendment and Firearms Freedom

In October 2009, Montana became the first state to enact a "Firearms Freedom Act" ("FFA") which explicitly invoked the Tenth Amendment and declared that firearms manufactured in Montana and which remained within Montana's borders were "not subject to federal law or federal regulation, including registration, under the authority of congress to regulate interstate commerce."[62] In other words, to the extent that a federal law purports to regulate firearms made and used only in Montana under the Commerce Clause, that federal law is null and void. Since the Montana FFA's passage, seven more states have passed similar FFAs of their own: Alaska, Arizona, Idaho, South Dakota, Tennessee, Utah, and Wyoming.[63] And at least 20 states in total have introduced such legislation.[64]

The original FFA was drafted and promoted by firearms enthusiast and Missoula, Montana, resident Gary Marbut. Though known as a supporter of gun rights, Marbut's law was a deliberate attempt to vindicate Tenth Amendment rights, not Second Amendment rights. "This is really about states' rights and federal power rather than gun control," he told the *Wall Street Journal*. There is "an emerging awareness by the people of America that the federal government has gone too far," he maintains, and the federal government's expansion of its power under the Commerce Clause is, he says, dependent on the "really weird interpretation" found in *Wickard v. Filburn*.[65]

Once the Montana FFA was signed by Democrat Governor Brian Schweitzer, Marbut declared his intention to manufacture a gun called the "Buckaroo," which would be based upon an 1899 Winchester model and intended for children ages 5 to 10. Orders poured in – including orders from Montana state legislators – but the Bureau of Alcohol Tobacco and Firearms warned Marbut that if he proceeded, they would consider him to be in violation of federal law.

Marbut therefore sued in federal court, and his case is pending before the U.S. Court of Appeals for Ninth Circuit. Hardcore

---

[62] Montana House Bill 246 (2009).
[63] "Firearms Freedom Act," Tenth Amendment Center.
[64] "Firearms Freedom Act," Tenth Amendment Center.
[65] Jess Bravin, "A Gun Activist Takes Aim at U.S. Regulatory Power," *Wall Street Journal* (July 14th 2011).

nullification advocates may observe here, as with the Health Care Freedom Acts, that going to federal court is likely to be a losing battle, as federal courts usually rule in favor of the federal government. It appears Marbut has more radical measures in mind as a backup plan. Should the Supreme Court ultimately strike down the Montana FFA, he has a bill in store called "Sheriffs First," which would allow Montana sheriffs to arrest federal agents who enter their respective counties without permission.

As of March 2013, the case is being heard by the Ninth Circuit Court of Appeals.

Taking Back the 'N' Word

A search of the Lexis-Nexis database of articles from major newspapers in the past several decades, reveals no references at all to nullification in the context of current events (as opposed to historical book reviews and the like) before 2009. Even at the height of interest in the Tenth Amendment during the 1990s, "nullification" does not seem to have found its way into the mainstream media or, for that matter, conservative media. Now, though, the term appears often.

No one knows for certain how it all got started, but it appears that online videos of speeches by libertarian historian Thomas Woods on the "Principles of '98" (that is, the nullification principles of the Virginia and Kentucky Resolutions of 1798) played a critical role. Woods began speaking and writing about nullification around the time that he released his *New York Times* bestseller *The Politically Incorrect Guide to American History* in 2005. He talked about it not because he expected anyone to pursue it again anytime soon—he assumed that was too much to hope for—but because he wanted to challenge the prevailing notion that the federal government should be trusted to determine the extent of its own powers.[66] He was therefore surprised to find, some time later, that some Tea Party groups were featuring the video of his speech on their websites—not just to provide historical background, but to suggest that nullification is something that could be used to limit government today.

---

[66] Except where noted, information related to Dr. Woods in this chapter is derived from an interview conducted with him on July 22nd 2011.

Woods's speeches and articles also caught the attention of Boldin and his colleagues at the Tenth Amendment Center. Thus, in early 2009, Boldin and the Tenth Amendment Center's deputy director, Bryce Shonka, decided that they should make a concerted effort to put the word "nullification" back into the national political conversation. Wherever states were standing up to the federal government in any way, Boldin and Shonka would make phone calls to reporters and send press releases discussing the event in terms of nullification, and the word began to appear in the nation's newspapers.

Although most people aren't used to hearing it—and although it carries a negative connotation for some who have heard of it—Boldin believes the word "nullification" provided a "marketable" hook to catch reporters' attention. Taking a make-lemons-into-lemonade attitude, Boldin even considers the negative association to be potentially beneficial because it may prompt journalists to give a Tenth Amendment-related story more attention than they otherwise would. It's a controversial term, and controversy, of course, draws readers' attention, too. "All publicity," says Boldin, perhaps only slightly joking, "is good publicity."

When he saw nullification making the news, Woods decided to make the most of it by quickly producing a new book on the topic, *Nullification: How to Resist Federal Tyranny in the 21st Century*, released by Regnery, a publisher that specializes in conservative books. With a cover image of Obama signing a bill into law surrounded by Democrat cohorts and the word "NULLIFICATION" stamped over it, the book was pitched squarely at Tea Party supporters looking for a solution other than electoral politics.

Nullification drew even more attention to the cause, especially when the Republican nominee for Attorney General of Connecticut, tea party favorite Martha Dean, not only mentioned the book but read directly from it in a televised debate with her Democrat opponent. To show that the concept was part of Connecticut's heritage, she read from a speech by nineteenth-century Connecticut governor Josiah Trumbull that is reprinted in the book: "Whenever our national legislature is led to overleap the prescribed bounds of their constitutional powers, on the State Legislatures, in great emergencies, devolves the arduous task—it is their right—it becomes their duty, to interpose their protecting shield between the right and liberty of the people, and the assumed power of the General

Government."[67] Unsurprisingly, since Connecticut is a heavily Democratic state, she lost the race.[68]

Attacks from Left and Right

With Tea Partiers and Tenthers challenging the Obama administration's agenda on several fronts, harsh attacks unsurprisingly began to come from the left. Attacks also came from the right.[69] Some of them challenged nullification on the basis of constitutional law. Others simply tried to smear it by associating it with racism and "neo-Confederate" ideology.

The left-wing Southern Poverty Law Center, which describes itself as a "nonprofit civil rights organization dedicated to fighting hate and bigotry, and to seeking justice for the most vulnerable members of society,"[70] featured a Tenth Amendment Center "Nullify Now" conference on its *Hatewatch* blog, even though it was unable to tie the TAC or its conference to anything having to do with racial hatred. Apparently, hatred of centralized government was offensive enough all by itself.[71]

On her primetime MSNBC program, leftist TV host Rachel Maddow ran a feature attacking nullification and the Tenth Amendment called "Confederates in the Attic." The segment began with images of a Civil War re-enactment. It then singled out such efforts as the Georgia Food Freedom Act, which would effectively legalize the sale of raw milk and other food products, which doesn't even explicitly nullify any federal law.[72] Near the end of her

---

[67] Thomas E. Woods, Jr., "Connecticut AG Candidate: I Favor Nullification," TomWoods.com (October 12th 2010). For the Trumbull quote in context, see Josiah Trumbull, "The States Are the Protecting Shield," (speech, Opening of the Special Session of the Legislature, February 23rd 1809), in Woods, *Nullification*, 191.

[68] "Election Results for Attorney General Summarized by Town," Connecticut Secretary of the State.

[69] See for instance Matt Spalding "Nullification Fails, Again (This Time in North Dakota)," *The Foundry* (May 3rd 2011); Michael Sabo, "The Tea Party and Nullification," Ashbrook Center (April 2011).

[70] "Who We Are," Southern Poverty Law Center.

[71] Robert Steinback, "Nullification Advocates Take Show on the Road," *Hatewatch* (April 26th 2011).

[72] "Rachel Maddow: Confederate Themes Back in Fashion" (video), *The Rachel Maddow Show* (April 12th 2011).

piece, Maddow brought on political-science professor Melissa Harris-Perry, who stated that she thinks "it would be foolish to imagine" that renewed interested in nullification "is uncorrelated with having an African-American president. Certainly the revival of notions of the Confederacy track pretty closely with any visible gains in African-American equality."

When he wrote his book *Nullification*, Thomas Woods anticipated attacks like these which raise the specter of segregation and slavery. Woods points out, as we have above, that there is of course nothing inherently racist or segregationist about the concept of nullification or decentralized government. In fact, it was used against slavery by Northern states that didn't want to enforce federal fugitive slave laws. Moreover, political decentralization has historically been the enemy of despotic regimes; notably, Woods points out, Hitler considered it essential to his plans to abolish Germany's decentralized governmental structure. Centralized power, Woods argues, is a much bigger threat to everyone's life and liberty than decentralization.[73]

Conservative attacks have tended more, though not exclusively, toward historical and constitutional arguments. Some specifically attempt to "warn" Tea Partiers away from such efforts, reflecting a split between more establishment-oriented Republicans and the more radical elements of the Tea Party.[74]

That anyone is talking about nullification at all, however, must be seen as a victory for the would-be nullifiers. Even if no major nullifications occur in the short run, the fact that it is part of the political spectrum should change the terms of the debate. If nothing else, it serves to make other Tenth Amendment enthusiasts seem more moderate, which should only please them and help their cause.

The Tenth Amendment's Prospects

How much Tea Partiers, Tenthers, and other would-be nullifiers can accomplish with the Tenth Amendment is unclear. True nullification measures—in which the state would interpose on behalf of

---

[73] See Thomas E. Woods, Jr., "When Zombies Attack," LewRockwell.com (October 21st 2010).

[74] See for example Julie Ponzi, "Nullification Is Not a Principle for the Serious Tea Partier," *No Left Turns* (April 20th 2011).

citizens by arresting federal agents engaged in unconstitutional activities—would require a state governor with exceptional courage. As we have seen from Texas's example, even a governor who purports to support the Tenth Amendment and Tea Party principles can't be counted on when standing up for states' rights would entail a faceoff with the feds and threaten his long-term political prospects.

In the short run, the Tenth Amendment movement will likely accomplish more in the way of education than anything else—education not only about the Constitution, but about the principle of decentralized government and liberty. It will lead more people to question whether it's appropriate for the federal government to be the ultimate arbiter of its own powers.

7

The Tea Party and Occupy Wall Street

From the beginning, Occupy Wall Street was seen as a leftist alternative to the Tea Party. The Occupy movement was initiated by the Canadian anti-capitalist activist group Adbusters and has led to "Occupy" protests and movements around the world. In the United States the first Occupy protest began on September 17th 2011 in Zuccotti Park, in New York City's Wall Street financial district.

Adbusters suggested September 17th as a starting date to coincide with America's Constitution Day, and the idea quickly spread online with help from the hacker group Anonymous. As with the recent citizen uprisings in Europe and the Middle East, social media played a vital role in spreading awareness of the "leaderless resistance movement," particularly on Twitter.

The Zuccotti Park event was prepared by weeks of planning meetings in New York, conducted in "People's General Assemblies." Among the leading activists was the anarchist David Graeber, often identified as the major intellectual influence in the Occupy movement. Graeber is both a distinguished scholar in the field of anthropology and a proud veteran of many violent left-wing demonstrations in Quebec City and Genoa, the Republican National Convention protests in Philadelphia and New York, the World Economic Forum in New York in 2002, and the London tuition protests and riots of 2011.

The Genoa Group of Eight Summit protest, for example, took place from July 18th to July 22nd 2001 and was the bloodiest protest in recent European history wounding hundreds of policemen while horrified civilians locked themselves inside their homes. It also led to the death of a young Genoese anarchist during rioting by masked protesters in black. The city of Genoa is still trying to recover from the damage inflicted by Professor Graeber's comrades.

Some have been scandalized at the organizations and individuals that have endorsed the Occupy protests. They include the American Nazi Party, the government of North Korea, the Islamic terrorist group Hezbollah, and Iranian Supreme Leader Ayatollah Khameni. But the Occupy folks, like the Tea Party, have no control over who voices support for them.[1]

On July 13th 2011 Adbusters demanded that a Wall Street occupation should begin on September 17th. Setting the date and publicizing it through the social media sparked activists in New York and elsewhere. A group of student activists and community organizers, "New Yorkers Against Budget Cuts," led the organization and execution of protests.

For three weeks in June and July, to protest city budget cuts and layoffs, the group had camped out across the street from City Hall in a tent city they called Bloombergville. They liked the idea of trying a similar approach on Wall Street. After talking to Adbusters, the group began advertising a "People's General Assembly" to "Oppose Cutbacks and Austerity of Any Kind" and plan the September 17th occupation. The internet group Anonymous also encouraged its followers to take part in the protests as well as other left-wing groups, including the U.S. Day of Rage and the New York City General Assembly.

The protest itself began on September 17th, a Facebook page for the demonstrations began two days later on September 19th, featuring a YouTube video of earlier events. Half a year later Facebook listed 214 Occupy-related pages.

The main media outlets of the movement are Adbusters, Coup Media Group—Revolutionary Human Media, along with "OccupyWallStreet.org—The revolution continues worldwide!"

Demands

The protesters were against capitalism, for public and private debt forgiveness, against social and economic inequality, against high

---

[1] Lachlan Markay, "Meet the Radical Group Handling 'Occupy Wall Street' Finances" (November 7th 2011), http://blog.heritage.org/2011/11/07/meet-the-radical-group-handling-occupy-wall-street-finances.

unemployment, and against corporate greed, corruption, and the undue influence of money and big corporations in politics. Enemy number one is the financial services sector. The protesters' slogan "We are the 99 percent" refers to the income inequality and wealth distribution between the wealthiest one percent and the rest of Americans. One of the "Occupier's" leaders Ivor O'Connor commented on NPR:[2]

> Our country will spiral down for another twenty years until it is obvious to all we've become a giant slum of a third world nation. All international currency will be based on something other than the dollar. All development done elsewhere. All factories elsewhere. And the economists will look back and sagely say it all started when Nixon took us off the gold standard. . . We missed what was being written between the lines. By the time America realized all that was left was a parasitic infrastructure of government workers feeding off other government workers it was too late to fix the country. An epic depression worse than the collapse of the USSR occurs. Fifty plus years of it.[3]

Many Occupiers shared the Tea Party's concerns on fiscal problems and its distaste for the Big Government–Big Business alliance and bailouts. Both believe that a catastrophe is looming but they differ in their approaches to how to deal with it.

The Tea Party believe in free market capitalism while the Occupiers profess anti-capitalism, though without any agreement on the system they would like to put in capitalism's place. Even the ideological leaders of the Occupiers running the major website of the movement have a pretty blurred vision of alternatives:

> There are some who believe that where there is a market economy, money, and competition, then that's automatically capitalism. That's not true. In capitalism there is of course a market economy, but that can exist in other systems as well.[4]

---

[2] NPR.org: Neal Conan, Host, "Occupy Wall Street: The Future And History, So Far," www.npr.org/blogs/itsallpolitics/2012/12/31/168196092/why-the-tea-party-stands-at-a-crossroads.

[3] "Capitalism IS the Problem." Posted on May 21st 2013, by OccupyWallSt at www. OccupyWallSt.org.

[4] http://coupmedia.org/occupywallstreet/occupy-wall-street-official-demands-2009.

Following Oskar Lange, Mikhail Gorbachev, and other adherents of the "market socialism" theory, Occupiers insist that

> What characterizes capitalism is that there is private ownership of the means of production. That's when you know you're dealing with a capitalist system. If this feature is absent, if it's not the case that some individuals privately own the means of production others are using, then it's no longer capitalism. If it instead was a system in which, let's say, the workers themselves controlled and managed the means of production democratically at the place where they worked, and that these institutions were operating in a market system, then that would be some kind of market socialism etc, not capitalism.

Apparently, though some Occupiers seem to have been influenced by modern theories of market socialism as propounded by such writers as John Roemer and David Schweickart, this influence is not reflected in any publications or websites of the movement that we've seen.

Many Occupiers are anarchists, socialists, left-leaning libertarians and other fellow travelers of all kinds who have participated in mass anti-capitalist, anti-government protests before. They have never reached any agreement on what kind of socialism and what kind of market are to be featured in the new world. We have been forced to conclude that the Occupy movement is even more ideologically diverse than the Tea Party movement, and this is reflected in an eclectic list of Occupy Wall Street demands summarized by Anonymous on the Coup Media Group—Revolutionary Human Media website:

> The Sovereign People's Movement, represented nationally through the people occupying the various Liberty Square locations across this great country, have laid out and democratically submitted and are currently voting on the list of following Demands to then be distilled into one Unified Common Demand of the people. First of all. There are no Official Demands of the Occupy Movement. That being said, multiple factions of the movement have been assembling to discuss and vote on the output and message for the movement. Below this list is a list of grievances that citizens have provided nationally and have voted on in solidarity to the movement.

Visitors to the website are invited to "Participate in Democracy and Vote on Occupy Wall Street Demands Here to Have Your Voice Heard." According to Steve Marshall, a webmaster of the

Coup Media Group—Revolutionary Human Media website, with whom we had a very pleasant conversation on February 17th 2012, all voters are identified by their IP addresses.

> Many have been vocal about the Demands of Occupy Wall Street. From Occupy Wall Street to Occupy SF, Occupy Dallas, and Occupy Austin, to Occupy Boston, and Occupy Seattle. We at Coup Media Group and CoupMedia.Org hear YOU, the 99%. We are also of the 99% faction. Some say we need demands, some say it is foolish to have demands of a broken system. This is a key note because it is indeed a realized point. So what do you think? Please voice your opinion. Whether you are at an Occupy location officially representing the 99% or only able to 'virtually' attend, we at CoupMedia.Org believe that it is your right to have your voices heard. So please, SPEAK UP AND BE HEARD. We stand in SOLIDARITY with all the Occupy movements.[5]

According to webmaster Marshall many of the following demands were brought in by visitors to the website and the most popular demand on that day was to investigate suspicious circumstances surrounding 9/11 as well as a "demand of investigation into the source of secret funding for CIA occupation programs since WWII, the cover up of the trillions of dollars that aided in the collapse of the Soviet Union and may have ultimately instigated the 9/11 attacks as well as their cover-up". As of the same day—February 17th 2012—this was backed by 120,059 votes according to the Coup Media Poll. According to Steve Marshall "Although these votes are not represented by the general assemblies, this demand has become the most popular demand by a significant vote amount that should be considered. Because of the overwhelming volume of votes to include, Coup Media is now including this into the official list of Occupy Demands."

Below Is the Original List of Proposed Demands of the Occupy Wall Street Movement for Global Revolution:

1. Eliminate Corporate Rights as Persons. Require Corporations to have Labor representatives on their boards of directors.

2. Repeal of the Patriot Act.

---

[5] http://coupmedia.org/occupywallstreet/occupy-wall-street-official-demands-2009.

3. Forced Acquisition of the Federal Reserve for $1 Billion USD by the US Congress.

4. Restructure Campaign Finance Legislation and Provide a real democratic system for US Elections and US Policy.

5. Real Health Care Reform. Make Healthcare affordable and available to all without a "Mandate."

6. End the War on Drugs.

7. Education Reform.

8. National Repeal of Capital Punishment.

9. End Gender Discrimination—Equal Pay.

10. Office of the Citizen.

11. The United States Must Comply with International Human Rights Law.

12. Rights of victims must take precedent in courts. Restitution for previous wrongdoing by courts and police.

13. Prosecutions of the guilty. We want indictments and prosecutions of all crimes committed by banks, brokerage firms, and insurance companies.

14. Environmental Responsibility Reform.

15. Repeal Rex 84 and H.R. 645 and the procedures to establish Martial Law.

16. Create a Board of Officers to Manage the Demands to monitor the importance of all demands, with experts who are knowledgeable on the proposed policies and necessary amendments.

17. Re-investigate the Attacks of September 11th 2001 with full media coverage and disclosure.

Prompted by the "Truth" movement, the last demand—to reinvestigate the attacks of September 11th 2001 is the most popular among those summarized above by Anonymous. "Truthers" believe that

No objective person can look at the absence of wreckage at the Pentagon and the WTC Building 7 collapse and not know something is terribly wrong with the official story. Without doubt, the leadership and many members of the mainstream media, Democrats, Republicans, FBI, CIA, MI6, Mossad, the Israeli, British, Russian, European, and Asian governments know the truth or are involved in the September 11, 2001 attack.[6]

According to a Rasmussen poll of May 4th 2007, 22 percent of all voters believe that President Bush and Vice President Cheney knew about the attacks in advance. A slightly larger number, 29 percent, believe the CIA knew about the attacks in advance. White Americans are less likely than others to believe that either the President or the CIA knew about the attacks in advance. Young Americans are more likely than their elders to believe the President or the CIA knew about the attacks in advance. "Truthers" tend to be Democrats and younger. Thirty-five percent of Democrats believe he did know, 39 percent say he did not know, and 26 percdent are not sure. Republicans reject that view and, by a 7-to-1 margin, say the President did not know in advance about the attacks. Among those not affiliated with either major party, 18 percent believe the President knew and 57 percent take the opposite view.[7] This issue, quite popular on the Left was never mentioned at the Tea Party meetings that we know of. It does not appear that any substantial number of Tea Partiers share conspiracy theories with the Left.

Black Blocs and Violent Protests

What began as a peaceful protest in Zuccotti Park turned pretty ugly, apparently due to the impatient behavior of some militants among the Occupiers. According to Peter Gelderloos of Counterpunch, more and more Occupiers are using the Black Bloc tactics which first appeared at the 1999 World Trade Organization protests in Seattle in the form of property damage and violent confrontation with police. Black Bloc followers wear black clothing,

---

[6] http://www.reopen911.org.
[7] Brent Baker, "Flashback: 35% of Democrats Think Bush Knew of 9/11 Attacks in Advance" (August 4th 2009), www.mrc.org/node/34936.

ski masks, scarves, bandanas, black helmets, or other black face-concealing items. The clothing is used to conceal marcher's identities and promote solidarity among the protesters.

According to the BBC, during the violent riots in Rome in October 2011 "militants dressed in black infiltrated the crowd and began attacking property." Offices of the Italian defense ministry and numerous cars including armored police vehicles were set on fire, in addition to attacks on ATMs and bank and shop windows. Violence erupted in "occupied" Oakland, California, Chicago, New York, Washington, D.C. and other cities in the United States and Europe. In the U.S. there have been over 6,846 arrests of Occupy protesters from September 17th 2011 to March 29th 2012 according to Occupyarrests.com. Peter Gelderloos writes:

> Labor union anarchists, anarcha-feminists, social anarchists, indigenous anarchists, Christian anarchists, as well as plain old, unaffiliated street youth, students, immigrants, parents, and others have participated in black blocs.[8]

President Obama and other Democratic Party leaders had encouraging words for the protestors. Drawing parallels between Martin Luther King Jr. and the Occupy Wall Street Movement, President Obama insisted that Dr. King "would have sympathized with activists demanding social justice from Wall Street."

The Democratic Congressional Campaign Committee (DCCC) adopted the goal of collecting 100,000 signatures for a "Standing with Occupy Wall Street" campaign. People can sign a solidarity pledge at the DCCC site and send it to Republican congressional leaders. The Occupy movement was "blessed" by the White House and the General Services Administration which instructed local law enforcement officials in Portland, Oregon, not to arrest members of the Occupy movement. "We now have a new GSA scandal—one that involves the Obama White House," said Judicial Watch President Tom Fitton. "These documents clearly show that federal agencies colluded with the Obama White House to allow the Occupy Wall Street protestors to violate the law with

---

[8] Peter Gelderloos, "Hedges' Hypocrisies: The Surgeons of Occupy," Counterpunch.org (February 9th 2012).

impunity. These documents tell us that the GSA and DHS can't be relied upon to protect federal workers or property." [9]

It is not clear, however, whether "Standing with Occupy Wall Street" campaign and Obama's support of Occupiers was an asset or liability for Democrats.

Conservative blogger Bruce McQuain writes: "It comes as no surprise then those media water carriers and spin doctors along with the administration see this as an opportunity to expand on the class warfare meme and shift blame and focus away from government."

Tea Partiers' Response to Occupiers

There were numerous attempts to identify Tea Partiers and Occupiers. Almost half of Americans identify themselves as supporters of one movement or the other. Contrary to popular perceptions, the Tea Party movement attracts more white-collar support than blue-collar, and the largest contingent of Occupy Wall Street supporters isn't young but rather middle-aged.

In a very broad sense both movements have something in common, namely a long lists of grievances and complaints. Both tend not to offer specific ideas and solutions. Both are products of discontent with the status quo and a desire to affect the national conversation. As in all the most powerful populist movements in history, it is common for members to know what they are against rather than provide specific detailed solutions to the problems or agree on detailed programs provided by others. Both groups are critical of the big government and totalitarian tendencies of the Obama Administration.

Kate Zernike wrote:

> More and more commentators—as well as President Obama—have likened the Occupy forces spreading across the country to the Tea Party movement. But as they have, conservatives and Tea Party activists have rushed to discredit the comparison and the nascent movement. They have portrayed the Occupy protesters as messy, indolent, drug-addled, and anti-Semitic, circulated a photo of one of them defecating on a police car, and generally intimated that

---

[9] www.americanthinker.com/blog/2012/08/gsa_scandal_just_got_a_lot_more_interesting.html#ixzz2UbGmpr3G.

Democrats who embrace them are on a headlong road to Chicago 1968.[10]

Rick Santelli rejected any similarities:

> While the vandals are on the street corners, the Tea Party conservatives, they're working state houses, the governorships, the mayorships, the Senate, the House. See, they understand, they've read the Constitution. If you want to make a difference, don't go break windows, okay? Break some phony arguments that things like austerity are going to put you in the hole. What put you in the hole is borrowing 38 cents of every dollar you spent. That's what put you in the hole, pure and simple. Everything else is political spin.

A bystander at the Occupy DC camp at McPherson Square told us pointing at the Occupiers' poster demanding debt forgiveness: "Debt forgiveness is an excellent idea, except for the fact that someone's debt is another's savings." Others go further: "Occupy Wall Street is one of the most egregiously immoral "movements" in the past several decades. Reports of rape, violence, public masturbation, and rabid anti-Semitism define OWS, writes blogger Aurelius. He compiled a set of 40 links to pictures, videos, articles and police reports. All of these materials look authentic.[11]

At the Tea Party meetings Occupiers are often compared with Chinese Red Guards—a mass paramilitary social movement of young people in the People's Republic of China, who were personally approved and supported by Mao Zedong in 1966 during the Cultural Revolution. Millions were murdered during the Cultural Revolution and it was a disaster for China. From the point of view of older leaders of the Occupiers, it was a brilliant piece of guerilla action on Mao's part in the power struggle he instigated, a lesson that many older radicals remember well since their first political apprenticeship in the tumultuous 1960s.

Anita Dunn, former communications director for the Obama White House, claimed that Mao Zedong and Mother Teresa were

---

[10] Kate Zernike, "Wall St. Protest Isn't Like Ours, Tea Party Says," *New York Times* (October 21st 2011).

[11] "40 Examples of OWS Violence, Perversion, and Anti-Semitism (With Pictures, Videos) Compilation. Posted by Aurelius (October 29th 2011), www.punditpress.com/2011/10/compilation-40-examples-of-ows-violence.html.

"two of my favorite political philosophers."[12] After a mass public outcry following Ms. Dunn's statement on conservative, libertarian and Tea Party blogs, Fox News, Glenn Beck's show, and numerous talk radio programs, Anita Dunn tried to fire back at her critics saying that "The use of the phrase 'favorite political philosophers' was intended as irony, but clearly the effort fell flat—at least with a certain Fox commentator whose sense of irony may be missing."[13]

It also fell flat with Tea Party members already deeply concerned by the president's friends and associates like Jeremiah Wright, William Ayers, and Van Jones. Anita Dunn is the wife of Robert Bauer, personal counsel to President Obama and the White House Counsel. *Newsweek* named Dunn and Bauer the new "power couple" in Washington.[14] It doesn't look as if Ms. Dunn's praise of the most murderous and ruthless dictator in history was taken out of context. Speaking before high school students she said:

> In 1947, when Mao Zedong was being challenged within his own party on his plan to basically take China over, Chiang Kai Shek and the nationalist Chinese held the cities that had the army. They had the airport. They had everything on their side, and people said, "How can you win? How can you do this? How can you do this, against all the odds against you?" And Mao Zedong said, "You know, you fight your war, and I'll fight mine." And think about that for a second. You don't have to accept the definition of how to do things, and you don't have to follow other people's choices and paths, OK? It is about your choices and your path. You fight your own war. You lay out your own path. You figure out what's right for you. You don't let external definitions define how good you are internally. You fight your war. You let them fight theirs. Everybody has their own path.[15]

Doesn't sound like a lot of irony either!

Many on the right and on the left are concerned with the civil liberties record of the Obama Administration. Jonathan Turley wrote:

---

[12] http://theobamafile.com/_associates/AnitaDunn.htm.

[13] Suzanne Malveaux and Ed Hornick, "Obama Aide Fires Back at Beck over Mao Remarks," CNN Politics (October 16th 2009).

[14] "Under Obama, There Will Be a New Elite in Washington," *Newsweek* (December 19th 2008).

[15] Scott Johnson, "What Anita Dunn Done," Powerline (October 20th 2009), www.powerlineblog.com/archives/2009/10/024751.php.

One man is primarily responsible for the disappearance of civil liberties from the national debate, and he is Barack Obama. While many are reluctant to admit it, Obama has proved a disaster not just for specific civil liberties but the civil liberties cause in the United States.[16]

President Obama approved an extension of controversial parts of the Patriot Act that were set to expire. "Federal wiretaps are at an all-time high, up 34% since 2009. The Obama administration has prosecuted five "whistleblowers" under the Espionage Act, more than all the other previous administrations combined. Under his watch, Private Bradley Manning has been held for over a year and has been tortured numerous times. Obama has used the excuse of "state secrets" to stifle investigations and dismiss cases against the Bush Administration and his own administration. The "material support" statute has been strengthened, allowing the federal government to criminalize legal actions of U.S. citizens if it falls under the increasingly vague umbrella of "supporting terrorist groups." Within weeks of taking office, although specifically vowing to not prosecute medical marijuana facilities legal under state law, the DEA launched multiple raids in California. These are only some of the more egregious examples of the Obama administration's abuse of the liberties that the Bill of Rights was designed to protect.[17]

The Occupiers' Coup Media Group—Revolutionary Human Media website author R.C. Christian placed an interview with libertarian Judge Napolitano arguing that the president is "dangerously close to totalitarianism" with his recent questioning of the constitutional powers of the Supreme Court and its decision-making to begin a review of Obamacare. "A few months ago he was saying the Congress doesn't count. The Congress doesn't mean anything. I am going to rule by decree and by administrative regulation," Napolitano emphasized. "Now he's basically saying the Supreme Court doesn't count. It doesn't matter what they think.

---

[16] Jonathan Turley, "Obama: A Disaster for Civil Liberties: He May Prove the Most Disastrous President in Our History in Terms of Civil Liberties," *Los Angeles Times* (September 29th 2011).

[17] http://www.policymic.com/articles/2760/defense-authorization-act-shows-obama-s-awful-civil-liberties-record.

They can't review our legislation. That would leave just him as the only branch of government standing."[18]

But most Tea Partiers are derisive at any suggestion they have common aims with Occupy. Darryl Chan, a blogger from Foster City, California, wrote:

> I don't remember the Tea Party folks setting up illegal tent cities and refusing to leave. The Tea Party movement rallies were places where families went; people exercised their right to free speech and were respectful of the laws. Occupy folks are calling police officers "pigs" and throwing paint in their faces . . . two very different ideological camps and two very distinct ways of exercising their free speech.

Tony DeSylva, a blogger from San Francisco, California wrote on his Facebook wall: "Yeah they have a few core grievances in common. . . . but look at how differently the two groups behaved. Tea Party people weren't camping out, pissing in the streets, robbing others and becoming violent. Don't compare this pathetic bunch to the Tea Partiers. Tea Party rallies left their space CLEANER than it was before they came. Yeah there were a few screwy people in the Tea Party rallies, as there will be in all large groups, but they were rare and when discovered they were shunned, cast out. There weren't a rash of people carrying guns at the Tea Party rallies either, give me a break."

Even inside the OWS you hear protests against violence from more level-headed traditional leftwing leaders like Chris Hedges:

> The Black Bloc anarchists, who have been active on the streets in Oakland and other cities, are the cancer of the Occupy movement. The presences of Black Bloc anarchists—so named because they dress in black, obscure their faces, move as a unified mass, seek physical confrontations with police and destroy property—are a gift from heaven to the security and surveillance state.

Hedges identified himself as an "uncompromising democratic socialist" in contrast to what he sees as "ruthless totalitarian

---

[18] R.C. Christian, "Judge Napolitano Argues 'Obama Is Dangerously Close to Totalitarianism',". (6th April 2012), http://coupmedia.org/politics/judge-napolitano-argues-obama-is-dangerously-close-to-totalitarianism-0604.

capitalism." Interestingly enough, on November 4th 2011, Hedges himself was arrested as part of the Occupy Wall Street demonstration in New York.

From the point of view of many Tea Partiers the true color of the Occupy Wall Street movement is shining through, both in actions and affiliations, and it is red. Increasing violence and anticapitalist extremism is anything but representative of the 99 percent of Americans the movement claims to stand for.

Heritage's investigative journalist Lachlan Markay reports that as the Occupy Wall Street begins taking in hundreds of thousands of dollars in donations, an organization known as the Alliance for Global Justice (AFGJ) has been retained to process the transactions. That group's activities and associations are cause for alarm:

> The AFGJ provides 'grassroots' support for organizations that pursue 'a socially, ecologically and economically just world,' according to its website. Among its initiatives are efforts to encourage American soldiers to desert and an anti-George Bush organization founded by members of the Revolutionary Communist Party. The organization's president, Katherine Hoyt, leads the Alliance's Nicaragua Network program, which supports the country's Marxist Sandinista political party—and was founded for the explicit purpose of overthrowing the country's government. . . . Another of AFGJ's affiliates: George Soros. His Open Society Institute has given the group $100,000. The Occupy Wall Street movement has other supporters, too, including Big Labor.[19]

The leading union federation the AFL-CIO took out advertisements supporting the protests and unions provided the protesters with food, blankets; office space, meeting rooms, photocopying services, legal assistance, and other facilities.

> The co-ordination represents a new chapter for the anti-Wall Street activists, who have expressed anger at establishment forces in both major political parties and eschewed the traditional grass-roots organizing tactics long deployed by labor unions. It also suggests an evolution for organized labor, which retains close ties to President Obama and the Democratic Party but sees the Occupy protests as a galvaniz-

---

[19] Mike Brownfield, "Morning Bell: Occupy Wall Street Gets More Violent," heritage.org (November 8th 2011).

ing moment. Some union officials concede that their efforts to highlight income inequality and other economic concerns have fallen short, scoring few victories with a White House that many on the left see as too close with Wall Street. "Our members have been trying to have this discussion about Wall Street and the economy for a long time," AFL-CIO President Richard Trumka said in an interview. "This movement is providing us the vehicle."[20]

The Tea Party was accused of being an astroturf organization sponsored and funded by the Koch Brothers and other right-wing groups. As Jonah Goldberg wrote, there was some truth to that. Conservative groups, though the ones opposed to Wall Street bailouts, did join the Tea-Party cause after it was up and running. But later Big Labor, progressive billionaires, and the left wing of the Democratic Party began backing the Occupiers in ever larger numbers. Where were the cries of astroturfing from the *New York Times* and *Washington Post*?

"The short answer is that what counts as the political center in this country still leans considerably to the left. These young, scruffy, utopian, urban protesters are what rebels are supposed to look and sound like."[21] Occupy Wall Street, Rand Paul suggested, was more of an emotional protest. "I think Occupy Wall Street was more of a generic sort of, 'We just hate people who have any money, and why can't they give it to us?' kind of thing."[22]

In his column "Tea and Anarchy" at the Renew America Tea Party site Dan Popp wrote:

> I consider myself a Tea Party guy. If the Tea Party movement is against government bailouts, out-of-control spending and high taxes, I'm in. So it disturbed me recently to read from a self-described "patriot" that she believes Occupy Wall Street and Anonymous "have a lot in common" with the Tea Party. Of course any two groups have some things in common, if only accidentally. I would probably find common ground with a socialist—if there

---

[20] Peter Wallsten, "Occupy Wall Street, Unions Get Their Activism Together," *Washington Post* (October 20th 2011).

[21] Jonah Goldberg, "Sorting Out the 'Extremists': The Difference between Wall Street Protestors and the Tea Party," nationalreview.com (October 7th 2011).

[22] Rand Paul, "Tea Party Is Like the American Revolution: The Occupy Movement More Like the French Revolution," *Washington Examiner* (March 13th 2013).

were a communist in the room. But Christians accepting National Socialism in order to fight back communism didn't work out so well in Germany in the 1930s. The enemy of my enemy is sometimes my enemy, too.[23]

---

[23] Dan Popp, "Tea and Anarchy," renewamerica.com (March 14th 2013).

8

Battling the Beast

Americans are gradually waking up to a surprising—and for most of us, uncomfortable—reality. We used to assume that the United States was one of the freest, least corrupt, least government-dominated economies in the world. As a direct and obvious result of this, it was also one of the richest. This is no longer true. Most European countries, for instance, are now less heavily regulated, less heavily taxed, less government-dominated, and therefore less corrupt than the United States.

Just to give a couple of examples of this broad picture:

> the United States has the highest corporate tax rate in the world at 39.2 percent. Our next-door neighbor Canada's rate is 26 percent, and the average European country's is 21 percent. If you're trying to decide whether to invest in Canada or in the United States, you will notice that you get to keep thirteen cents more out of every dollar that you earn in Canada rather than in the United States.[1]

Or, to get another indicator of the government burden, the U.S. government spends more, per head of population, than 93 percent of national governments in the world, and over three times more than the average national government in the world. France spends 12 percent less than the U.S., and Germany 15 percent less.[2] Because of measures already in the pipeline, these differences are

---

[1] John R. Lott, *At the Brink: Will Obama Push Us Over the Edge?* (Regnery, 2012), 201.

[2] Lott, *At the Brink*, 209–210. These numbers are for non-defense spending. Including defense makes them higher.

sure to expand dramatically with each passing year, as more and more countries become better places to invest than the U.S., and eventually, better places to live.

A country's standard of life is mainly determined by the social and legal framework that has characterized it in recent decades or even centuries. The United States has a comparatively high standard of life mainly because, for many decades, it had a freer, less government-dominated economy than most of the world (with a few exceptions like Switzerland, which has long been economically freer than the U.S.). We can therefore expect to see, in the next few decades, more and more countries throughout the world becoming richer, happier, and nicer places to live than the United States. This is already decided by the economic policies of the last few decades and cannot now be changed. What can be changed is the more distant future, thirty or forty years ahead, the future our children and grandchildren will eventually inherit from us.

The fact that European countries are mostly economically freer than the U.S. arises partly because the U.S. has been moving more quickly to expand the role of government in our lives. But it is also due to the fact that some European countries which introduced ambitious welfare states fifty, sixty, or more years ago, have been cutting them back. They have discovered the pathologies and impoverishment inevitably generated by state welfare systems. Long-lived welfare states in Western Europe are all in crisis, and some of them are being trimmed down—notably in Sweden, once considered a welfare-state paradise by American leftists.

The U.S. is now set on a course of rapidly ballooning increases in government spending. Because there is a limit to the amount of taxation people will stand for, the deficit—the difference between government spending and the amount raised in taxes—is also exploding, and hence the government's debt keeps growing too.

This problem is occasionally understood by perceptive individuals from anywhere in the political spectrum. According to Steven Cohen, writing in the *Huffington Post*:

> In Congress, Republicans continue to sign pledges to 'starve the beast' and lower taxes, while simultaneously insisting on large defense and domestic spending programs. In our State Houses, Governors are doing their best to keep their distance from county and municipal fis-

cal problems. We have developed a culture of fiscal irresponsibility that is shocking, stupid, and short-sighted.[3]

While attention in Washington has been focused on the federal debt and the failure of the Congressional 'super committee', we have already seen a number of local governments head toward bankruptcy. Some are filing for Chapter 9, others are seeking state approval to go bankrupt, and a number are just starting to explore their options. Broke localities have included Alabama's Jefferson County, the city of Harrisburg, Pennsylvania, the town of Central Falls, Rhode Island, and the town of Hamtramck, Michigan.

The Tea Party is primarily a popular response to the exploding deficit and exploding debt, and there has been discussion about the best strategy for tackling these problems. As one approach, the Tea Party Debt Commission was formed by FreedomWorks. FreedomWorks was one of the first organizations to recognize the potential strength of the Tea Party movement and come out in support. FreedomWorks has formed the commission with twelve commissioners and held nine hearings across the country where it gave presentations on the budget deficit and solicited ideas on how to cut it.

Plans for the commission were set at a four-day Tea Party activist 'boot camp' that FreedomWorks hosted in June of 2011, where about 150 activists from thirty states learned about the nuts and bolts of politics, from running a campaign to crafting policy.

"The third iteration of the Tea Party is all about understanding the legislative process and the tough choices," explained FreedomWorks president and indefatigable Tea Party writer and activist Matt Kibbe. The Tea Party started as a protest movement and then morphed into a get-out-the-vote effort during the 2010 midterms, which ushered in the Republican House majority. "Now, 'we the people' must govern," says Kibbe. "That's a responsibility all of these activists feel because they helped get these guys elected."[4]

The FreedomWorks website, FreedomConnector, presented users with a series of choices about what to cut from the budget.

---

[3] "The Culture of Fiscal Irresponsibility," *Huffington Post* (November 21st 2011).

[4] www.cbsnews.com/8301-503544_162-20074797-503544.html.

FreedomWorks reported it found broad support for repealing Obamacare and eliminating entire federal departments, but much less enthusiasm for changes to Medicare and Social Security. Medicare and Social Security, however, are the biggest contributors to the nation's deficit. Still, the Tea Party Debt Commission says that its proposals add up to $6 trillion in savings over ten years.

A FreedomWorks memo on the preliminary findings said that more than forty thousand people visited the Web site to make recommendations for cuts. The most popular idea, supported by 93 percent, was repealing Obamacare. After that, the most popular ideas were reducing duplicative purchases of Pentagon supplies (90 percent), eliminating the Department of Education and privatizing Fannie Mae and Freddie Mac (81 percent each), and reducing discretionary spending to 2008 levels (76 percent). When it comes to cutting Medicare, Medicaid and Social Security, visitors to the site were "more cautious," and "prefer reductions in peripheral elements," like tightening eligibility for Social Security disability payments and reducing subsidies to teaching hospitals.

Here we see Tea Party ideas bumping up against one of the hard realities of politics. People want lower taxes but they also want some of the benefits these taxes pay for. Medicare, Medicaid, and Social Security are such an enormous slice of the budget that the fiscal crisis can't be fixed without tackling them (unless we can suddenly increase the birth rate or overnight bring in millions of young tax-paying immigrants). Social Security benefits could be means-tested or could become available later in life (say, one month later each year for the next thirty-six years, all announced in advance), but either of these very modest proposals would meet with opposition from many voters.

Against Obamacare

One of the most vital developments in the history of the Tea Party movement is its opposition to Obamacare.

Obamacare mainly refers to the Patient Protection and Affordable Care Act (PPACA), passed by Congress and signed into law by President Barack Obama on March 23rd, 2010. The Tea Party owes much of its continued support and enthusiasm to its firm commitment to the complete repeal of Obamacare. The Tea

Party proclaims that Obamacare will seriously damage healthcare provision, will add to the national debt, and will be detrimental to individual liberty.

The Health Care and Education Reconciliation Act of 2010 is a complementary law to PPACA that was enacted by means of the reconciliation process, in order to amend the PPACA. This law also includes the Student Aid and Fiscal Responsibility Act, which was attached as a 'rider', effectively nationalizing the student loan industry.

PPACA is horrendously complicated and many analysts still can't agree on just how it will play out. It increases insurance coverage of pre-existing conditions, expands access to insurance for over thirty million Americans, and mandates an increase in total national medical expenditure financed by a combination of taxes, fees, and penalties imposed on individuals and on the health care, pharmaceutical, medical insurance, and medical devices industries.

The list of 'new and improved' taxes in the Obamacare package is staggering. According to Grace-Marie Turner of the Galen Institute, here are just a few of the most egregious Obamacare taxes that hard-working Americans will soon be facing:

- The"breath tax": The infamous "death tax" now has a new sibling: the $17 billion "breath tax." The new health overhaul law requires everyone in America who breathes to have health insurance by 2014; some will get subsidies, but most will have to pay a fine if they don't buy the health insurance required by the federal government. Internal Revenue Commissioner Douglas Shulman said that enforcement of the individual mandate will come by seizing tax refunds and "collection, if need be."

- Taxes on medical devices: surgical scissors, wheelchairs, intravenous bags, dental retainers and braces, CT scanners, stretchers, exam room tables, heart stents, pacemakers, surgical gloves, spine boards at every local pool, scales at a doctor's office or health club, any diagnostic test for any disease or condition—all will be among the products and procedures subject to Obamacare's special $20 billion medical device tax beginning in 2013. This tax will make these medical supplies more expensive, will drive up the cost of health care and health insurance for Americans, will threaten jobs in the medical device industry, and confiscate money needed for new innovative breakthroughs.

- The new tax on health insurance providers: Even though soaring health costs are the problem Americans most wanted government to solve, Obamacare promises to drive costs even higher by instituting a new $60 billion tax on health insurers. Insurers and health plans can be expected to pass along this tax to policyholders through higher premiums. So starting in 2014, Americans will be forced to buy health insurance, and the federal government will be actively making it more expensive.

- Medicare Payroll Tax: Starting in 2013, Obamacare increases the Medicare payroll tax for many small business owners and others earning more than $250,000 a year. This tax hike will place yet another burden on small business owners who the country needs to create jobs and lead the economy to prosperity. This job-killing payroll tax is estimated to raise $86.8 billion over seven years.

- A new tax on Investment: In addition to the Medicare payroll tax hike, investment income will now be subject to a tax of 3.8% starting in 2013 for those in higher income categories. Even middle-class homeowners who realize a capital gain of $250,000 or more on the sale of their home will be hit by this Medicare tax, which will drain another $123.4 billion out of taxpayers' pockets and into the government's coffers over seven years.

- A new drug tax: Obamacare's new tax on brand-name drugs kicks in next year and is estimated to raise $27 billion over nine years. The public can expect to have these costs passed on to them in the form of higher drug prices and higher insurance costs.[5]

It seems puzzling that Obamacare imposes so many measures that will indisputably and immediately push up health care costs. We can only guess that the framers of the law were in such a scramble to come up with something they could window-dress as deficit-

---

[5] *Washington Examiner* (April 13th 2010).

neutral, that they just stuck in these horrible new taxes wherever they could think of it.

The PPACA represents the largest tax hike in U.S. history and despite President Obama's campaign promise that no one making $250,000 or less would see a tax increase, Congress's Joint Committee on Taxation has confirmed that these tax hikes will hit millions of middle- and working-class families who are struggling to make ends meet. (But there will be complex and difficult-to-predict consequences: some people will receive a windfall and find themselves immediately better off.)

According to well-documented research by Americans for Tax Reform in Washington, D.C., besides the penalty tax for lawbreakers who fail to carry health insurance (which the CBO says will cost taxpayers $39 billion from 2013 to 2019), there is the Medicine Cabinet Tax, the Health Savings Account withdrawal penalty, the Flexible Spending Account Cap of $2,500, the Tax on Medical Device Manufacturers, a tax on Indoor Tanning Services, a Blue Cross/Blue Shield tax, an excise tax on charitable hospitals, a tax on Innovator Pharmaceutical Companies, a tax on health insurers, the elimination of a tax deduction for employer-provided retirement prescription drug coverage in co-ordination with Medicare Part D, and other tax-related measures, such as the $500,000 annual executive compensation limit for health insurance executives, and employer reporting of insurance on W-2 and Corporate 1099-MISC IRS forms, which creates additional compliance burdens for all businesses and makes additional penalties likely.

Aside from the sheer burden of Obamacare, there is the problem that it is so complicated, companies can't figure out just how much it will cost them. This deters them from making employment commitments until the situation has clarified, adding to the slowness of recovery from the recession. The distinguished African-American economist and Tea Party supporter Thomas Sowell explains:

> If employers knew that Obamacare would add $1,000 to their costs of hiring an employee, then they could simply reduce the salaries they offer by $1,000 and start hiring. But, since it will take years to create all the regulations required to carry out Obamacare, employers today don't know whether the Obamacare costs that will hit them down the road will be $500 per employee or $5,000 per employee. Many businesses work their existing employees overtime or hire temporary

workers, rather than get stuck with unknown and unknowable costs for expanding their permanent work force.[6]

Why Obamacare?

Why the desperate urgency to reconfigure the entire health care industry in such a way that even its originators find it hard to predict most of the consequences?

A major segment of the American left is passionately committed to the ideal of a Soviet-style health care system, and although Obamacare is not quite that, it is seen by the left as a major step in that direction (as it might indeed eventually turn out to be).

Most propaganda for Obamacare maintains that the U.S. health care system comes out badly in comparison with other countries, and that it has a scandalous problem of millions of people with no health insurance. But in fact the U.S. health care system is comparatively good, while the problem of the uninsured is exaggerated and can be fixed rather simply without recourse to anything as earth-shaking as Obamacare.

INTERNATIONAL HEALTH CARE COMPARISONS

Michael Moore is one of the most effective socialist propagandists in America. In his movie, *Sicko*, he unfavorably compares health care in the U.S. with health care in France and Canada—no, wait, he compares U.S. health care for older patients with complex and incurable diseases to French and Canadian health care for young women having babies. Had he done the reverse—compared healthcare for young women having babies in the United States to health care for older patients with complex and incurable diseases in France and Canada—the movie would have been the same, except that the US health care system would look wonderful, and the systems in Canada and France would look dismal.

The United States has one of the highest rates of infant mortality in the developed countries—partly because it counts all dead infants, including premature babies, which is where most of the fatalities occur. Most countries do not count premature-infant deaths. Some don't count any deaths that occur in the first sev-

---

[6] *The Patriot Post-Chronicle* (August 31st 2011).

enty-two hours after birth. Some countries don't even count any deaths from the first two weeks of life.

In Cuba, which boasts a very low infant-mortality rate, infants are only registered when they are several months old, thereby leaving out of the official statistics all infant deaths that take place within the first several months of life. The Cuban health care system is still being sold by the American left to the American public as a shining success of government planning. On Yuri Maltsev's visits to Cuba, he has more than once been told: "The only real health care in Cuba is to swim to Miami."

The appalling state of medical care in the Soviet Union, despite its huge number of doctors, is now well known. After seventy-four years of medical socialism, 57 percent of all Russian hospitals did not have running hot water, and 36 percent of hospitals in Russia had no running water at all or even proper sewage disposal. Now Oleg Kulikov, a member of the Russian Duma (parliament), comments:

> It is fascinating: we are returning to capitalism in health care by increasing the share of private payments and health care provision while Obama has suggested a system which we can accurately define as communist or socialist. They are assuming positions that we've abandoned.[7]

In Britain, with its National Health Service, the waiting list for surgeries is nearly 800,000 out of a population of 55 million. State-of-the-art equipment is nonexistent in most British hospitals. Britain pioneered in developing kidney-dialysis technology, and yet the country has one of the lowest dialysis rates in the world. The Brookings Institution reports that every year 7,000 Britons in need of hip replacements, between 4,000 and 20,000 in need of coronary bypass surgery, and some 10,000 to 15,000 in need of cancer chemotherapy are denied medical attention. Britain allows completely private medical treatment provided it is kept strictly separate from the National Health Service, and recourse to the private sector keeps growing, as Britons give up on the NHS. Purchasers of private health care in Britain naturally have to pay for it, in addition to paying their taxes to pay for the 'free' NHS.

---

[7] Speech at the Moscow State Duma, 2010.

Americans often don't understand that in countries with many decades of experience of ambitious welfare-statism, popular discontent with these systems is endemic and is growing. American leftists think of Sweden as an almost ideal welfare state. Yet Sweden has seen the growth of opposition to its inefficient welfare state, and is now moving toward privatization of government services, school choice, and reduction in marginal taxes and corporate income tax.

According to a BBC report,

> the Swedish system is far from perfect. Patients routinely complain about waiting lists—the government has recently introduced a six-month waiting guarantee—and it is common to find hospital doctors scrambling around trying to find beds for patients.[8]

As a result of Swedish people's dissatisfaction with the socialized health care system, a piecemeal market-led orientation in the health care market has been occurring. Especially in county councils with non-socialist majorities, the development of private health care provision is now encouraged.[9]

According to the *European Journal of Public Health*,

> Ideas about privatizing health care in Western Europe were triggered by the crisis of the welfare state, . . . Historically, the negative experiences, which opened the door to privatization, were rigidity of public institutions and their inability to change or adapt to different stimuli from their environment, including the population's and patients' expectations.[10]

In European policy circles there is now a lot of goodwill for reforming welfare state health care systems by privatization:

---

[8] Nick Triggle, BBC news release, "How the NHS Could Learn from Sweden" (28th November 2005).

[9] A.H. Glenngård, F. Hjalte, M. Svensson, A. Anell, and V. Bankauskaite, *Health Systems in Transition: Sweden* (Copenhagen: WHO Regional Office for Europe on behalf of the European Observatory on Health Systems and Policies, 2005), 103.

[10] Tit Albreht, "Privatization Processes in Health Care in Europe: A Move in the Right Direction, a 'Trendy' Option, or a Step Back?" *European Journal of Public Health* 19:5, 448–450. Albreht is not friendly to privatization but the quoted statement illustrates its current topicality.

[Privatization] has proven it is worth the effort as it eliminates waste, saves resources, reduces government budget deficits and debt, and creates a better health care system for those who need it most.[11]

In Canada Dr. Jacques Chaoulli sued the Quebec government, arguing that the actual Canadian implementation of publicly-funded health care is not effective at delivering an adequate level of care. The Canadian Supreme Court decision on the case resulted in a change in the Quebec government's policy on wait times and opened up the possibility of privatization of health care delivery. As Dr. Chaoulli commented:

Challenging a powerful state monopoly of medical services is not easy, but as I had reached the point where I could no longer tolerate seeing my patients suffer and die while on waiting lists, I had to do something.[12]

It is an automatic feature of any system which abolishes or restricts rationing by price that it will give rise to other forms of rationing. In many cases, this means rationing by bureaucratic discretion or simply by long wait lists. Age discrimination soon becomes apparent in all government-run or heavily regulated systems of health care. In Soviet-sphere countries with socialized health care systems patients over 65 were considered worthless parasites and those over 75 were often denied even elementary forms of healthcare, unless they belonged to the ruling elite.

Now we in the United States are being prepared for discrimination against the elderly. Ezekiel Emanuel is director of the Clinical Bioethics Department at the US National Institutes of Health and an architect of Obama's health care plan. He is the brother of Rahm Emanuel, mayor of Chicago and Obama's former White House chief of staff. Foster Friess reports that Ezekiel Emanuel has written that health services should not be guaranteed to individuals who are irreversibly prevented from being or becoming participating citizens. An obvious example is not guaranteeing health services to patients with dementia.[13]

---

[11] Ian Wootto, "Privatisation in the Healthcare Industry," in *Proceedings of the AEMH Conference, Brussels* (7th May 2009), 13.

[12] Jacques Chaoulli, M.D., "The Long Road to Freedom in Canadian Medicine," *Journal of American Physicians and Surgeons* 10: 3 (Fall 2005), 91.

An article co-authored by Emanuel appeared in the highly prestigious medical journal *The Lancet* in January 2009. The authors write that unlike allocation of health care by sex or race, allocation by age is not invidious discrimination; every person lives through different life stages rather than remaining at a single age. Even if 25-year-olds receive priority over 65-year-olds, everyone who is 65 now was once 25. So, treating 65-year-olds differently because of stereotypes or falsehoods would be ageist and ethically unacceptable, while treating them differently because they have already had more life-years is not![14]

Alternatives to Obamacare

The pre-Obamacare system of healthcare is not as bad as often made out, and will soon be looked back on fondly as a comparatively happy era. International comparisons of health care systems show that people are decidedly happier with their health care in the U.S. than in countries with socialized systems such as Canada. In fact Canadians as a whole have about the same degree of satisfaction with their health care as *uninsured* Americans. In terms of consumer satisfaction with the quality of their health care, the U.S. ranks first in the world.[15]

One problem often cited is the number of people without health insurance. However, many uninsured in the U.S. are uninsured simply because they want to be. For example, they are between jobs for a few months and don't think it worth their while to buy health insurance before they start their new job. Furthermore uninsured persons routinely get medical treatment without any problem. Only 6.2 percent of U.S. residents are both uninsured and dissatisfied with their health care.[16]

At a tiny fraction of the cost of Obamacare, with its vast Kafkaeque bureaucracies, it is easily possible to provide low-income people with medical insurance vouchers or tax credits, thus solving the

---

[13] Foster Friess, "Can You Believe Denying Health Care to People with Dementia Is Being Considered?" (July 14th 2009); Ezekiel J. Emanuel, "Where Civic Republicanism and Deliberative Democracy Meet," *Hastings Center Report* 26: 6.

[14] Govind Persad, Alan Wertheimer, and Ezekiel J. Emanuel, "Principles for Allocation of Scarce Medical Interventions," *The Lancet* 373:9661.

[15] Lott, *At the Brink*, 23–40.

[16] Lott, *At the Brink*, 37–38.

problem of the uninsured without devastating the established health care industry.

More radical and sweeping free-market reforms have their advocates. Economist Hans-Hermann Hoppe has proposed a battery of measures including eliminating licensing requirements for medical schools and doctors—Hoppe believes that competing voluntary accreditation agencies would take the place of compulsory government licensing, giving more consumer freedom and lower costs along with protection against fraud. Hoppe also favors abolition of the Food and Drug Administration and deregulation of the health insurance industry, which is currently obliged to provide coverage for some risks which are not really insurable, thus raising premiums for everyone.[17]

Since the Tea Party was in the vanguard of opposition to Obamacare, it must be chalked up as a serious failure that they were unable to present a cogent and convincing case against it. Many of the 90 percent of voters who were satisfied with their health care somehow accepted as an abstract proposition that health care had major problems which needed radical changes. Obama's preposterous assertions that everyone would be able to keep the health insurance they already had were never seriously scrutinized. The misleading references to international comparisons and to "the millions of people without health care" (meaning without health insurance but not at all without health care) were perpetrated by the left with no serious challenge.

Gun Control: New Life for the Tea Party

The Tea Party movement advocates strict adherence to the United States Constitution including the Second Amendment right to keep and bear arms. As ratified by the States and authenticated by Thomas Jefferson, Secretary of State, the Second Amendment reads:

> A well regulated militia being necessary to the security of a free state, the right of the people to keep and bear arms shall not be infringed.

---

[17] Hans-Hermann Hoppe, "A Four-Step Health-Care Solution," *The Free Market* 11: 4 (April 1993).

Numerous Supreme Court's rulings have upheld the literal interpretation of the Second Amendment. The Court's 2008 decision in *Heller v. District of Columbia* confirmed that the Second Amendment means what it says. *McDonald v. Chicago*, which applied the Second Amendment rights to the states, made clear that what government cannot do is deny the individual interest in self-defense. Martin Luther King, Jr. preached nonviolence but knew that passive resistance could not be relied on for his own family's protection. King owned several guns but was subjected to the worst kind of gun control—and deprived of his basic right to defend himself and his family—when police in Alabama denied him a concealed carry permit in 1956.

After the mass gun murders at a movie theater in Aurora, Colorado in July 2012, another at a Sikh temple in Wisconsin in August of the same year, and yet another at a Connecticut elementary school in December of 2012 many leading Democrats, including President Obama, proposed a system of licensing and registration. The most radical of these proposals was a bill introduced by Senator Dianne Feinstein on January 24th 2013 in the wake of the Newtown, Connecticut, school shooting for the Assault Weapons Ban of 2013. This bill was supposed to stop the sale, transfer, importation, and manufacturing of military-style assault weapons and high-capacity ammunition feeding devices. Later the bill became a part of a broader gun control bill, which also included the so-called Manchin-Toomey proposal on background checks. These were centerpieces of the proposed legislation with senators Joe Manchin and Pat Toomey attracting four Republican votes.

Both Feinstein's plan to ban dozens of so-called assault weapons and Manchin-Toomey proposal on background checks were defeated. The Senate votes on April 16th 2013 rejected President Obama's gun control policies. "All in all, this was a pretty shameful day for Washington," Obama said, promising that "this effort is not over."[18]

Liberal stand-up comedian and television host Bill Maher attacked the Second Amendment in the following way: "I'm so sorry, but this is the problem with the gun debate—it is that it's a constant center-right debate," Maher said. "There's no left in this

---

[18] www.washingtonpost.com/blogs/post-politics/wp/2013/04/17/senate-to-vote-on-amendments-to-gun-bill-with-background-check-plan-in-doubt.

debate. Everyone on the left is so afraid to say what should be said, which is the Second Amendment is bullshit. Why doesn't anyone go at the core of it?"[19] Go back a few decades and any self-respecting leftist would not have wished to disarm the proletariat in the face of the bourgeois state, but Maher is too young to remember that.

The Democrats' attempt to introduce effective measures of gun control re-energized the Tea Party activities in all fifty states as it was perceived to violate individual liberties, including the right of self-protection and resistance against criminals and over-reaching government. Most Tea Party activists believe that firearms are an important tool in the exercise of this right. They see a new threat to the Second Amendment in the United Nations passage of the "Small Arms Treaty" vigorously supported by the Obama Administration and especially former Secretary of State Hillary Clinton as well as other leading Democrats.

One of the leading figures in the Tea Party in Florida and a columnist for the *Sun Sentinel* and *Florida Voices* Steven Kurlander believes that Obama's efforts to introduce new gun control laws re-energized the Tea Party. Kurlander wrote:

> When President Obama was re-elected, eulogies were being written for not only the vanquished Republican Party, but a Tea Party movement that had lost its efficacy, too. Even as the results were still coming in, and it became apparent that President Obama was going to win a decisive victory, particularly in the Electoral College, the Tea Party was declared DOA as a result of the traumatic loss. The Democratic Congressional Campaign Committee issued a statement that the Tea Party movement, which had morphed into a political powerhouse in 2010, was "over." In fact, it really didn't look like the Tea Party had much of a future, with a number of favorites, like Florida Rep. Allen West, having been beaten. . . . But such prophetic views have proven short-lived. Weeks after it was pro-nounced lifeless, the Tea Party has gained a critical, second wind. It's drawing new strength from the momentous outrage arising from major gun control initiatives being proposed by President Obama and Democrats in the wake of the Sandy Hook massacre, as well as new gun control initiatives in many state capitals.[20]

---

[19] www.teaparty.org/bill-maher-the-second-amendment-is-bullsht-23012.
[20] "Second Amendment Politics: Despite Rumors to Contrary, Tea Party Is Far from Dead," *Sun Sentinel* (January 24th 2012).

In our view the Tea Party was nowhere near dying anyway, but Obama's assault on the right to bear arms certainly gave the movement a stimulating shot in the arm.

In his *New York Times* interview of December 25th 2012 Everett Wilkinson, chairman of the Florida Tea Party in Palm Beach County, said the number of active Tea Party groups statewide "has diminished significantly in the last year or so, certainly in the last couple of months," with only a third of what there once was. "A lot of people gave their heart and soul to trying to get Obama out; they're frustrated," he added. "They don't know what to do. They got involved with the electoral process, and that didn't work out."[21]

A week after that, following the tragedy in Newtown, Connecticut, and President Obama's aggressive stance on guns, Wilkinson declared:

> Obama's gun grab has thrown gasoline on the fire for liberty. He has awakened the American people to his socialist agenda. Obama is the greatest recruiter for the Tea Party. A tougher President Obama indeed has taken the offensive to bring significant changes in gun control, and has shown an apparent willingness to push it as part of a perceived liberal mandate given to him by American voters. In nuanced language in his second Inaugural Address, the president made it clear he was taking no prisoners in a new fight to expand federal restrictions on the individual ownership of automatic and semi-automatic weapons. In response, Americans are buying guns like crazy and gun owners are coming out of the woodwork to join the Tea Party and to embrace the movement's stance against what is now being termed 'Obamaism'—a twenty-first-century threat of despotism framed by these proposed gun restrictions.[22]

The Tea Party movement once again captured the frustrations of millions of Americans with perceived infringements of constitutional rights and liberties.

The most influential leader of the Tea Party Senator Rand Paul promised to defeat the UN's Small Arms Treaty and asked Tea Partiers "to turn the heat up on the U.S. Senate now before it's

---

[21] Trip Gabriel, "Clout Diminished, Tea Party Turns to Narrower Issues," *New York Times* (December 25th 2012).

[22] Kurlander, "Second Amendment Politics."

too late!" The overwhelming majority of the Tea Party movement opposed the gun control policies and rhetoric of the Obama Administration and considers self-defense to be a fundamental and unalienable human right.

Attempts to pass new gun controls laws and regulations have led to dramatic increase in demand for guns and ammunition. "A San Francisco gun shop dealer said keeping 9 millimeter ammunition on store shelves is pretty much a lesson in futility. A box of 9mm ammunition "has a shelf life of about five minutes," said Steve Alcairo, the general manager of High Bridge Arms. Ammunition manufacturers, meanwhile, say they have expanded operations and are making bullets around the clock.[23]

Economist John Lott, a frequent speaker at Tea Party events, has written seven books, including the pathbreaking and rigorously reasoned *More Guns, Less Crime*, showing empirically that widespread gun ownership reduces the quantity of gun-related crime. The data for Lott's impressive study came from the FBI's crime statistics for all 3,054 U.S. counties.[24]

Evidence has continued to accumulate to support Lott's thesis.[25] Whenever guns are banned, gun violence increases, and the more guns are restricted, the more gun violence there is. Turning areas (such as areas around schools) into 'gun-free zones' increases the likelihood that shootings will occur there. These empirical findings should be what we expect, when we consider that thousands of crimes are deterred every day by the prospective victim producing a gun, and that any realistic gun control measures will disarm the law-abiding population but not the criminal class.

Tea Partiers therefore respond to reports of shootings rather differently than leftists. Tea Partier 'Danelle' posted her reaction to the murder of the British soldier Lee Rigby by Muslim extremists at the Williamsteaparty.com:

> This sad story, if nothing else, should impress upon you the purpose and importance of our Second Amendment rights and the need to

---

[23] Cheryl K. Chumley, "California Gun Shop Owner: 9mm ammo 'Has a Shelf Life of about 5 Minutes'," *Washington Times* (May 27th 2013).

[24] John R. Lott Jr., *More Guns, Less Crime: Understanding Crime and Gun Control Laws*. Third edition (University of Chicago Press, 2010).

[25] Lott, *At the Brink*, 123–138.

protect it at all costs from tyrannical and unlawful powers that be. Disarmed British citizens witness to this murder can do nothing more than stand and look on in horror and/or run screaming from the scene. Even the police that shot a suspect are now being investigated for firing their weapons during the incident. Is there where you want to be America!!!? Grow a backbone for Christ's sake and stand up to this corrupt Government we are coddling here in the U.S.! Personally, I'd rather die in a pile of brass amid a gunfight with these animals than be disarmed and hacked to death by meat cleavers.[26]

Rand Paul reflected some fairly typical Tea Party opinion when he wrote:

Ever since its founding 65 years ago, the United Nations has been hell-bent on bringing the United States to its knees. To the petty dictators and one-world socialists who control the UN, the United States of America isn't a "shining city on a hill"—it's an affront to their grand designs for the globe. These anti-gun globalists know that so long as Americans remain free to make our own decisions without being bossed around by big government bureaucrats, they'll NEVER be able to seize the worldwide power they crave. And the UN's apologists also know the most effective way to finally strip you and me of ALL our freedoms would be to DESTROY our gun rights. That's why I was so glad to hear that the National Association for Gun Rights is leading the fight to stop this assault on our Constitution![27]

Sharron Angle who ran in 2012 against Senate Majority Leader Harry Reid on the Tea Party platform and with the Tea Party support has appealed to the Second Amendment. Angle has said, "What is a little bit disconcerting and concerning is the inability for sporting goods stores to keep ammunition in stock. . . . That tells me the nation is arming. What are they arming for if it isn't that they are so distrustful of their government? They're afraid they'll have to fight for their liberty in more Second Amendment kinds of ways?" and "That's why I look at this as almost an imperative. If we don't win at the ballot box, what will be the next step?

---

[26] "British Soldier Beheaded and Your Second Amendment Rights." Posted on May 22nd 2013 by Danelle, http://williamsteaparty.com/2013/05/22/british-soldier-beheaded-amendment-rights.

[27] www.nagr.org/UN_lp_survey2.aspx.

Angle also stated that the Second Amendment exists for us "to defend ourselves. And you know, I'm hoping that we're not getting to Second Amendment remedies." On Lars Larson's radio show, she stated:

> You know, our Founding Fathers, they put that Second Amendment in there for a good reason and that was for the people to protect themselves against a tyrannical government. In fact Thomas Jefferson said it's good for a country to have a revolution every twenty years. I hope that's not where we're going, but, you know, if this Congress keeps going the way it is, people are really looking toward those Second Amendment remedies and saying, "My goodness, what can we do to turn this country around?[28]

Attacks on Personal Freedom

On December 20, 2011 seven Occupy D.C. protesters were arrested outside the White House as they protested the law Congress passed a week before permitting the indefinite detention of American citizens. "This was the latest of three consecutive protests against the NDAA outside the White House this week; eleven were arrested at a protest Monday night. Protester Marshall Scott said the group plans to continue the nightly protests until Obama vetoes the bill. In an editorial, the *Salt Lake Tribune* called NDAA 2012 "the most direct assault so far on the concept found in the Declaration of Independence that humans are endowed with certain inalienable rights" and called it a "disgusting turn of events."

A letter in the *Gazette* (Cedar Rapids, Iowa) denounced Senator Charles Grassley for supporting NDAA 2012, telling him that "I cannot begin to fathom why you would support circumventing the Constitution. To say that I'm disappointed in you is an absolute understatement." Brian Morton of Baltimore's *City Paper* pointed out "one of my main problems with the latest defense authorization bill: The language in it leads one to think that there is no end to this conflict. . . . we are now prisoners to fear."[29]

The law allows the federal government to detain and imprison US Citizens without trial—indefinitely. If any U.S. Citizen is deemed to provide "substantial support," which is not defined at

---

[28] http://en.wikipedia.org/wiki/Sharron_Angle.

all, to any "associated" group (also not defined at all) that the president deems a "threat" (also not defined) those Citizens can be arrested and held without trial, without recourse, without end. Even worse, one provision in the bill specifies that detention doesn't necessarily have to occur domestically—nor does it have to be in a foreign prison run by the U.S. Tea Party activists believe that this is even worse than the Patriot Act.

Some leading Democrats surrounding Obama are already trying to present Tea Party and other opposition to Obama Administration as "harmful" to the U.S. national security, society, and economy. One of them, former White House Budget Director Peter Orszag, argued that we have too much democracy. Orszag wrote that "the country's political polarization was growing worse—harming Washington's ability to do the basic, necessary work of governing." His solution? "We need to minimize the harm from legislative inertia by relying more on automatic policies and depoliticized commissions for certain policy decisions. In other words, radical as it sounds, we need to counter the gridlock of our political institutions by making them a bit less democratic."[30]

Orszag's view is typical of Obama White House alumni. Last year, former auto czar Steve Rattner wrote in his book, *Overhaul*, "Either Congress needs to get its act together or we should explore alternatives. . . . If our country wants to do a better job of solving its problems, it needs to find a way to let talented government officials operate more like they do in the private sector."

Perhaps know-it-all bureaucrats can be forgiven for harboring such contempt for the voting public. But elected officials cannot. That's why similar comments by the Democratic Governor of North Carolina, Bev Perdue, were more troubling. "I think we ought to suspend, perhaps, elections for Congress for two years and just tell them we won't hold it against them, whatever decisions they make, to just let them help this country recover," Perdue told a Rotary Club gathering in suburban Raleigh. "I really hope that someone can agree with me on that."

Perdue's office at first claimed her comments were made in jest. The subsequent release of the audio recording conclusively

---

[29] www.ufppc.org/us-a-world-news-mainmenu-35/10771-news-protesters-against-disgusting-ndaa-2012-arrested-at-white-house.html.

[30] "Too Much of a Good Thing," *New Republic* (October 6th 2011).

demonstrates otherwise. These remarks were used by the Tea Party activists to fight her bid for another term. Given Perdue's apparent disdain for the American constitutional system, the Tea Party of North Carolina insisted that the voters of the state should remind her in the November 2012 elections who's the boss.[31] On January 26th 2012, facing sinking approval ratings, Perdue announced that she would not seek re-election in the 2012 gubernatorial election.

The Beast Bites Back

In May 2013, the report by the Treasury Inspector General for Tax Administration described in detail the use of "inappropriate criteria" to screen political advocacy groups by the Internal Revenue Service (IRS). An IRS unit for tax exempt organizations created the 'Be On the Lookout' list for Tea Party organizations. These groups faced lengthy delays and demands for disclosure of private information in consideration of their applications. This led to both political and public condemnation of the agency and triggered further investigations.

One of the most visible tax defense lawyers in America, Michael Minns, summarized the essence of the scandal:

> Let's boil this scandal down to simple words; words like "Tea Party" and "Patriot" and "Constitutional"; words that when used in paperwork to become tax exempt organizations, keep the people filing from being treated fairly. And, . . . everyone should be treated fairly . . . and with a First Amendment Right to speak and write and congregate . . . what we say or write should have no bearing on whether or not we are treated equally. Who disagrees with that? Something is wrong if some words (speech) are tax deductible and some words aren't. Something is wrong if the government gets to decide which ones are deductible and which ones are not. It's a heinous encroachment on the 1st Amendment.[32]

It's not the political targeting of conservatives and libertarians that should worry you, as former IRS commissioner Doug H.

---

[31] http://washingtonexaminer.com/opinion/2011/09/obama-style-democracy-bureaucrats-know-best#ixzz1ZMqW2GvN.

[32] Michael Minns,"The Real IRS Scandal: The Tea Party Is Small Potatoes" (June 5th 2013), http://personalliberty.com/2013/06/05/the-real-irs-scandal-the-tea-party-is-small-potatoes.

Shulman told the House Committee on Oversight and Government Reform. It's that the IRS is underfunded.[33] The same argument is presented by the IRS official report with self-descriptive title: "The IRS Is Significantly Underfunded to Serve Taxpayers and Collect Tax."[34]

At the time of the harassment of the Tea Party groups the "underfunded" IRS spent over $50 million on conferences including $4 million for an August 2010 gathering in Anaheim, California, for which "the agency did not negotiate lower room rates, even though that is standard government practice, according to a statement by the House Oversight and Government Reform Committee. Instead, some of the 2,600 attendees received benefits, including baseball tickets and stays in presidential suites that normally cost $1,500 to $3,500 per night. In addition, 15 outside speakers were paid a total of $135,000 in fees, with one paid $17,000 to talk about "leadership through art," the House committee said."[35] An additional $50,000 was spent to produce videos, including one in which IRS agents were instructed how to line dance and a training video that replicated the set of "Star Trek."[36]

In emotional testimony before the House Ways and Means Committee on June 4th 2013, representatives of the Tea Party groups told of waiting up to three years for their applications to be approved and having to answer questions about their political views. The Tea Partiers described IRS demands for details about employees' and group officials' political activities and backgrounds, for comments they'd posted on Tea Party websites, for videos of meetings and information on what kind of political views and statements were expressed by speakers at Tea Party rallies and meetings. Many applications submitted over three years ago are still waiting to be considered. "I'm a born-free American woman," Becky Gerritson, president of the Wetumpka Tea Party of

---

[33] www.nationalreview.com/corner/349076/former-irs-chief-irs-underfunded-handling-obamacare-ian-tuttle.

[34] http://www.taxpayeradvocate.irs.gov/userfiles/file/Full-Report/Most-Serious-Problems-IRS-Significantly-Underfunded.pdf.

[35] Alan Fram, "Congressional Report on Expensive Conferences Latest Black Eye for IRS," Associated Press (June 2nd 2013).

[36] http://washingtonexaminer.com/irs-refuses-to-turn-over-documents-on-targeting-to-senate/article/2531142.

Alabama, tearfully told the lawmakers. "I'm telling my government, 'You've forgotten your place'."[37]

On January 21, 2010, the U.S. Supreme Court decided
Citizens United v. Federal Election Commission, which overturned
many previous restrictions on political campaign spending and
allowed nearly unlimited and often anonymous spending by corporations and other groups to influence elections. Some Tea Party
leaders began forming political action committees as offshoots of
their 501(c)-tax-exempt organizations. By the November elections
of 2010, tax-exempt non-profit groups had spent in excess of $100
million on the mid-term elections, more than double the expenditure from a similar point in the election cycle four years earlier.

Most figures on the left question the non-partisan status of the
Tea Party and no doubt they are right. Earl Blumenauer pointed
out that many of the conservative groups have taken positions on
highly charged political issues. "Let's stop this charade of pretend-
ing to be just social welfare organizations. Admit they are political
and treat them as such," Blumenauer said.[38] We can see no flaw in
this line of reasoning. It's very difficult to define what does and
what doesn't qualify for defense of the public good and social welfare. What is wrong, however, is to select one segment of the political spectrum and discriminate against groups based on details of
their ideology and their attitude to the Obama administration.

All kinds of blatantly leftist groups get the tax exemptions these
Tea Party groups were seeking. The leftist organization Public
Campaign receives "major funding" from the pro-Obamacare
alliance Health Care for America NOW!, which is comprised of the
national trade union center AFL-CIO and labor unions AFSCME,
SEIU, and the "progressive" activist organization Move On,
among others. Another leftist group, Priorities USA, created and
aired numerous pro-Obama, anti-Romney TV ads featuring a former steel worker Joe Soptic who blamed Romney for his wife's
death from cancer. Rush Limbaugh and others have noted that
Soptic is apparently wearing the same shirt for campaign ads of
both the Priorities USA and official Democratic Party Obama For

---

[37] http://www.washingtonguardian.com/irs-officials-enjoyed-luxury-
rooms-conference-1.

[38] http://www.washingtonguardian.com/irs-officials-enjoyed-luxury-
rooms-conference-1.

America, Obama's 2012 campaign organization, that were allegedly taped months apart. Priorities USA is a self-described as a social welfare 501(c)4 and is not required to disclose individuals, corporations, or union organizations that have donated in an effort to affect the 2012 election. It's no different from Crossroads GPS, the Karl Rove-affiliated neoconservative group that Senate Majority Whip Dick Durbin asked Shulman in a letter to investigate. Yet Karl Rove and his neocon group escaped the "special scrutiny" the IRS reserved for the Tea Party groups.

After the IRS scandal unraveled former Republican senator and presidential candidate Fred Thompson sarcastically observed that

> In St. Louis, armed Homeland Security agents monitored Tea Party members protesting the IRS. Good idea. When people think their government is out to get them, the best response is to send the government out to get them.[39]

News of the IRS victimization helped both to re-energize the Tea Party and to revive its popularity in the country. Tea Party members held rallies at all fifty statehouses, regional IRS offices, and federal buildings to protest the IRS, drawing media attention. The Tea Party rallies provided a forum for the Tea Party hopefuls for 2014. In Georgia, for example, Karen Handel and Bob Barr at a time when their candidacies would have otherwise drawn little attention were in the news again.

> Barr, a former Libertarian Party presidential candidate, Congressman and federal prosecutor who served as one of the impeachment managers indicting President Bill Clinton, is using the IRS as fodder for his congressional comeback campaign amid demands to impeach President Barack Obama. And Handel, Georgia's former secretary of state, used the rally to revive the call for ethics reform she used in 2010 to come within a whisker of winning the GOP gubernatorial nomination. Suddenly, she has a ready-made platform in her quest for the U.S. Senate next year.[40]

---

[39] http://patriotpost.us/editions/18508.

[40] "Jones: Scandals Threaten to Dampen Democrats' Momentum" (May 26th 2013), http://onlineathens.com/opinion/2013-05-26/jones-scandals-threaten-dampen-democrats-momentum.

The way some more pessimistic Tea Partiers see it, the slow-motion coup d'état in Washington is not slow-motion any more. Attacks on the personal liberties of Americans, including the wire-tapping, harassment, and prosecution of journalists, the use of the IRS to target political critics, the Benghazi scandal and cover-up, the employment of drones even against civilians, the National Defense Authorization Act (NDAA), with its provision that anyone whom the government doesn't like may be held indefinitely, including U.S. citizens arrested on American soil, and the National Security Agency (NSA), possessing the most advanced array of equipment and scientific personnel, authorized to listen to whomever they want to, . . . now we at last see the real meaning of "Change you can believe in."

Epilogue
The Future of the Tea Party

The Tea Party is a popular response to the ongoing crisis of big government. The Tea Party is not going away because the crisis of big government is not going away.

The most unmistakable symptom of the deepening crisis is the expanding federal deficit and the exploding federal debt. It is now too late for this problem to be cured by judicious compromise measures. Sweeping, painful cuts in government programs can no longer be avoided. Even the most leftwing of governments will be compelled by an irresistible avalanche of dire circumstances to make these cuts. There is no alternative.

With the downfall of the Soviet Union, the late twentieth century saw the end of socialism, ultimately because it was unworkable. The early twenty-first century will see the end of welfare statism, the theory that the government can look after everyone from cradle to grave, protect them from their own dysfunctional desires, make the distribution of incomes conform to some arbitrary notion of fairness, and generally rush in to cure any discomfort that anyone might think to complain about. Welfare statism, like socialism, will be abandoned because it is demonstrated to be unworkable. The downfall of socialism taught us that human well-being requires capitalism. The downfall of welfare statism will teach us that capitalism requires limited government.

The future collapse of the welfare state, just like the recent collapse of socialism, unfortunately means a painful transition for many but can only lead to ultimate improvement for most—and is in any case inescapable. The painful transition will be rendered shorter and less painful to the extent that people who understand

193

what's going on move swiftly to cut back the size of government and the scale and scope of its toxic meddling in people's lives. To prepare the way so that the transition is quicker, less agonizing, and more easily accepted is the historic role of the Tea Party.

Traditionally, crises of over-government often culminate in runaway inflation. The government spends its way out of its problems by creating additional money, which drives up prices. When people begin to expect rapid price inflation, this very expectation accelerates the rate of price increases, as people have an additional motive for not holding onto money. They become preoccupied with converting money into goods as quickly as they can. The price index rises by three digits, and then four digits, then five, each year. The money system collapses and people revert to barter. Savings are annihilated. Modern industry, which absolutely requires monetary calculation in stable units, and benefits greatly from sophisticated, flexible financial markets, is devastated. Mass unemployment and impoverishment ensues while industrial plant lies idle.

Some economists now believe that the future collapse will not take the form of runaway inflation (technically called 'hyperinflation'). Because of the evolution of technology and financial markets, it is no longer true that modern governments can benefit greatly by depreciating the currency. According to these economists, some increase in inflation is to be expected, but hyperinflation itself will be avoided. Hyperinflation will still occur in a few very poor third-world economies, but in most of the world, with digital technology and today's exquisitely sensitive financial markets, the inflationary consequences of government activity become much more obvious much more speedily, and this reduces the incentive for politicians to inflate their way out of a desperate situation.

Jeffrey Rogers Hummel, a libertarian economist at San Jose State University, has proposed that the impending collapse of the welfare state will take the form, not of hyperinflation, but of a general government default on obligations to lenders. The government finances its operations by issuing U.S. Treasury securities, a form of borrowing at interest. The government has to borrow a steadily increasing amount just to pay the interest on its earlier borrowings. If the government reaches a point where (for example) it either has to abolish all of Social Security and Medicare at one stroke, overnight, or abruptly increase the money supply several hundredfold, or default on its obligations to holders of Treasury securities, Hummel believes the government will choose to default.

The effective abolition or massive reduction of Social Security, Medicare, and other government programs will have to follow shortly afterwards, but will be postponed by a few months, and can be blamed on the conspiracy of malevolent investors who will no longer buy risky Treasury securities at low interest rates. We do not mean to imply that the immediate and total abolition of all tax-funded government welfare is essential (though that is what libertarians would love to see). What *is* essential is that all such programs be fully funded and actuarially sound (just as they are in private pension funds), and that government borrowing be strictly curtailed.

Prior to the actual occurrence of the default, increasing suspicion that the government may default will drive up the risk premium on Treasury securities, meaning that the effective interest rate on these securities will increase. Given the government's abject dependence on borrowing more billions every day, this creates further pressure to default. Because of this, default itself may be quite sudden and 'unexpected', meaning that those in the know (including those in the Tea Party) will expect it while the comedians in the White House and at MSNBC and CNN won't have a clue. Hummel estimates that default could occur at any time in the next twenty years.[1]

If Hummel turns out to be mistaken, the collapse of the welfare state will take a different, though equally dismal, course. What will definitely not happen is that the growth of government spending continues for the next thirty years without an economic and political earthquake which would make the recession of 2008–2012 seem like a storm in a teacup.

A surge of economic growth, such as that made possible by cheaper energy through fracking, could postpone the default and resulting collapse, though only by a few years, and possibly not even that, because any indication that we are 'growing ourselves out of the deficit' would immediately prompt Washington politi-

---

[1] "Why Default on U.S. Treasuries Is Likely," www.econlib.org/library/Columns/2009/Hummeltbills.html

cians, in their present frame of mind, to ratchet up their spending and borrowing even more.

Most people today view the Tea Party as extreme and unco-operative in its insistence on reducing the growth of government spending and borrowing. But we may soon come to look back upon the present Tea Party, especially its delegates in Washington, as way too timid.

The Tea Party has been a considerable force acting to moder-ate the growth of government spending. But more than mere moderation of the rate of growth of spending is required. Actual cuts have to come. Whether the Tea Party is up to the task is still to be decided.

We very much hope that Tea Partiers will have the courage and resolve to persevere in their struggle against the Moloch state. Only when the classical liberal principles of personal freedom, lim-ited government, and balanced budgets have been securely rein-stated can we look forward to lasting prosperity without fear.

Index

ABC, 69, 79, 142
abortion, 15, 45–46, 74, 79,
  106–07, 111
ACLU, 100
Adamson, Chris, 98
Adbuster, 151
Afghanistan, 39–40, 112
AFL-CIO, 165, 189
AIG bailout, 55
Alabama, 132, 169, 180, 189
Alaska, 8, 102, 132, 145
Alliance for Global Justice, 164
Amar, Akhil Reed, 127
Amato, John, 50
American Civil Rights Institute, 81
American Family Association, 107,
  109
American Legislative Exchange
  Council (ALEC), 136
American Majority, 89–90
American Museum of Natural
  History, 100
American Nazi Party, 152
American Recovery and
  Reinvestment Act of 2009, 58, 62
American Spectator, 9
Americans for Limited Government,
  88
Americans for Prosperity, 16, 72, 73,
  85, 88–89, 98–99, 119
Americans for Tax Reform, 173
Amtrak, 60

anarchocapitalism, 34
Angle, Sharron, 95, 184
Anonymous, 151, 154, 156
Antle, James, 9
Arizona, 15, 68, 93, 132, 135–36,
  145
Arizona Academy of Family
  Physicians, 136
Arizona Chamber of Commerce, 136
Armey, Dick, 4, 26, 83, 91
Articles of Confederation, 36, 124
Assault Weapons Ban, 180
Association of Community
  Organizations for Reform Now
  (ACORN), 69, 89
AT&T, 92
Atlanta, 96
Austin, 99, 155
Austrian Business Cycle Theory, 37
Austrian school of economics, 37, 39
auto bailout, 57–58
Ayers, William "Bill," 69, 161

Babeu, Paul, 68
Bachmann, Michele, 14, 16, 79, 90,
  92–93, 110, 114
bailouts, 1, 13, 25, 50, 54–58, 70,
  74, 80, 105, 153, 165
Bair, Sheila, 14
Baker, Peter, 112
Bank of America, 69

Barnes, Fred, 41
Barnett, Randy E., 133–34
Barr, Bob, 190
Bartlett, Bruce, 14
Bastiat, Frédéric, 67, 115
Bauer, Robert, 161
BBC news, 158, 176
Bean, Danielle, 10, 110
Beck, Glenn, 4, 29, 56, 75, 87, 96, 110–11, 114, 117–120, 161
Benghazi , 190
Bennet, Robert, 8
Beren, Steve, 71
Biden, Joe, 62
Bike, Bill, 22
blowback, 40, 43
Blumenauer, Earl, 189
Boehner, John, 12, 14
Boldin, Michael, 130–31, 138, 147
Bolick, Clint, 135
Boortz, Meal, 80 .
Boston, 26–27, 32, 141, 155
Boston Tea Party (1773), vii, 32, 120
Boston, Rob, 109
Bovard, James, 114
Bozzi, Joe, 31
Brookings Institute, 175
Brown, Scott, 2–3, 14, 95
Buchanan, Pat, 1, 115
Buckley, William F. Jr., 44–45
Budget Control Act of 2011, 13, 93
Bureau of Alcohol Tobacco and Firearms, 145
Burger King, 57
Bush, George Walker, 3, 40–42, 46, 53, 55–57, 61, 68, 74, 108, 113, 130–32, 139–140, 157, 164

Cain, Herman, 14, 16, 79–80, 82
Caldara, Jon, 73
California, 60, 88, 129, 158, 162, 163, 188
Cameron, Carl, 43
Campaign for Liberty, 46–47, 142
Canada, 64, 151, 167, 174, 177, 178

Cao, Joseph, 14
Capitalism Magazine, 108
Captain Morgan Rum, 57
Carender, Keli, 26, 70–72
Carter, Jimmy, 41
Castillo, Susie, 141
Castle, Michael, 9,102
Cato Institute, 25, 47
CBS, 79
Center for Disease Control, 60
Chaffetz, Jason, 93, 102
Chan, Darryl, 163
Chaoulli, Jacques, 177
Cheney, Dick, 5, 157
Chertoff, Michael, 140
Chicago, 25, 26, 49, 73, 90, 141, 158, 160, 177, 180
Chicago School of Economics, 37
Chicago Tribune, 31
Christian, R.C., 162
Christian Coalition, 111
Christian Science Monitor, 114
Chrysler, 57
Citizens for a Sound Economy, 25, 88, 90, 99
Citizens United v. Federal Elections Commission, 189
Clinton, Bill, 53, 130, 190
Clinton, Hillary, 29, 46, 181
CNN, 2, 29, 68, 79, 94
Coakley, Martha, 2
Cohen, Steven, 168
Cohlmia, Melissa, 99
Collins, Susan, 14
Colorado, 6–7, 72, 130, 180
Commerce Clause, 125–26, 133, 137, 145
Common Cause, 100
Connecticut, 147, 180, 182
Connerly, Wardell, 81, 88
Constitution, U.S., 1, 21,28, 35, 70, 75, 78, 115–17, 123–150, 160, 185
Constitution Party, 6
Coulter, Ann, 42
Counterpunch, 157
Coup Media Group: Revolutionary Human Media, 151, 154, 162

CPAC, 101–02, 109, 115–16
CPB, 78
crisis, 2008 financial, 53–54
Crist, Charlie, 9, 102
Cruz, Ted, 15, 93
Cuba, 48, 131
Curry, Judith, 64

Daily Reckoning, 50
Dallas, 155
Daniels, Mitch, 112
Dean, Martha, 147
debates: 1996 Presidential, 131;
    2008 Republican Primary, 29, 33,
    42–44, 54; 2010 Connecticut
    Attorney General, 147; 2010
    South Carolina Gubernetorial, 6;
    2012 Republican Primary, 94
debt ceiling, 12–13, 93, 116
default on U.S. Treasury securities,
    19, 20, 193–94
defense spending, 16
deficit (federal), 11, 16, 19–21, 36,
    74–75, 82–83, 168–170, 172,
    177, 193–96
Delaware, 9, 102
DeMint, Jim, 11, 16, 93, 102,
    113–14
Democratic Congressional Campaign
    Committee, 158, 181
Democratic Party, 4, 6–8, 18, 21,
    69, 83–84, 103, 164–65, 186
Dent, Charlie, 14
Denver Post, 72
Department of Commerce, 36
Department of Education,
    36,41,170
Department of Energy, 36,63,59
Department of Health and Human
    Services, 59
Department of Homeland Security,
    59,141
Department of Interior, 36
Department of Labor, 59
Der Spiegel, 11
DeSylva, Tony, 163

Detroit, 49
Dewherst, David, 144
Diageo PLC, 57
Dodge, Andrew Ian, 106, 112
Dole, Bob, 131
drug legalization / decriminalization,
    12, 100–01, 106, 129, 131, 141,
    156, 162
Dunn, Anita, 160–61
Durbin, Dick, 22, 190

The Economist, 56
education reform, 12, 36, 156, 170,
    171
Eisenhower, Dwight, 44
elections: 2008, 2, 4, 27, 31–33, 39,
    42–44; 2010, 1–13, 22, 84, 102,
    121; 2012, 1, 8–9, 14–19, 22, 39,
    61, 89, 93–94, 102, 119
Emanuel, Ezekiel, 177
Emanuel, Rahm, 61, 177
Emergency Economic Stabilization
    Act of 2008, 55
Environmentalist / Green move-
    ment, 62, 63, 97, 156
Espionage Act, 162
European Union, 140, 167–68

Facebook, 29, 88, 92
Falwell, Jerry, 45
Faneuil Hall, 32
Fannie Mae, 170
Fast and Furious, 69
Fawkes, Guy, 30, 118
Federal Reserve, 20, 27, 33, 36, 37,
    38, 39, 47, 51, 55, 62, 66, 73, 75,
    156
Feinstein, Dianne, 180
Firearms Freedom Act, 145–46
First Amendment, 78
Fischer, Bryan, 107
Fitton, Tom, 158
Flake, Jeff, 15, 93
Florida, 6–9, 30, 46, 87, 89, 93,
    102–04, 182

Fogel, Apryl Marie, 89
Food and Drug Administration, 179
Foreign Policy (journal), 112
Foundation for Economic Education, 25
Founding Fathers, 50, 70
Fox News, 19, 43–44, 79, 101, 103, 117, 120
fracking, 196
France, 174
Freddie Mac, 170
Freedom Works, 16, 85, 88, 90–91, 92, 114, 119, 169–170
Fried, Charles, 135
Friedman, Milton, 37–38
Frum, David, 5, 113
Fugitive Slave Laws, 128–29

Gadsden Flag, 32
Galbraith, John Kenneth, 66
Garofalo, Janeane, 79
gay marriage, 107
GayPatriot.com, 80
Gelderloos, Peter, 157–58
general welfare clause, 125
Genoa Group, 151
George Mason University, 19
Georgetown University, 133
Georgia, 136, 190
Georgia Food Freedom Act, 148
Georgia State University, 60
Germany, 165, 167
Gerritson, Becky, 188
Gerson, Michael, 113
Gillespie, Nick, 9, 12
Gingrich, Newt, 14, 16, 17, 121
Giuliani, Rudolph, 14, 30, 43, 46
global warming, 62–64
Gobson, Chris, 14
Goldberg, Whoopi, 142
Goldberg, Jonah, 165
Goldman Sachs, 51, 56
Goldwater Instititute, 135
Gonigam, Dave, 50
Gonzalez v. Raich, 129

government, 3, 11, 13, 20, 25, 34, 50–52, 55, 109, 175; big, 1, 3, 5, 21, 27, 41–42, 53, 112, 114, 115, 153, 159, 167–68, 184–85, 189–190, 193–94; corruption, 68–70, 167; debt, 168, 193–95; expansion of, 6, 42, 53, 105, 168; as job creator, 66–67; limited, vii, 9, 10, 12, 18, 20, 21, 35–37, 41, 86, 88, 89, 96, 101, 105, 109, 115, 116–18, 119–120, 123–150; shutdown, 12; smaller, 1–9, 10, 16, 22, 40, 45, 100, 105–06, 110; spending, 12, 16, 19, 20, 41, 46, 53–54, 58–60, 65, 168
Gorbachev, Mikhail, 154
Graeber, David, 151–52
Graham, Lindsey, 5,14
Grassfire Nation, 92
Grassley, Charles, 14, 185
Grayson, Trey, 8,102
Great Britain, 175–76
Green, Joshua, 75
Green technology, 62–63
Grimm, Michael, 14
Gross, Terry, 79
Ground Zero mosque, 94
gun rights / gun control, 22, 145–46, 179, 185
Guy Fawkes Day, 30, 118

Hagel, Chuck, 27–28
Haley, Nikki, 6, 17, 82, 102, 121
Handel, Karen, 190
Hannity, Sean, 42–43
Hardball, 29
Harris-Perry, Melissa, 149
Harvard Law School, 135
Hayek, Friedrich A., 11, 37, 66
Hazlitt, Henry, 66
Health Care and Education Reconciliation Act of 2010, 171
Health Care Freedom Act; *see* Obamacare
Hedges, Chris, 163–64
Heller v. District of Columbia, 180

Heritage Foundation, 16, 164
Hezbollah, 152
Hickenlooper, John, 7
Holder, Eric H. Jr., 69
Holdren, John, 140
Hollywood, 59
Homeland Security, 139, 190
homosexuality, 45
homosexuals in the military, 95
Hoppe, Hans-Hermann, 179
Horn, Norman, 142
Horowitz, David, 118
Houghton, Amo, 14
House Ways and Means Committee, 188
Housing and Urban Development, 36
Hoyt, Katherine, 164
HUD, 59
Huebert, Jacob, vii
Huelskamp, Tim, 18
Huffington Post, 50, 168
Hummel, Jeffrey Rogers, 194–95
Huntsman, Jon Jr., 14, 61
Hussein, Saddam, 40

Idaho, 7, 132, 136, 145
Illinois, 73
immigration, 11, 68
Independent Institute, 72–73
independent party candidates, 6–7
Indiana, 15, 93
inflation, 19, 20, 54, 68, 193–94
Institute for Global Economic Growth, 67
Iowa, 3, 23, 46, 78, 121, 185
Iran, 113, 115–16, 152
Iraq, 40, 42–43, 94, 118
IRS, 20, 22, 27, 51, 73, 173, 187–190
Israel, 45, 157

Japan, 114
Jefferson, Thomas, 127–28, 179
Jeffords, Jim, 14

Johnson, Gary, 20
Jones, Van, 161
just war, 40
Justice Department, 69

Kaloogian, Howard, 94
Kansas, 18, 98, 132, 136
Kasich, John, 6
Kennedy, Ted, 2
Kentucky, 3, 8, 102
Kentucky Resolutions, 128, 146
Key, Charles, 131
Keynes, John Maynard, 58
Keynesianism, 66–67
Khameni, Ayatollah, 152
Kibbe, Matt, 16, 26, 169
King, Martin Luther, Jr., 180
Koch brothers, 19, 47, 72, 83–84, 88, 97–101, 165
Korea, 114
Kremer, Amy, 102, 107
Kristol, Bill, 103
Kristol, Irving, 45
Krugman, Paul, 4, 58, 61, 80, 83–86
Ku Klux Klan, 128
Kulikov, Oleg, 175
Kurlander, Steven, 181

Lange, Oskar, 154
Larson, Lars, 185
Lee, Edward, 29
Lee, Mike, 8, 93
LePage, Paul Richard, 6
Libertarian Party, 20, 28, 73, 99, 190
Liberty Belle, 70–72
Liberty First, 96
Limbaugh, Rush, 42, 71, 189
Lincoln, Abraham, 94
Lindzen, Richard, 64
Lizza, Ryan, 79
Los Angeles Times, 9, 28, 110, 130
Lott, John R., Jr., 64, 183
Lott, Trent, 11, 102
Louisiana, 132, 136

Ludwig von Mises Institute, 39
Lyman, Trevor, 30–31

Maddow, Rachel, 113, 148
Madison, James, 124, 128
Maes, Dan, 7
Maher, Bill, 181
Maine, 6, 106, 112
Malkin, Michelle, 72
Manchin, Joe, 180
Manning, Bradley, 162
Markay, Lachlan, 164
Marshall, Steve, 154–55
Martin, Jenny Beth, 96, 107, 117
Marxism, 54, 69, 164
Massachusetts, 2–3, 32, 95, 135
Matthews, Chris, 4, 30
McCain, John, 14, 53, 55
McDonald v. Chicago, 180
McGlowan, Angela, 81
McIntyre, Mike, 6
McLaughlin and Associates poll, 28
McQuain, Bruce, 159
Meckler, Mark, 57, 96
Media Matters, 101
Medicaid, 170
Medicare, 18, 19, 59, 170, 172, 195
Medicare Part D, 41, 130, 134, 173
Medvedev, Dmitry, 69–70
Meetup.com, 29, 32–33, 47, 73, 74, 92
Meyer, Ron, 116
Miami Herald, 29
Michigan, 8, 38, 144, 169
Miller, Joe, 8, 95, 102
Minnick, Walter, 7
Minns, Michael, 187
Mises, Ludwig von, 37, 47
Mississippi, 81
Missouri, 136
Mollahan, Allen, 7
monetarist school of economics, 37
money bomb, vii, 31–33, 118
Montana, 111, 145–46
Moore, Michael, 174–75
Morris, Philip, 92

Morton, Brian, 185
Mother Teresa, 160–61
Mourdock, Richard, 15, 93
Move On, 189
Murdoch, Rupert, 97
Murkowski, Lisa, 8, 102
Murphy, John E., 143

NAACP, 96
Nader, Ralph, 1
Napolitano, Andrew (Judge), 162–63
Napolitano, Janet, 136, 139–141
NASCAR, 57
Nashville, 33, 95, 113
National Defense Authorization Act
   (NDAA), 13, 116, 117, 185, 191
National Health Service, 175–76
National ID / Real ID, 11, 129, 131
National Public Radio (NPR),
   56–57, 78–79, 153
National Review, 42, 44, 81
National Rifle Association, 25
National Security Agency, 191
National Tea Party Convention, 113
National Tea Party Federation,
   91–92, 94, 96, 102
NBC, 4, 25, 29, 47, 79, 105, 113,
   148
Nebraska, 27 132
Necessary and Proper Clause, 125
Neighborhood Stabilization
   Program, 60
neoconservatism, 3, 22, 42, 45–46,
   112–13
Nevada, 46
New Deal, 44, 126
New Hampshire, 33, 46, 144
New Jersey, 7,144
New York (state), 7, 28, 43
New York City, 94, 151, 158
New York Journal, 124
New York Magazine, 30
New York State Theater, 100
New York Times, 4, 5, 11, 29, 56,
   58, 70, 73, 80, 83, 97, 98, 114,
   146, 165

New Yorker, 99
Nichols, John, 31
9/11 issues, 30, 42, 34; Commission
  Report, 43; terrorist attacks, 30,
  42, 43, 53
9/12 project, 87–88, 95
No Child Left Behind Act, 41,
  130–31
Noonan, Peggy, 14
Norquist, Grover, 18, 110
North Carolina, 6–7, 186–87
North Dakota, 132, 138
North Korea, 152
Northwestern University, 60
Novack, Eric, 135
November 5th Money Bomb, 30–31

Oakland, 158, 163
Obama, Barack H., 2, 3, 15, 20–21,
  42, 48, 51–56, 58, 61–64, 68, 69,
  72, 103, 108, 112, 132, 135, 140,
  147, 158, 164, 170, 181, 186
Obamacare (Patient Protection and
  Affordable Care Act / Health
  Care Freedom Act), 7, 16, 22, 82,
  133–37, 138, 162, 170–79, 189
Occupy Wall Street, 1, 68, 105,
  151–165, 185
O'Connor, Ivor, 153
O'Donnel, Christine, 9, 95, 102
Ohio, 6, 15, 27, 31, 60, 85–86
Ohio Liberty Council, 85
Oklahoma, 111, 131–32, 136
Olbermann, Keith, 4
Oliverio, Michael, 7
O'Neill, Paul, 14
Orszag, Peter, 186
Osama bin Laden, 43
Our Country Deserves Better, 93, 94

Palin, Sarah, 95, 113–14, 117–19
Pataki, George, 28
Patient Protection and Affordable
  Care Act; *see* Obamacare
Patrick, Dan, 144

Patriot Act, 13, 33, 100–01, 116,
  130, 155, 162, 186
Patriot Action Network, 92
Patriot Caucus, 96
Paul v. Virginia, 133
Paul, Rand, 3, 8–9, 12, 23, 26,
  32–33, 93, 102, 113, 165,
  183–84
Paul, Ron, vii, 4, 8, 13–15, 16,
  26–40, 42–44, 46–47, 50, 51,
  54–55, 56, 72, 73, 92, 93, 103,
  105, 113, 114, 118–120, 121,
  123, 130
Paulson, Henry, 51, 55–56
PBS, 78, 100
Pennsylvania, 144,169
Pentagon, 170
People's General Assembly, 151
Perdue, Bev, 186
Perkins, Tony, 109
Perot, Ross, 1
Perry, Rick, 16, 143, 144
Pew Poll, 56
Pfaff, Jim, 73
Philadelphia, 124, 151
Phillips, Judson, 95
Politico, 31, 86, 92
polls: auto bailout opposition, 57;
  Gallup, 6, 29, 58; global warming
  belief, 63; 9/11 speculation, 157;
  Republican Primary (2008), 29;
  stimulus support, 62; Tea Party
  Leadership / Participation, 84,
  114, 117–18; Tea Party support /
  demographic, 77; Tea Party sup-
  port (2010), 2; Who passed
  TARP?, 56
Popp, Dan, 165
Porkulus Protest, 70–71
Powell, Colin, 14
Prentice, Paul, 66
Priorities USA, 189–190
private law society, 34
Proposition 215, 129
Public Broadcasting Act of 1967, 78
Pugh, Tim, 121
Putin, Vladimir, 70

Quebec City, 151, 177

racism, 77–78
Rahn, Richard, 21, 67, 69, 78–79
Raimondo, Justin, 15
Rand, Ayn, 82
Rasmussen, Scott, 26
Rattner, Steve, 186
Read, Leonard E., 34
Real ID Act, 129, 131
Reason magazine, 9
Redistributing Knowledge, 71
Reed, Scott, 103
Reich, Robert, 18
Reid, Harry, 184
Religious Right, 11, 18, 22–23, 42,
    45–46, 79, 82, 88, 106–112
Republican Liberty Caucus, 142
Republican National Committee, 43,
    151
Republican National Convention, 151
Republican Party, 3–5, 18, 21–22,
    29, 42–46, 83–84, 92, 94,
    101–03, 108, 115, 168, 181
Republican Party Platform, 17, 41
Restoring Honor Rally, 88, 96, 110,
    119
Rhode Island, 169
Rice University, 60
Rich, Frank, 11,97
Richards, Jay, 109
Rigby, Lee, 183
Rockwell, Lew, 10, 118–19
Roe v. Wade, 45–46
Roemer, John, 154
Romney, Mitt, 5, 14–18, 44, 102,
    120, 135, 189
Roosevelt, Franklin Delano, 41,
    125–26
Roosevelt, Theodore, 1
Rothbard, Murray N., 34, 45, 47, 99
Rove, Karl, 4–5, 9, 11, 22, 80, 102,
    190
Rubio, Marco, 9, 82, 95, 102
Rugy, Veronique de, 19
Russia, 69–70, 157, 175–76

Russo, Sal, 94
Ryan, Paul, 15, 17
Ryun, Ned, 90

Salon, 117
Salt Lake Tribune, 185
Sam Adams Alliance, 90
same-sex marriage, 45
Sandys, Jonathan, 118
Santelli, Rick, vii, 25–27, 47–51,
    73–74, 105, 108, 160
Santorum, Rick, 121
Saudi Arabia, 43
Scarborough, Rick, 111
Schier, Steven, 111
Schiff, Peter, 39
Schiller, Ron, 79
Schoen, Douglas, 26
Schwarzenneger, Arnold, 14
Schwartz, Anna J., 38
Schweickart, David, 154
Scioto River, 27
Scott, Marshall, 185
Scott, Rick, 6
Seattle, 26, 70–71, 155
Seattle Sons and Daughters of
    Liberty, 72
Senior, Jennifer, 30
sequestration, 18–19
Shipley, Jeff, 3
Shonka, Bryce, 147
Shulman, Douglas H., 22, 171,
    187–88
Silva, Mark, 31
Simpson, David, 142
Skokpol, Theda, 82
Smart Girl Politics, 96
Smith, Chris, 14
Snowe, Olympia, 14
socialism, 21, 54, 78, 154, 175, 193
Social Security, 18, 92, 134, 170, 195
Solyndra Corporation, 62–63
Soptic, Joe, 189
Soros, George, 100–01, 164
South Carolina, 6, 17, 46, 102, 121,
    128, 132

South Dakota, 111, 132, 145
Southern Poverty Law Center, 148
Soviet Union; *see* U.S.S.R
Sowell, Thomas, 173
Spinner, Steven, 63
Steele, David Ramsay, vii
Steele, Michael, 43
Steinhauser, Brendan, 103
stimulus, 55, 59, 61, 64–65, 67
Stockman, David, 14
Strauss, Joe, 144
Strickland, Ted, 6
Student Aid and Fiscal Responsibility Act, 171
student loans, 59
Sullivan, Patricia, 103–04
Summers, Lawrence, 49
Supreme Court, 135, 137–38, 146, 162–63, 180, 189
Sweden, 168, 176
Switzerland, 168

Taft, Robert, 44
Taliban, 40
Tancredo, Tom, 6–7, 72–73
TARP, 50, 55–57, 61, 70
Tax Day Protest (2009), 88, 96, 105
Tax Day Protest (2010), 114
Tea Party (1773), 27, 32
Tea Party Caucus, 13, 92–93, 103
Tea Party Debate (September 12th 2011), 94
Tea Party Express, 7, 92–95, 102, 107
Tea Party Nation, 95
Tea Party Patriots, 57, 84, 94–96, 102, 106, 112, 117
Temporary Assistance for Needy Families, 59
Tennessee, 33, 132, 136, 145
Tenth Amendment Movement, 123–150
terrorism, 30, 40, 42–43, 69, 106, 112, 118, 142
Texas, 15, 18, 44, 60, 93, 111–12, 142–43, 150

Thomas, Cal, 70
Thompson, Fred, 28, 190
Time magazine, 119
Toomey, Pat, 180
Transportation Security Administration (TSA), 139
tricorne hats, 32, 123
TrueMajority.com, 56
Trumbull, Josiah, 147
Trumka, Richard, 165
Trump, Donald, 16
Truth Tour, 94
Turley, Jonathan, 162
Turner, Grace-Marie, 171

unions, labor, 158, 164, 189–190; public sector, 89, 98, 100
United States v. South-Eastern Underwriters, 133–34
United Auto Workers Union, 58
United Nations, 181,184
University of California at San Francisco, 140
University of California, Berkeley, 60
University of Texas at Austin, 112
U.S. Forest Service, 60
U.S.S.R., 44, 98, 153, 155, 175, 193
Utah, 8, 93, 102, 132, 145

Vander Plaats, Bob, 23
Verizon, 92
Vietnam War, 45
Viguerie, Richard, 114
Virginia, 128, 136
Virginia Resolutions, 128, 146
Vision America, 111
Vogel, Kenneth, 86, 92
voluntarism, 34
Von Drehle, David, 119
voter fraud, 85

Wake Forest University, 60
Walker, Scott, 23, 89–90, 98, 100

Wall Street Journal, 61, 62, 66, 73, 145
Wallace, George, 1
war, 10–11, 29, 39–42, 45–46, 112–17, 119–120
Ward, Kenric, 103
Washington D.C., 47, 49, 72, 88, 92, 129, 158, 160, 173, 185
Washington Post, 8, 10, 11, 28, 56, 84, 102, 110, 114, 117, 165
Washington State, 60, 70–71
Watts, Anthony, 64
Weather Underground, 69
Weekly Standard, 41–42, 103
Welch, Matt, 9, 12
welfare state, 51, 67, 74, 168, 176–77, 193
West, Allen, 15, 82, 93, 115–116, 181
West Virginia, 7
Wickard v. Filburn, 126, 145
Wierzbicki, Joe, 94

Wilber, Kirby, 71
Wilkinson, Everett, 87, 182
Williams, Mark, 94
Williams, Vanessa, 82
Wilson, Woodrow, 45
Wisconsin, 23, 89, 90, 98, 100
Woods, Thomas Jr., 128, 138, 146–47, 149
World Trade Organization, 157
World War II, 44
Wright, Jeremiah, 161
Wyoming, 132, 145

Young America's Foundation, 116

Zedong, Mao, 160–61
Zernike, Kate, 26, 70, 80, 83, 159
Zuccotti Park, 151, 157